Magic & Modernism
Art from Cornwall in Context 1800-1950

Rupert White

ANTENNA
www.antennapublications.org.uk

Copyright © 2023 Rupert White
All rights reserved.

First Edition 2023

...the Cornish coast, the prospect of seeing it, the very thought of its existence, has the exhilaration of a rapturous prayer. There the earth is exquisitely clean, the bright sea bubbles like champagne, and its mere mists are rainbow-hued dreams; the sky has flung off its dingy robe and is naked, beautiful, alive. (Havelock Ellis, 1914)

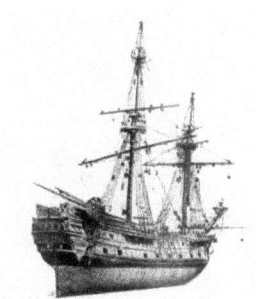

In memory of Dr Alan M. Kent who, in 2014, commented supportively on an early draft.

Foreword

When Rupert White asked me to write the foreword for 'Magic & Modernism', it was an affirmation that the Cornish creatures called 'piskeys' still flicker their lanterns and light our way.

Rupert and I met on April 1st 2023 on a rainy afternoon at his residence in Cornwall. I drove out to see him with only a day left before my flight back to California, making this only my second visit to Cornwall in 10 years.

The first trip was in 2014, just months after my start with the legendary Pixies. The band had asked me to go on a world tour which started January 10th in the US, replacing bassist/singer Kim Deal who had unexpectedly quit. Unflinchingly, I accepted the offer and committed to the tour dates which included most countries in every continent around the world.

It was a transitional period for all of us Pixies, and transitions beckon signs to help validate our choices. Before committing myself fully I needed to know that these 'Gigantic' pixie-shoes I was being asked to fill were indeed the right fit.

That summer, on July 9th, during our UK/EU tour, Pixies were scheduled to perform at the Eden Sessions at the Eden Project. This was the band's first time in Cornwall. As we crossed the Tamar River Bridge I can remember Black Francis saying: 'We have arrived at our next beehive'.

Disheveled and disoriented, Pixies and crew exited our dimly-lit tour bus into a brightly lit day at Fowey Hall Hotel. Fowey Hall sits overlooking the Celtic sea with views over the river mouth. It was the setting for classic children's book 'The Wind in the Willows' by Kenneth Grahame.

Toad, Mole, Rat and Badger embodied the timeless scenery which sprinkled Pixie dust on my expedition, later that day, around the idyllic fisherman's town of Polperro. I wandered through the narrow cobbled streets that led down to an antique shop full of Cornish treasures. I purchased a mysterious brass charm of a naked figure no larger than my thumb with writing above her that reads 'Joan the Wad' and then made my way back to Fowey Hall.

After the Eden Session concert at the Eden Project I climbed back up into my bunk in the bus and began researching the mysterious 'Joan the Wad, Queen of the Piskeys!' The word 'Pixies' derives from the Cornish word 'piskeys' which made all of this too serendipitous to ignore. It seemed to be the sign I was looking for. Soon after I became a permanent member of the Pixies and we have been prospering since.

Joan the Wad paved many paths connecting me to Rupert. His article 'This Charming Man: FT Nettleinghame and his Piskey Empire' took me to his book 'The Re-enchanted Landscape' which introduced me to surrealist/occultist Ithell Colquhoun, and finally led me back to Cornwall and to this new book, in which Joan, Nettleinghame and Colquhoun, as well as Kenneth Grahame, all make welcome appearances again.

It's safe to say, I have been 'piskey-led'.

Paz Lenchantin
Bassist/singer and co-songwriter of Pixies

Preface

Cornish Studies literature has tended to play down, and even ignore, the presence of artists in Cornwall. Perhaps they have been seen as occupying a privileged, detached position, or as outsiders sealed off from the everyday lived experience of the people[1].

If artists are perceived in this way, however, it is partly because many art books, particularly those relating to Modernism in St Ives, have presented it so. Existing narratives have tended to describe the activities of the artists as if they relate only to art-history and to aesthetic concerns that belong to an exclusive, even elitist, art-world.

This book is a first attempt to relate the story of art in Cornwall to a wider range of cultural forces and ideas, as a way of grounding the international in the local, and thus reconciling the two.

In describing this wider context I hope to show the ways that artists, alongside writers, folklorists and Cornish-revivalists, ultimately contributed to the creation of a new post-industrial Cornwall.

This, of course, is the Cornwall that we live in now.

---

[1] Amy Hale describes Cornish visual art as 'an uncomfortable topic for scholars of Cornwall' (Hale, 2020). Also see interview 'On Ithell Colquhoun, Celticity and Surrealism' with Amy Hale on artcornwall.org.

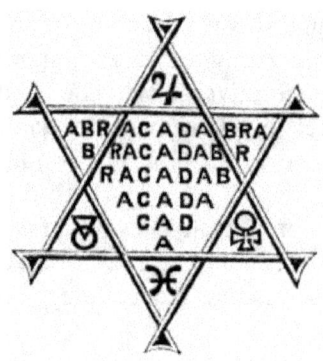

Introduction: British culture 'at war with itself'

The depopulation of rural districts has been often the theme of the moralist: and it is the favourite subject of the poet's regret. In glancing over the deserted village, the poetic eye is suffused with sorrow: and the possessors of lord-ships or manors, demolishing cottages, throwing down small enclosures, and reducing numerous tenements into one wide demesne; excite in some bosoms suspicion and alarm. (Richard Polwhele, 1806)

With their Celtic background the Cornish have far less in common with the entire English nation than they have, for example, with their cousins in Wales, Scotland and Ireland....Cornwall, in the face of all the mass centralisation of our modern society, has remained stubbornly different...its position of being the most westerly of all English counties at once puts it literally, out on a limb...it is a place apart, a world of its own, full indeed of a spirit and atmosphere of 'the very long ago' (Denys Val Baker, 1973)

Britain saw a huge expansion in its economic power and imperial might during the 19th century. The base of its economy changed from agriculture to industry and commerce, and between 1801 and 1911 the proportion of the population living in urban areas grew from twenty per cent to eighty percent. The mass movement of the populace was hastened by the process of 'enclosure', (where common-land went into private ownership), the promise of jobs in factories, and the collapse of farming in the 1870's (Marsh, 1982).

The rapid growth of the cities created new social problems, however, with writers like Leo Tolstoy, John Ruskin, William Morris and Charles Dickens critical of the consequences of urbanisation and industrialisation. There was concern that cities affected the quality of human relationships, damaged communities, and created squalor, poverty and moral degradation[2].

In explaining the trajectory of Britain's economic development in the last 200 years, some have suggested that The Great Exhibition of 1851 marked the turning point in attitudes towards economic expansion and industrialism in British culture. In place of a proud triumphalism, it ushered in the modern era of ambivalence and doubt: a nation that, in cultural terms, has been 'at war with itself' ever since (Wiener, 1981)[3].

Many of the most radical social reformers of the late Victorian era – socialists like Ruskin and anarchists like Bakunin – considered that a return to a simpler, natural lifestyle, that included manual labour, was the solution to many of industrial society's problems, and could be of benefit to both rich and poor alike.

For artists and writers, the focus of attention shifted from depictions of the landscape, to interest in the people who lived in that landscape, and in their lifestyles and beliefs, which were valued and celebrated in their own right, particularly if there was a sense that they represented folk traditions or rural industries unchanged for centuries.

Alongside this nostalgic tendency there was a progressive and liberal impulse, partly driven by a reevaluation of what should be considered 'natural', in which typically modern personal and sexual freedoms were embraced, and alternative forms of spirituality were explored.

These concerns, rather than being random or accidental, are all interlinked, and seen in hindsight can perhaps be most easily encompassed by the term: 'ruralism'. Ruralism, of course, can be demonstrated to have manifested in many other parts of Britain but it is also clearly present in the response of writers and artists to Cornwall, and is exaggerated perhaps because of Cornwall's 'otherness'. Cornwall,

---

[2] Though not referring to cities, or large conurbations, in Cornwall similar concerns were raised especially by the Methodists and those involved in the Temperance Movement who were responding to conditions brought on by industrialisation (White, 2019).
[3] The architect Pugin, for example, described the Crystal Palace as a 'glass monster', and the product of a 'soulless age'. His own contribution, the Medieval Court, is now regarded as having spearheaded the Gothic revival in art and architecture.

with its uniquely Celtic credentials, was, after all, relatively remote and untouched by urbanisation[4].

Before the Second World War, I would suggest these 'ruralist' tendencies therefore appear as:
a) the preservation of folk songs, folk stories and folk traditions (cf Robert Hunt and Robert Morton Nance)
b) painterly depictions of landscapes, rural life and traditional industries (eg Newlyn art colony),
c) the revival of handicrafts (eg Newlyn Copper, The Leach Pottery, Pinwill Sisters),
d) sympathy with medievalism, Catholicism and Celticism including, importantly, the Cornish language revival,
e) an interest in primitive or untutored 'folk art' (including Cedric Morris, Christopher Wood, Alfred Wallis),
f) writing expressing or espousing new forms of 'natural' subjectivity particularly in the sphere of personal and sexual relations (eg Havelock Ellis and D.H. Lawrence).

In the post war period, the ambivalence towards industrial and technological progress that had become so characteristic of British culture, came to be embodied in the most celebrated works of the St Ives colony of modernist artists.

Many other aspects of the pre-war 'ruralist' agenda also evolved in the post-war period. These ideas and values reinforced Cornwall's rural 'otherness' and, for better or worse, contributed both to Cornwall's contemporary self-image, and to aspects of the expanded tourist industry that we see today.

---

[4] Relative to the rest of the UK, Cornwall industrialised and deindustrialised very early. It also had an unusual pattern of settlement, which resulted in no large urban centres, and a highly dispersed population. This is why Cornwall was, and is, considered 'rural' by most (Payton, 2004).

1. Mineral collectors

Landscape (painting) in the West was itself a symptom of modern loss, a cultural form that emerged only after humanity's primal relationship to nature had been disrupted by urbanism, commerce and technology. For when mankind still belonged to nature in a simple way, nobody needed to paint a landscape (Andrews, 1999)

In 1719 the poet Alexander Pope, using the proceeds from his best-selling translations of Homer, built a grand Palladian house in Twickenham. During the following two decades he created an elaborate underground grotto there, and lined its walls with 'three or four tunnes' of stones, gems and minerals from the mines of Cornwall.

The samples were sent to him by William Borlase, Rector of Ludgvan near Penzance, and the original request came via mutual friend: *I beg that you spare no cost in collecting a quantity, three or four tuns, of the finest spar mundick, copper and tin ores…and let them be packed up in hogsheads, and sent to London by one of the tinships* (Pool, 1986).

Borlase sourced collections of minerals for others including the botanist Linnaeus. He also inspired Phillip Rashleigh of Menabilly in Cornwall, to create his own grotto[5].

As was typical of his generation, Pope's sensibilities as well as his house in Twickenham, were shaped by his classical education, the Grand Tour, and by pastoral notions of the landscape derived from classical poetry.

---

[5] Rashleigh (1729-1811) made his grotto in the 1780s (see photo). His collection of minerals, which was housed at Menabilly, was ultimately purchased and presented to the RIC in 1902. Rashleigh produced two catalogues of the collection, the first, from 1797, was illustrated by Truro-born enamel painter and watercolourist Henry Bone. Later Menabilly was, famously, leased to Daphne Du Maurier for 25 years from 1943.

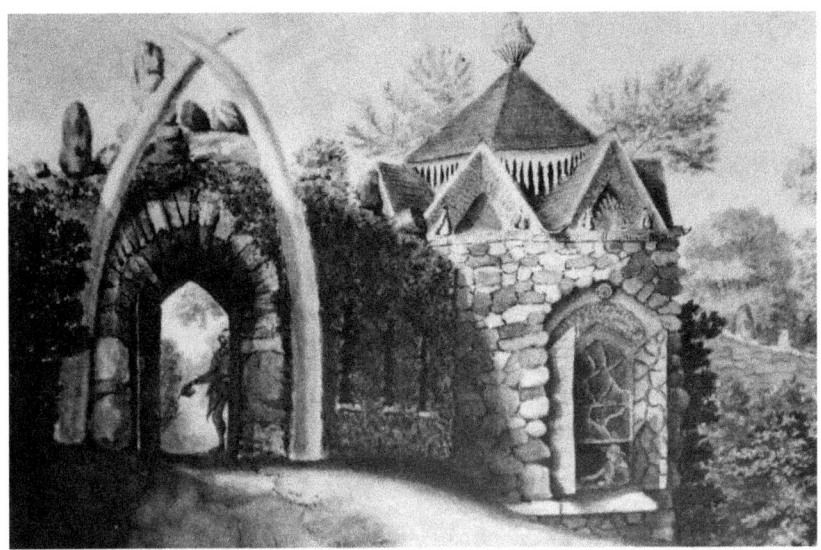

Rashleigh's Menabilly Grotto from a painting by G Boney 1806. The entrance arch was embellished with a whale's jawbone. Much later Menabilly was Daphne Du Maurier's home, and inspiration for 'Manderley'.

Joshua Reynolds, born in Plympton in 1723, went on his own Mediterranean Grand Tour in 1749. He had worked for several years as a portrait painter in Plymouth, based in a studio in the docks (now Devonport), where his patrons included the aristocratic families of Mount Edgcumbe and Port Eliot on the Cornish side of the Tamar[6].

For Reynolds, however, it was not enough to sustain a career, and he was to say later of Plymouth that it had *'the fewest admirers of pictures and prints... of any town of its size that I knew of.'* After settling in London he became the first, and most celebrated, President of the Royal Academy in 1768, and his success was partly thanks to the connections of Lord Edgcumbe, who helped him find commissions for his portraits.
Like Pope, Reynolds tended to look to the classical world, and to Italy and figurative painters like Michelangelo, for inspiration. However, in

---

[6] Several other Devonshire-born artists emerged from this same milieu, including Reynolds' own biographer James Northcote (b1746), his tutor Thomas Hudson (b1701) and, later Benjamin Robert Haydon (b1786) and Samuel Prout (b1783) the itinerant watercolourist.

the 1700s new aesthetic categories emerged, and with them new ways of evaluating art and experience. The 'sublime' was one: *Whatever is fitted in any sort to excite the ideas of pain, and danger, that is to say, whatever is in any sort terrible, or is conversant about terrible objects, or operates in a manner analogous to terror, is a source of the sublime; that is, it is productive of the strongest emotion which the mind is capable of feeling. I say the strongest emotion; because I am satisfied the ideas of pain are much more powerful than those which enter on the part of pleasure.* (Burke, 1759)

The 'picturesque' was another: *A piece of Palladian architecture may be elegant in the last degree. The proportion of its parts-the propriety of its ornaments-and the symmetry of the whole may be highly pleasing. But if we introduce it in a picture, it immediately becomes a formal object, and ceases to please. Should we wish to give it picturesque beauty, we must use the mallet, instead of the chissel; we must beat down one half of it, deface the other, and throw the mutilated members around in heaps. In short, from a smooth building we must turn it into a rough ruin. No painter, who had the choice of the two objects, would hesitate which to chuse.* (Gilpin, 1794)

Though here the writer, William Gilpin, is writing about architecture, his main interest was in landscapes. His books, all of which proved popular, described tours of the remote regions of Britain in search of picturesque views that matched the gorgeous if formulaic Italian paintings of Frenchman Claude Lorraine.

Gilpin visited Cornwall in 1775, but did not publish a response until 1808. Although impressed by the *'handsome town of Launceston'* he was indifferent regarding the rest of Cornwall; or at least what little he saw of it *'From Launceston we travelled as far into Cornwall as Bodmin, through a course naked country, and in all respects as uninteresting as can well be conceived. Of wood, in every shape, it was utterly destitute....We should have wished also to have heard the winds howl among the bleak promontories of the Lands-end; to have seen, through a clear evening, the light fall indistinctly on the distant isles of Scilly; and to have viewed the waves beating round the rocks of that singular*

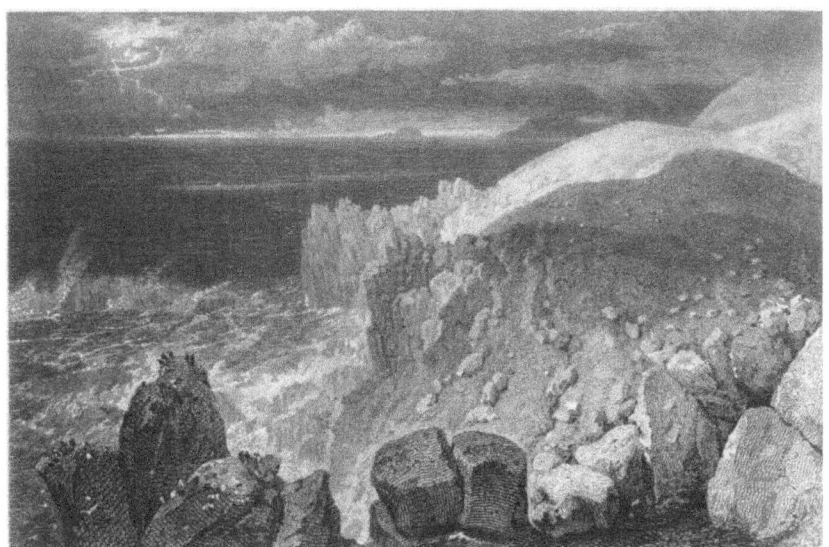

'Land's End, Cornwall'. Published in 'Picturesque Views on the Southern Coast of England' (1826) following JMW Turner's 3 month tour of Cornwall in 1811.

situation, Mount St Michael....But to travel over desarts of dreariness in quest of two or three objects seemed to be buying them at too high a price...

Because it was the elegant tree-framed paintings of Claude that provided the standard by which to recognize the picturesque, coastal and moorland landscapes apparently left him cold. Writers like Gilpin and Burke helped elevate the status of landscape art, however, which previously had been considered inferior to figurative art by Renaissance painters, and leading lights of the emerging British School: that is to say Joshua Reynolds and his contemporaries. They also encouraged the public to see the British landscape anew.

JMW Turner was one of the first to embrace and explore the potential of this new 'homegrown' landscape genre reproducing both a Claude-like 'picturesque' in his earlier paintings, and a triumphant 'sublime' later. Having been commissioned to illustrate the book 'Picturesque Views on the Southern Coast of England', Turner visited Cornwall in 1811, and stayed here for three months. He toured the Duchy, largely on foot, visiting and painting in Saltash, Looe, Fowey, Lostwithiel, St Mawes, Falmouth, Penzance, Mount's Bay, Land's End, St Ives, Redruth, Bodmin, Wadebridge, Padstow, Tintagel, Boscastle and Bude.

With paternal links to the South West (his father was from Devon), he returned to the Tamar Valley on a number of other occasions. His early debt to Claude is still evident, for example, in the tranquil 'Crossing The Brook', a depiction of the Tamar Valley painted in oil in 1815.

Turner was one of an extended generation of topographical artists who braved the rudimentary roads of Cornwall in the years before turnpikes. Samuel and Nathaniel Buck (c.f. 'Buck's Antiquities' 1734, which included studies of Tintagel, Pengersick, Pendennis and Launceston Castles), Joseph Farrington ('Britannia Depicta', 1813), William Daniell, Clarkson Stansfield and Thomas Allom (Devon and Cornwall Illustrated, 1832) all produced engravings for reproduction in travel books during the Georgian era[7]. During this period the idea of 'scenic pleasure touring' began to take hold among an English leisured class, who had started looking at the British landscape differently.

On his visits to Devon, Turner is known to have been accompanied by local artist Ambrose Bowden Johns, with whom he stayed. Johns (b. 1776) was, like James Leakey (b. 1775), one of the first of a large number of artists resident in Devon who would make extensive studies of its landscape. (Johns exhibited a Devonshire view at the RA as early as 1814.)

At the time, in the context of an expanding empire and war with Napoleonic France, the enthusiasm for Italian and classical art, architecture and poetry was receding. Native traditions - including folk tales - were described and celebrated instead, and in the case of Ossian, invented from new.

William Borlase, twenty years after finding gems for Pope's Augustan grotto, anticipated this changing situation in the introduction to his definitive 'Antiquities historical and monumental of the County of Cornwall' (1754; 2nd edition 1769): *It is the usual observation of*

---

[7] Sam Smiles has estimated that sixty topographical books relating to Devon and Cornwall were produced between 1800 and 1820 alone (Smiles, 2006)

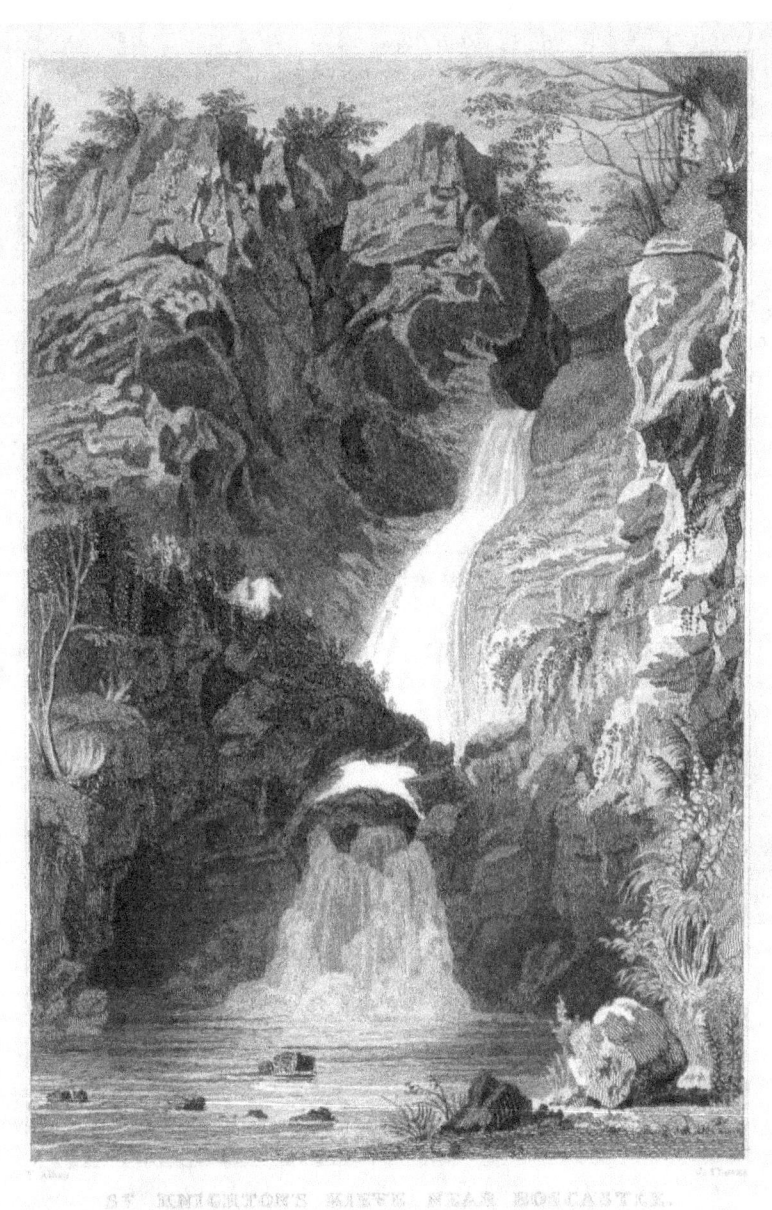

St Knighton's Kieve (now St Nectans Glen) near Boscastle. Published in 'Devon and Cornwall Illustrated' (1832) by Thomas Allom.

Foreigners that the English Travellers are too little acquainted with their own Country...Gentlemen return captivated with the Medals, Statues, Pictures and Architecture of Greece and Italy, they have seldom any relish for the ruder products of Ancient Britain.

The rise of Romanticism, therefore, saw the re-evaluation of more local European traditions. The word 'Celt' is derived from the Greek 'Keltoi', which was first used in the 5th century BC by Greek geographers to describe non-Greek speaking barbarians in North and Western Europe. It was re-introduced by George Buchanan in his *Rerum Scoticarum Historia* as early as 1582, however it was not until a century later that more sustained narratives appeared in the form of Paul Yves Pezron's *'L Antiquite de la Langue et de la Nation des Celtes'*, and importantly, Edward Lhuyd's *Archeologia Britannica* of 1707.

In this latter book, published in 1707, Lhuyd, who was director of the Ashmolean museum in Oxford, compares the vocabulary of 'Cornwal' with that of the other Celtic regions and demonstrates the close relationship of 'the original languages of Britain and Ireland' and of Brittany, calling them collectively 'Celtic'. He also speculates as to the migratory movements that would account for the distribution of the languages. From then on language was used as the principal cultural identifier at a time when national identities were changing[8] (Cunliffe, 2003).

Lhuyd's work was diligent and moderate: however more speculative books followed. The first volume of William Stukeley's *History of the Ancient Celts* appeared in 1740. Drawing from the writings of Julius Caesar, Pliny and Tacitus, Stukeley proposed that, rather than having been built by the Romans, Stonehenge and Avebury had been instead built by Celtic Druids: *Tho' Stonehenge be the proudest singularity of this sort, in the world, as far as we know: yet there are so many others, manifestly form'd upn the same, or kindred design, by the same measure, and for the same purpose, all over the Britanic isles; that we can have no room to doubt of their being made by the same people, and that by direction of the British Druids. There are innumerable, from the land's*

---

[8] The Treaty of Union with Scotland was signed in the same year that Lhuyd's book was published (1707)), and the concept of 'Britain' and 'The British' was gaining currency.

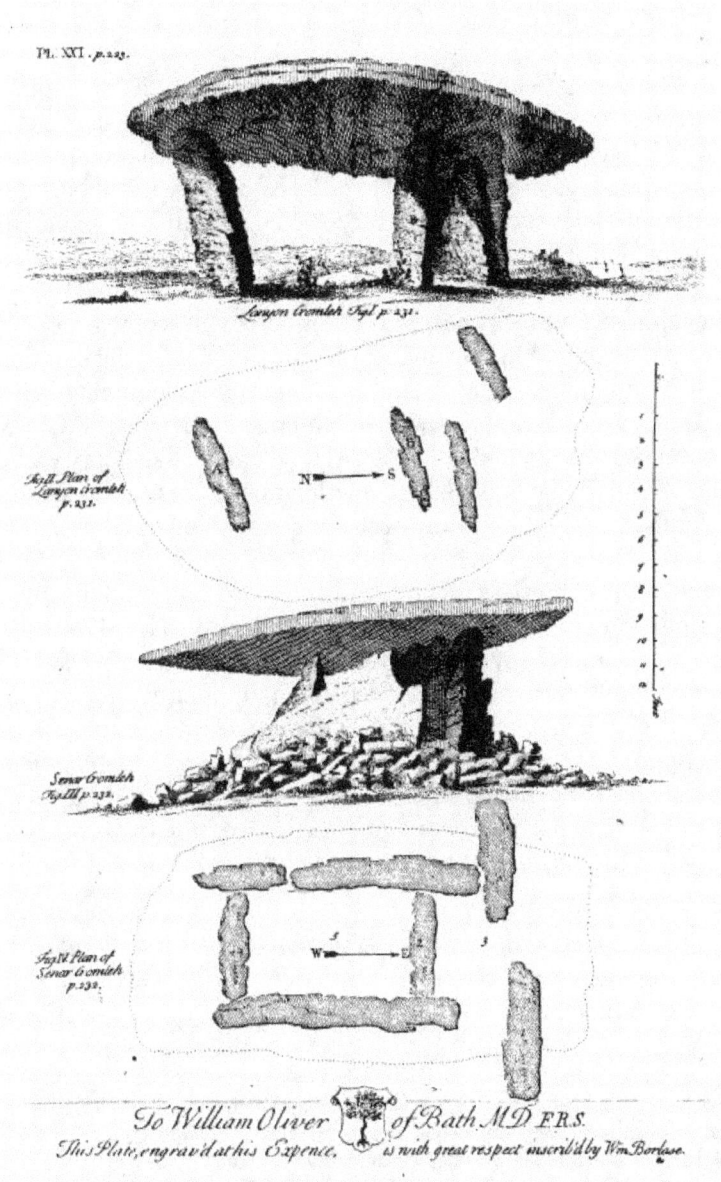

Lanyon and Zennor Cromlechs (or Quoits) from Borlase's *Antiquities* (1754). The 12.5 tonne capstone slipped off Zennor Quoit at some time after this drawing was made.

end in Cornwall, to the utmost northern promontory in Scotland, where the Romanpower never reach'd.

Most of Stukeley's fieldwork was carried out in the 1720's at a time when Freemasonry was spreading widely throughout British society and beyond. With its regalia and rituals, Freemasonry had started as a medieval stone-mason's guild, but by the 18th century it had become a supranational secret society attractive to scientists, atheists and all those who sought alternatives to existing religious dogma and institutions.

Stukeley, himself a Freemason, was described by his contemporaries as a deist (or pantheist). In his writing he, heretically, denied the doctrine of the Holy Trinity in referring to God as a unitary 'Divine Being'. He believed this was the God that was worshipped by Druids and Greek Neo-Platonists alike, and that the large stone circle at Avebury embodied this idea. Similarly he believed the interlocking circles of Stonehenge to represent the Neo-Platonic view of the universe (Hutton, 2009).

Reverend William Borlase, the mineral collector, follows Stukeley's lead in his pioneering book on Cornwall's antiquities (Borlase, 1754). However, as a more conventionally religious Anglican he is less sympathetic to the Druids, who he depicts in lurid terms: *It is in vain to enquire at what time this island of Britain first receiv'd its inhabitants ....this cannot be suppos'd to be very long after the dispersion of mankind at Babel...Like the people of Canaan and Moab (the Druids) dyed their altars with human gore. Groves they chose to worship in, as the Canaanites did...performing their sacred rites only under the consecrated oak*[9].

Pliny says that the Britans were so excessively devoted to all the mysteries of magic that they might seem to have taught even the Persians themselves that art ...It was general custom to chuse for their places of

---

[9] Borlase, as an Anglican rector, had an extensive knowledge of the Old Testament and of classical civilisations. Early in his book he suggests that Druids, like other Gentiles, strayed from the one true faith, ie that we can understand the Druids better by comparing them with other 'idolatrous' religions of the Mediterranean and Middle East. More than a third of the book consists of interesting but ultimately spurious descriptions of these other cultural practices, religious rites and architecture. For example, every unusual rock or rocky outcrop is imagined by Borlase as having been used by the druids for their gory ministrations and rituals; with Karn Bre (now Carn Brea) particularly singled out.

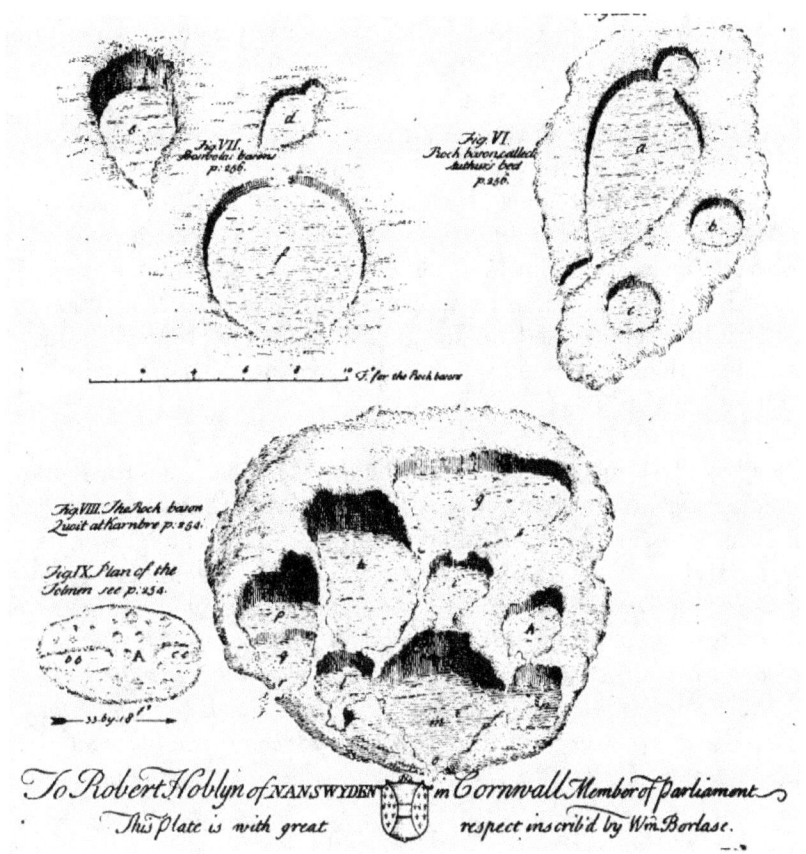

Rock 'basons' from Borlase's Antiquities (1754). Borlase believed the depressions in the rocks were carved by druids - and used in their 'horrid' rites.

worship Woods which stood on the tops of hills...The trees of this grove were all consecrated by sprinkling them with the blood of human victims...

That Altar which was for offering human victims must have been very different from what they used on less solemn occasions: there are many flat large rocks on Karnbre-hill which probably might have been appropriated to this horrid rite...of such holocaust Altars we have some I think remaining still in the higher parts of the parish of Gullval...

Borlase's work was widely read and contributed greatly to early

Romantic constructions of Cornwall[10]. Elsewhere the growing reaction against Neo-Classicism took other forms, with 'Gothic' another key strand within Romanticism that frequently intersected with Celticism. One of its early adopters, Horace Walpole was for 14 years MP of Callington in North Cornwall. Walpole published the counter-Enlightenment Gothic novel 'The Castle of Otranto' in 1764, having built his extraordinary house 'Strawberry Hill', in Twickenham only a few streets away from Pope's. Both Walpole's house, which was the antithesis to Pope's, and his novel were a tribute to pre-Reformation Northern European art and architecture, with the latter set in a Gothic castle, featuring strange and supernatural elements taken from medieval literature[11].

As well as Pre-Raphaelite painting, which was another manifestation of Medievalism, Gothic architecture was persuasively championed by art-critic and left-wing thinker Ruskin, notably in 'The Stones of Venice' (1851-53): *I am not sure when the word 'Gothic' was first generically applied to the architecture of the North but I presume that, whatever the date of its original usage, it was intended to imply reproach, and express the barbaric character of the nations among whom that architecture arose...the word Gothic became a term of unmitigated contempt, not unmixed with aversion. ..It is true, greatly and deeply true, that the architecture of the North is rude and wild; -but it is not true, that, for this*

---

[10] At the time William Borlase was writing, cultural change of a different order was taking place. Borlase was known to be actively opposed to the rise of Methodism in Cornwall in the 1700s: a process that started in 1743 when the Wesleys first visited. He saw Methodism as being, like Druidry, a repository of superstition and backwardness. Certainly the Methodists clung tenaciously on to fear of the devil. This was reflected in their attitudes to a range of related phenomena. For example, in 1768, following the Witchcraft Act of 1736, Wesley wrote '...the giving up of witchcraft is in effect giving up the bible' (Davies, Witchcraft Magic and Culture 1999).
[11] The term 'Cornish Gothic' has been used more recently in relation to the work of Daphne Du Maurier, the influential novelist who moved to Cornwall in the late 1920s. (cf Horner and Zlosnik *Daphne du Maurier: Writing, Identity and the Gothic Imagination*, (MacMillan Press, 1998). In the same book, Ella Westland says that 'By the 1790s it was no longer necessary to leave Britain in search of a rugged landscape which would inspire ecstasy, tranquility, sweet melancholy or Gothic horror .... The transformation of Cornwall in the English imagination depended on rocky shores and surging seas taking their place with dark forests and snowy summits as approved sites for romantic sublimity'.

reason, we are to condemn it, or despise. Far otherwise: I believe it is in this very character that it deserves our profoundest reverence.

Ruskin goes on to damn Classical architecture, on the basis that it was made by slaves, not free men: *Pagan in its origin, proud and unholy in its revival, paralysed in its old age... an architecture invented, as it seems, to make plagiarists of its architects, slaves of its workmen, and sybarites of its inhabitants; an architecture in which intellect is idle, invention impossible, but in which all luxury is gratified and all insolence fortified.*

He contrasts this with the characterful, 'savage', nature of medieval gothic: *In the mediaeval, or especially Christian, system of ornament, slavery is done away with altogether; Christianity having recognized, in small things as well as great, the individual value of every soul. But it not only recognizes its value; it confesses its imperfection, in only bestowing dignity upon the acknowledgment of unworthiness... go forth again to gaze upon the old cathedral front, where you have smiled so often at the fantastic ignorance of the old sculptors: examine once more those ugly goblins, and formless monsters, and stern statues, anatomiless and rigid; but do not mock at them, for they are signs of the life and liberty of every workman who struck the stone; a freedom of thought, and rank in the scale of being, such as no laws, no charters, no charities can secure; but which it must be first aim of all Europe at this day to regain for her children.*

Gothic-revival architecture went on to become the dominant style during the Victorian period. This is clearly evident in many late 19th century Cornish buildings, especially the Cathedral in Truro, built between 1880 and 1910 in the Perpendicular style, to designs by the Gothic revival architect John Loughborough Pearson.

2. Art in industrial Cornwall

Visual art and architecture made in Cornwall in the Georgian period reflects many of the cultural changes outlined in the previous chapter. For example there is clear evidence of a move from portrait painting to landscape painting occurring in the early 1800s.

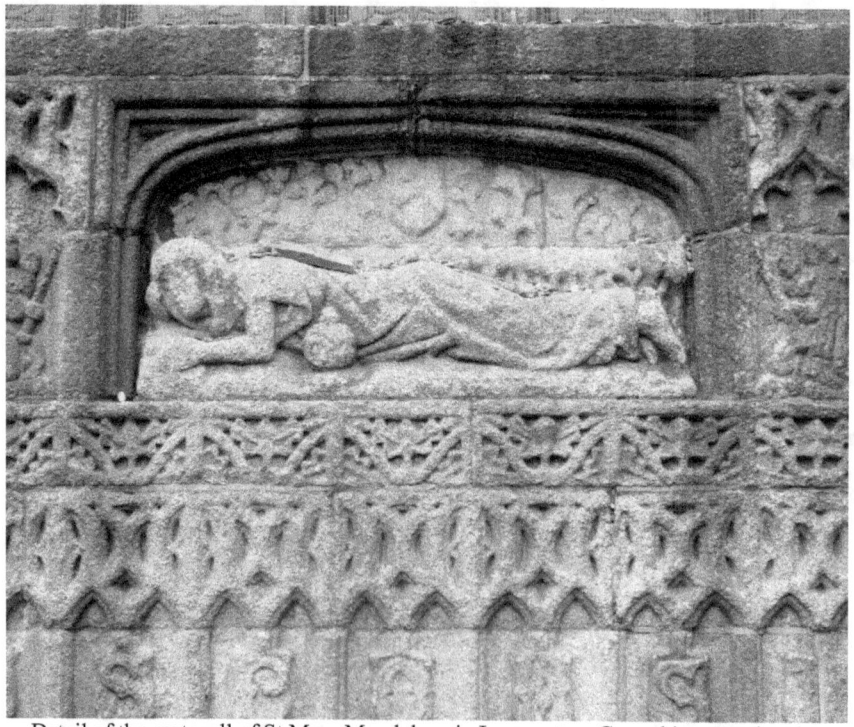

Detail of the east wall of St Mary Magdalene in Launceston. Carved into granite, the central image is of Mary prostrate before Christ. She has a bottle of spikenard oil next to her. (photo the author).

Most of the artworks produced in Cornwall prior to the 1700s had been made by anonymous craftsmen, and had 'savage' qualities as valorized by Ruskin. Here we could include the ornate carvings in stone on the outside of St Mary Magdalene, Launceston, and the mural of St Christopher in Breage church, for example[12].

Many 17th and 18th century portrait painters, sought out by those that could afford them, remain anonymous as they, too, did not always sign their works. This included James Gandy (b. 1619 – noted to be an inspiration to Joshua Reynolds), and his son William, both from Exeter, who would have travelled into Cornwall to find commissions (Pycroft, 1883).

Cornwall did not become a place conducive to supporting larger numbers of professional artists until after the railway came, but prior to this, just as Joshua Reynolds had done, a number of Cornishmen made the move to London either for apprenticeships, or to study at the Royal Academy which opened in 1768.

John Opie (b. 1761) (pronounced Oppy) who was born and grew up near Mithian, St Agnes, became the most renowned. After receiving some basic schooling, he was working as a carpenter when, aged 12, his ability to draw a good likeness was discovered by John Wolcot, a doctor living in Truro. Wolcot, who was some years older, acted as his manager and obtained hundreds of commissions from his patients, many of whom were Cornish landowners and aristocracy[13]. This, for example, included John St Aubyn of St Michael's Mount, who, in the 1770s secured a portrait of Dolly Pentreath (the Cornish language speaker) from Opie.

During these years, Opie developed his talent for portrait painting, learning by copying prints and etchings, and always aiming for as true a likeness as possible. When Opie was a boy there were no public or commercial galleries in Cornwall, and so the opportunity to look at other artists' work must have been limited. However, he would have visited

---

[12] The church bench ends at Altarnun, carved in the early 1500s, are not anonymous however, and include the following attribution: Robart Daye: Maker of this Worke.
[13] An Opie portrait of poet and historian Richard Polwhele survives from this time.

Dolly Pentreath by John Opie (detail). Now in St Michaels Mount, it would have been painted when Opie was still a teenager.

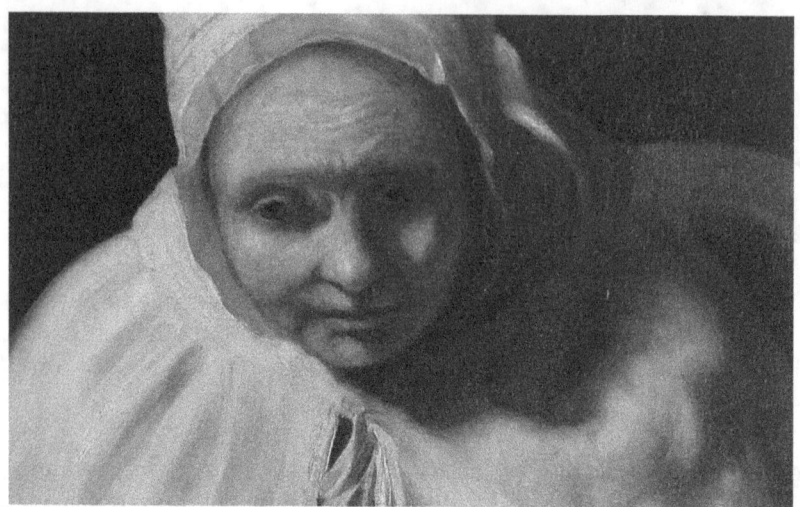

Advert for 'Harry's Museum': bookshop, artshop and music shop in Truro in 1801 in the first edition of The Royal Cornwall Gazette and Falmouth Packet.

the country houses of his patrons and there was also a network of bookshops and stationers in all the main towns in Cornwall, where he could have seen art books and prints of various kinds.

When he was twenty, Opie left for London, where he was introduced by Wolcot to Joshua Reynolds as completely untutored[14] (Hendra, 2007). Wolcot himself went on to become the well-known satirical writer, Peter Pindar, whilst Opie became Professor at The Royal Academy. His lectures there in the early 1800s were attended by the young JMW Turner, and the other landscape painters, like Farington, who helped arrange Opie's funeral when he died prematurely at the age of 46.

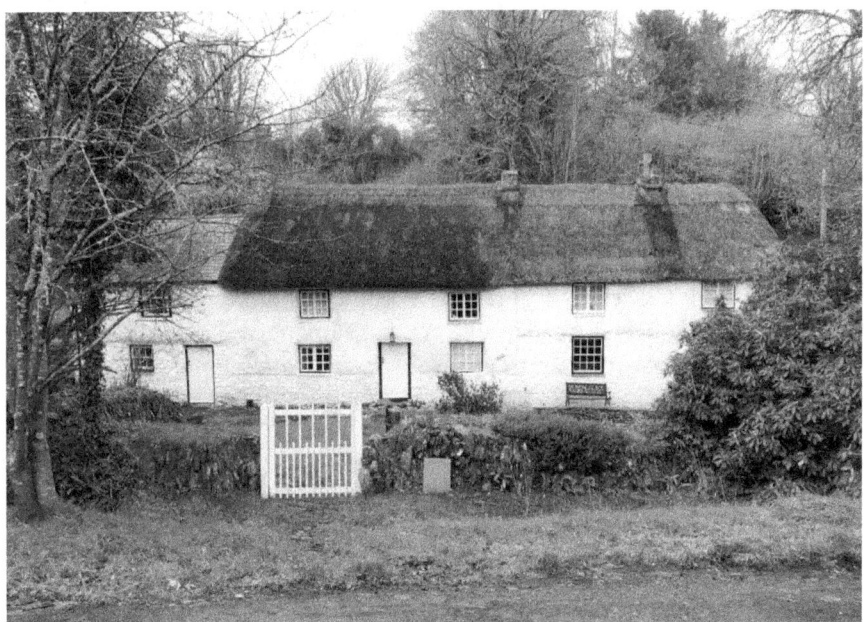

Harmony Cottage, Blowinghouse, Trevellas nr St Agnes. Birthplace and family home of John Opie (and Edward Opie). A commemorative slate plaque has been placed near the gate by the St Agnes Old Cornwall Society.

---

[14] Opie is alleged to have had a strong Cornish accent and crude manners. He also had a formidable intellect and, as well as rival artists, he was also close to a number of writers like proto-feminist Mary Wollstonecraft. His second wife, Amelia, was also a successful novelist and poet.

Henry Bone (b. 1755) and Joshua Cristall (b. 1767) were near contemporaries of Opie. Both were born in Cornwall (Truro and Camborne respectively), and were apprenticed in porcelain works as teenagers. Bone, who became best known as an enamellist and miniature painter, was also acquainted with Dr John Wolcot. Though based out of Cornwall for most of his career he received some important local commissions, including providing illustrations to Rashleigh's books on minerals. Cristall, similarly, is known to have visited Cornwall on several occasions after moving away. The Cornish landscape studies now in St Michael's Mount are some of his earliest known works (c1794), and would have been completed during the time he was training at the RA schools.

John Bryant Lane, born in 1788, is another who followed a similar though less exalted path as Opie more than twenty years later. Lane was 'discovered' by wealthy land-owner and MP, Francis Basset, Baron De Dunstanville of Tehidy, whilst still a schoolboy in Truro. Basset paid for him to attend the Royal Academy schools, and like Opie, Lane became a portrait painter, who would on occasion also tackle historical or biblical subjects. In 1808 Basset paid Lane for a large oil painting that would provide the altarpiece for the Trevenson Church on the Tehidy Estate, which he built to serve the growing mining community in Pool. It was exhibited at the Royal Academy (RA) that same year, before Basset, who had gone on his own 'Grand Tour' of Italy in 1777, supported his protégé to set up a studio in Rome in 1817. Lane only produced one substantial work, 'The Vision of Joseph' during his ten years there. Bizarrely, when it was finished, the Pope thought that it portrayed Joseph with a pair of horns, and as a result Lane was expelled from the country.

Neville Northey Burnard, famous in Cornwall for sculpting the Lander Monument in Truro (erected in 1852), was the son of a stonemason who learnt his craft studying the ornate carvings in the churches of East Cornwall: the exterior of Launceston and Fowey and the interior benches of the church in his own home village, Altarnun. Born in 1818, Burnard was in the first wave of local artists to show at the Royal Cornwall Polytechnic Society (RCPS) in Falmouth which opened in 1834 (he was 16 at the time), and as a result of this exposure was introduced to Queen Victoria by Sir Charles Lemon, MP, first President of the Polytechnic (Martin, 1978).

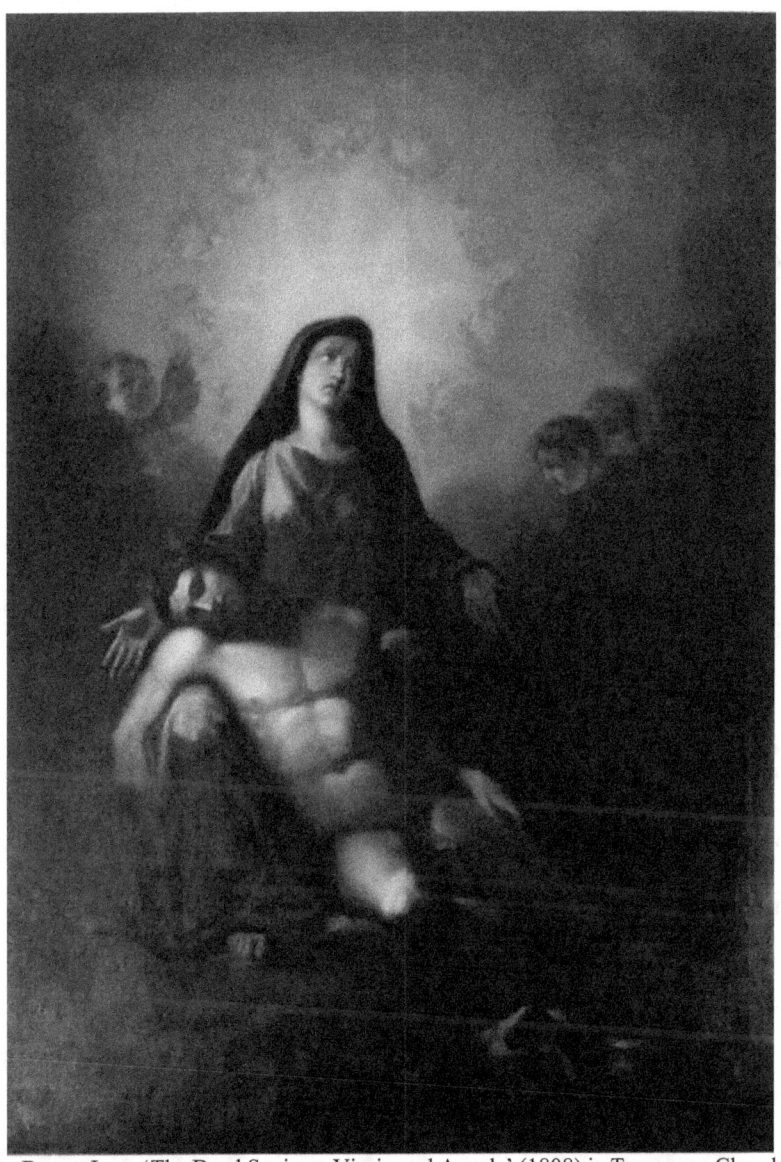

John Bryant Lane 'The Dead Saviour, Virgin and Angels' (1808) in Trevenson Church. It was rescued from a chicken coop in Penzance and restored in 2013. Photo the author.

The Polytechnic, or Poly as it is now known, was set up in 1834 as an educational establishment by local industrialists and philanthropists. It followed hard on the heels of the Royal Institution of Cornwall[15] but tended to be highly eclectic, and included paintings and sculpture by local artists alongside more scientific exhibits in its annual exhibitions. Its records, in the form of annual reports, are exhaustive and well preserved, and provide the best source of information on artists resident in Cornwall in the early to mid 19th century.

The names that crop up most frequently in the reports are the RCPS annual prize winners. As well as Burnard, those awarded prizes in the 'professional' categories are James George Philp, Philip Mitchell, Richard T Pentreath and, to a lesser extent, John Grenfell Moyle and Edward Opie (b 1810 – great-nephew to John).

Two painters based in Plymouth were also fairly regular contributors to the exhibitions in the mid 1800s. They were William Williams (b1808), originally from Penryn, and Nicholas Matthew Condy, son of landscape painter and namesake Nicholas Condy. Both also showed at the Royal Academy (RA). (Williams showed landscapes painted around the South West, whilst Condy junior showed paintings of boats).

Not all were fully professional. J.G. Moyle (b1817)[16], for example, was a doctor who worked on the Isles of Scilly, whilst R.T. Pentreath, was noted in the judges' reports as being 'barely tutored'. Philip Mitchell (b1814), another of the Polytechnic 'regulars' was born in Devonport, but moved to Falmouth aged 14 *'and there became acquainted with Philp and Williams, and with them he used to go a-sketching'* (Pycroft, 1883).

---

[15] Founded in 1818 as the Cornwall Literary and Philosophical Institution, the Royal Institution of Cornwall (RIC) was one of the earliest of seven similar societies established in England and Wales during the 19th century. These voluntary bodies typically founded a library and museum, offered a lecture programme and scientific demonstrations, and gave instruction to the local working class population, well before state education was available.

[16] See artcornwall.org 'The Sailing Surgeon'.

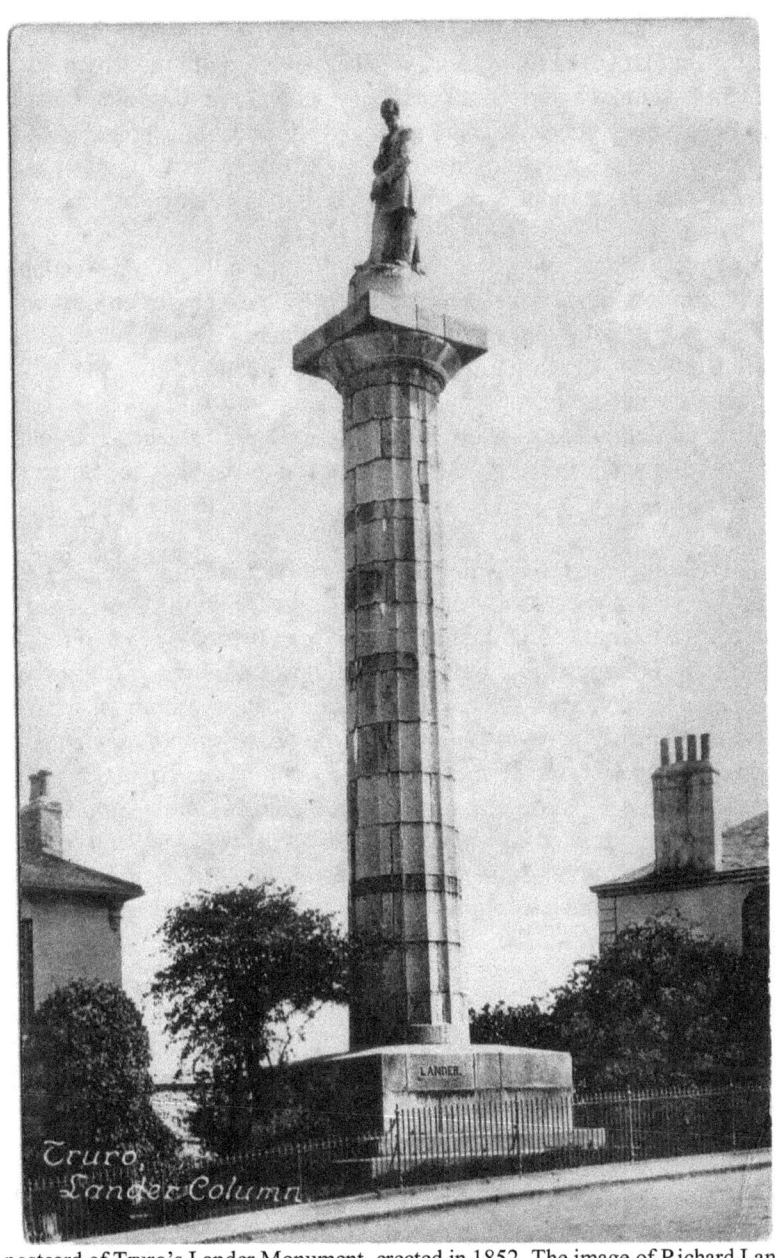

A postcard of Truro's Lander Monument, erected in 1852. The image of Richard Lander was carved by Neville Northey Burnard.

Later (1839) he is mentioned in adverts for Truro Grammar School as the 'Painting and Drawing tutor', and, indeed, according to the Royal Cornwall Gazette, he appears to have supplemented his income by teaching for many years, offering private tuition from his house in Lemon Villa before later moving back to Devon, and teaching in Plymouth and Tavistock Grammar School.

Many of these artists managed to show regularly at the Royal Academy (RA) in London, despite the fact that travel by coach between London and Penzance took up to a week. As a young man Pentreath worked as a servant for the St Aubyn family of St Michael's Mount, also, like Opie and Cristall benefitting from their support and patronage. He showed portraits and depictions of Mounts Bay at the RA on consecutive years between 1844 and 1852. His address at the time was Clarence Street, Penzance[17].

The Polytechnic's judging panel, led by Charles Lemon, frequently loaned pictures in their own collections to the exhibitions there. This included, for example, an oil painting by Titian owned by G.C. Fox. The report of 1841 suggests that through no fault of their own, most of the local artists were viewed as very much second rate by comparison: *In Italy and even in France and Germany....the possession of admirable works adorning ecclesiastical buildings or the influence of endowed academies of the Fine Arts....have matured so much of taste and skill as to reduce mere crudeness and imbecility to their proper estimation...In England....in the hurry of commercial competition and the manly activity of public life, there seems to have been little leisure and certainly has been small apparent zeal for the study of the Beautiful.*

There is therefore a strong sense that aesthetic standards were set elsewhere, still based on a Classical or Italian standard, and skills and technical prowess. In both regards, the Cornish artists were considered to

---

[17] J.G. Philp showed at the RA, but this was more than 10 years after he exhibited at the Poly, during a period when he lived in London. Edward Opie moved between the West Country (St Agnes and Plymouth) and London, having been brought up, like John Opie, in Harmony Cottage in Mithian. He showed 49 pictures at the RA between 1839 and 1886, many of them country scenes set in Cornwall.

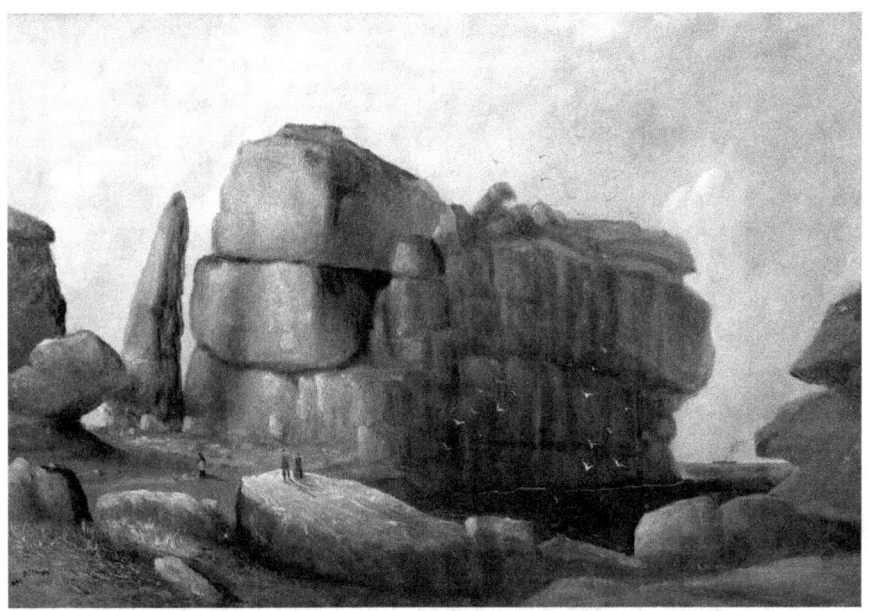

J.G. Moyle 'Tooth Rock, Penninis Head' 1892 (photo the author).

be lagging behind, never in a position to develop a distinctive style or voice of their own.

Inspired by the example of the Polytechnic, other 'learned' institutions in Cornwall mounted occasional exhibitions. The Royal Cornwall Gazette reports effusively on a Royal Institution of Cornwall exhibition in Truro during the summer of 1840, consisting of more than 200 pictures, curated by 'Mr Philip Michell' and (the architect) 'Mr P. Sambell'.

The exhibition was ostensibly a failed attempt to raise funds for the Royal Institution of Cornwall (RIC), but it was also an opportunity for the dignitaries associated with the Poly, as well as other local landowners, like Sir H. Vivian and Lady Basset to show off their art collections. Paintings by Opie senior and junior, were included, and as well as G C Fox's ubiquitous Titian, there were three Rembrandts, and a Van Dyck on show as well as lesser artists of Renaissance Italy and Spain. It may be significant that, for reasons best known to the organizers, the works were *'for the greater part ...not the production of living artists'*.

The newly formed 'Truro Institution' also put on an ambitious exhibition in 1847 which, in its eclecticism and inclusion of scientific models and curios, seems to have been a reprisal of the Polytechnic shows. Thanks are expressed for contributions by NN Burnard, together with 'Mr Chadwick, the sculptor of Exeter', 'Mr Philp of Falmouth', 'Mr Caunter for a Head of Christ', and to 'Mr (Robert) Whale for several pictures'. 'Mr (William) Williams of Plymouth' was also singled out for praise for the painting 'Morning after the Storm'. (RCG 22nd October1847)

> rance of the country, and so nearly exhausted its resources.
> PAINTINGS.—The exhibition opened this day, at the Royal Institution, contains some very valuable paintings by the great masters, sent in from the best collections in the county. There is also a large number of paintings in oil and water colours by modern artists, many of which will be found to possess considerable merit.—The selection and arrangement of the pictures has occupied for many weeks the diligent attention of the Committee, and the active and unwearied exertions of Mr. Philip Michell, artist, and Mr. P. Sambell. Considerable expense has been bestowed on this experiment on the taste of the Cornish public for one of the most interesting of the Fine Arts; and we hope that it will not prove to have been bestowed in vain, but that on the contrary the proceeds of the exhibition, at the almost nominal price of admission, will leave some surplus for the benefit of the Institution.
> TRURO.—On Sunday last, His Serene Highness the Hereditary Prince of Saxe Coburg-Gotha, eldest brother

Royal Cornwall Gazette (RCG), 1840

In September 1853 Penzance School of Art opened under headmaster Henry Geoffroi (Hardie, 2009). For more than twenty years it occupied the Regent House Academy building (or Old Regents House), until 1881, when it went to purpose-built premises on Morrab Road[18].

A second art-school had opened in Truro in October 1854 in a room in the Town Hall buildings, under a different master, Mr Gill. In 1874

---

[18] Proceeds from the profits of the Great Exhibition of 1851 were used to set up the Government Science and Art Department in Kensington in 1853. The new department, and its grants, helped support a network of new art and design schools in the provinces, including those in Penzance and Truro. Falmouth School of Art, meanwhile, was founded later, in 1902 by Anna Maria Fox, one of the family of Foxes heavily involved with the Poly.

Geoffroi took on the mastership of both schools, however, after the Truro school had run into difficulties: *'the little life it possessed entirely died out about twelve months ago…when Dr Barham (president)…succeeded in persuading Mr Geoffroi to undertake the mastership* (RCG Jan 2nd 1875).

Both schools provided prize-winners at the Poly, and exhibitions largely of works sent down from the South Kensington Department of Science and Art.

It is worth noting again that, compared with Opie's generation, mid-century Cornish artists (eg the group of artists involved with the Polytechnic in its earliest years) were much more likely to paint landscapes. Thus by the 1840s, depictions of unspoilt, picturesque views had become common-place amongst artists resident in Devon and Cornwall.

It has been argued that the Cornish, at least for a century or so, saw their self-identity as strongly bound to the mines, the mining industry, and to the technological innovations of scientists like Trevithick and Davy which it inspired. It is notable, however, that during the 1800s, whilst boats, fishermen, harbours, and coasts are plentiful, very few images of industrial (mining) Cornwall were produced either by resident or visiting artists.

Undoubtedly, St Michael's Mount was the most popular landscape subject. Thomas Luny, born in Cornwall in 1759 but mainly based in London and Devon, completed at least six substantial oils depicting the island (though his magical scenes with their dramatic skies and seas appear to have been painted from memory). Farington captured three different views of it for his 'Britannia Depicta', Opie – not known for his landscapes – is known to have painted it at least twice, and even Pentreath's portrait of Dolly Pentreath includes this distinctive landmark.

In contrast, apart from a celebrated painting by James Clarke Hook (1864), who came as a visitor, there are few significant 19th century painted images of miners or mines.

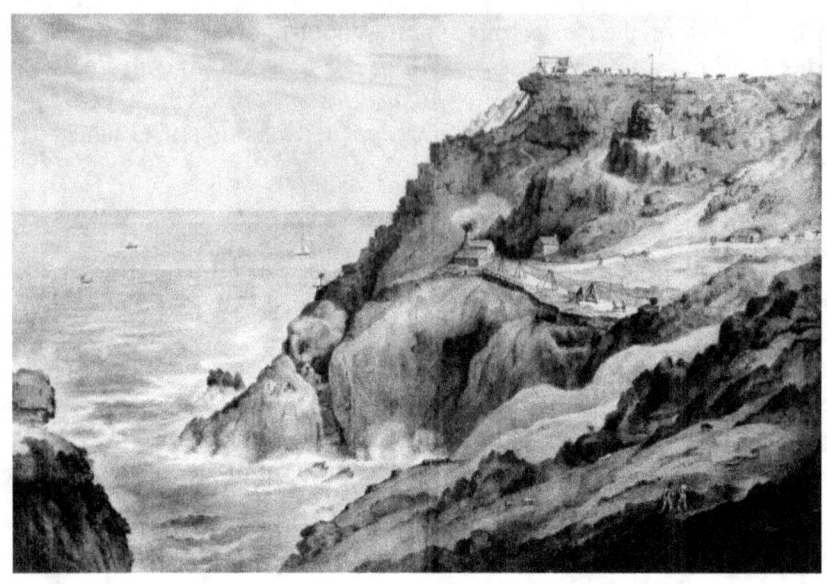

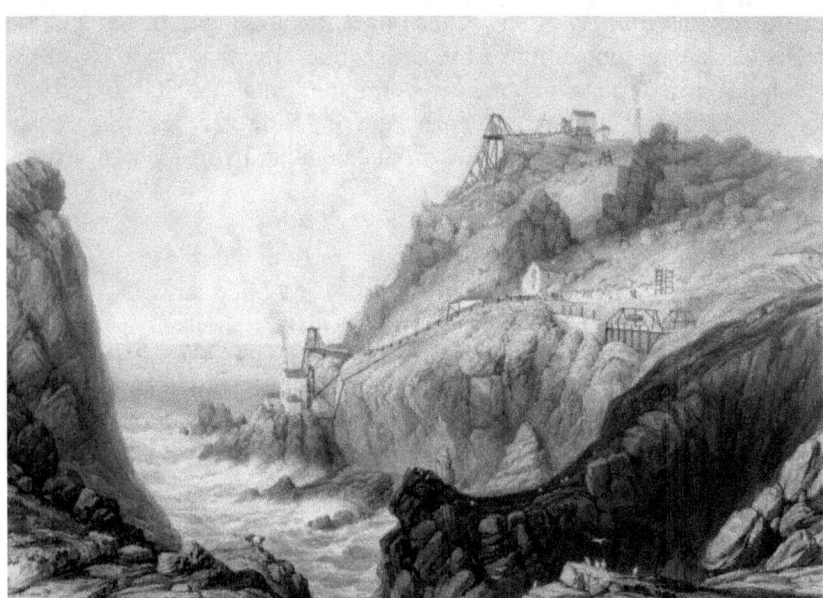

Botallack Mine by I. Tonkin 1822 (above top). Tonkin advertised for subscribers to this print in the Royal Cornwall Gazette (RCG). Some years later Philip Mitchell made an etching of Botallack from the same vantage point (in 1840 – above bottom).

The most obvious explanation is that they weren't considered suitable subjects for painting: that is, they did not conform to what had become established conventions regarding the picturesque or sublime. It is somewhat surprising that wealthy mine-owners and industrialists in Cornwall didn't commission more works, however.

Writers were perhaps marginally more inclined to acknowledge those parts of Cornwall that had become industrialized. John Harris, who was born in 1820 near Camborne, was sent to work in Dolcoath mine at the age of 12. As a writer he offers unique insights in this regard. His autobiography describes his first precarious descent into the mine workings: *descending the ladders, nearly sixty or seventy in number, was a fearful task...My father went before with a rope fastened to his waist, the other end of which was fastened to my trembling self. If my hands slipped from the rounds of the ladder, perhaps my father might catch me, or the sudden jerk might pull us both into the darkness to be bruised to death on the rocks...Sometimes the ladder went down through the middle of a huge cavern, warping and shaking at every step...sometimes we had to climb over craggy rocks jutting into the void, where a slip of the foot would be our doom...*

In 1857 Harris left the mines and moved to Falmouth to take up a position as a Bible-reader. Here he became acquainted with the Fox family, and visited their home at Penjerrick. Harris has been viewed as the first poet anywhere in the world to engage with processes of industrialization (Kent, 2000), and his poem, The Mine, published in 1860 matches Turner in its evocation of sublime terror:

> *Hast ever seen a mine? Hast ever been*
> *Down in its fabled grottoes, wali'd with gems,*
> *And canopied with torrid mineral-belts,*
> *That blaze within the fiery orifice?*
> *Hast ever, by the glimmer of the lamp,*
> *Or the fast-waning taper, gone down, down,*
> *Towards the earth's dread centre, where wise men*
> *Have told us that the earthquake is conceived,*
> *And great Vesuvius hath his lava-house,*
> *Which burns and burns for ever, shooting forth*
> *As from a fountain of eternal fire?*

Harris is sometimes compared to his near contemporary Robert Hawker (Harris was 17 years his junior), another Cornish poet, who lived and worked as an Anglican clergyman, like Borlase, resistant to the rise of Methodism[19].

Methodism took root in the mining communities of West and Mid Cornwall, partly because of new patterns of settlement that the industry brought with it. This is probably why Hawker, based in less industrial North Cornwall, rarely speaks of the mines. His focus is elsewhere (Kent, 2000).

His Grail poem 'The Quest of the Sangraal', was published in 1864. Arthur - a Celtic king who possibly fought against the Anglo-Saxons during the 5th century - first appears as a literary figure in ballads derived from Geoffrey of Monmouth's 12th century 'History of the Kings of Britain'. This, the 'Matter of Britain', also identifies Tintagel in North Cornwall as the site of Arthur's conception and birth, and Slaughter-bridge (near Camelford) the site of his demise at the hands of Mordred.

Lord Alfred Tennyson, author of 'Idylls of the King' (1859-1885), the key text in the Victorian revival of King Arthur, visited Cornwall on a number of occasions wanting to see these sites for himself. In 1848 whilst staying in Bude, he sought out Robert Hawker at his vicarage in Morwenstow. Together they travelled to Tintagel, as Hawker's journal explains: *'Seated on the brow of the Cliff, with Dundagel full in sight, he revealed to me the purpose of his journey to the West. He is about to conceive a Poem - the hero King Arthur - the Scenery in part the vanished Land of Lyonesse, between the Mainland and the Scilly Isles. Much converse then and there befel of Arthur and his Queen, his wound at Camlan and his prophesied return. Legends were exchanged, books noted down and references given.'*

---

[19] Henry Jenner (1904) suggests that the rise of Methodism in Cornwall was due to the imposition of the Book of Common Prayer: *Had the Book of Common Prayer been translated into Cornish and used in that tongue… the Cornish as a body might have been of the Church of England, instead of remaining of the old religion until the perhaps unavoidable neglect of its authorities caused them to drift into the outward irreligion from which John Wesley rescued them.*

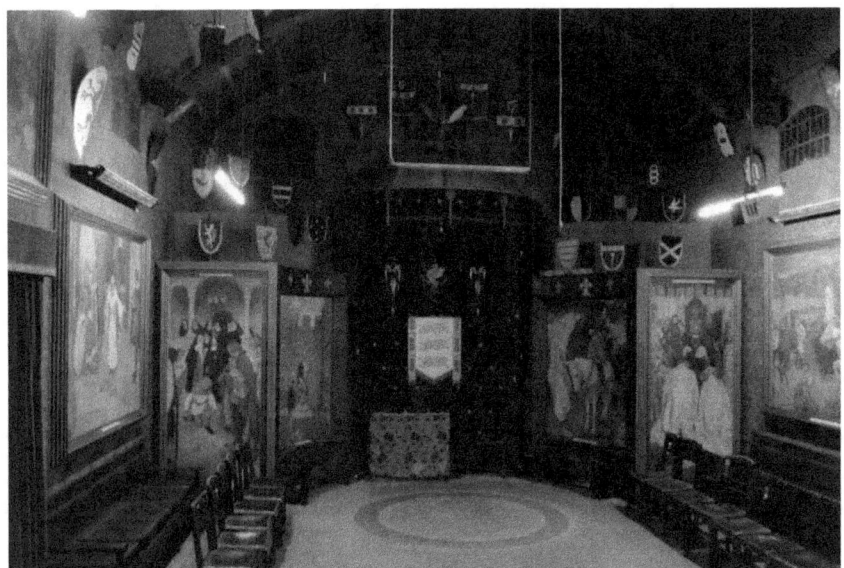

King Arthur's Halls, Tintagel. Opened in 1933, having been built by custard magnate Frederick Glasscock, it is currently open to the public as a tourist attraction. It houses paintings by William Hatherell and stained glass windows by Veronica Whall. Photo the author.

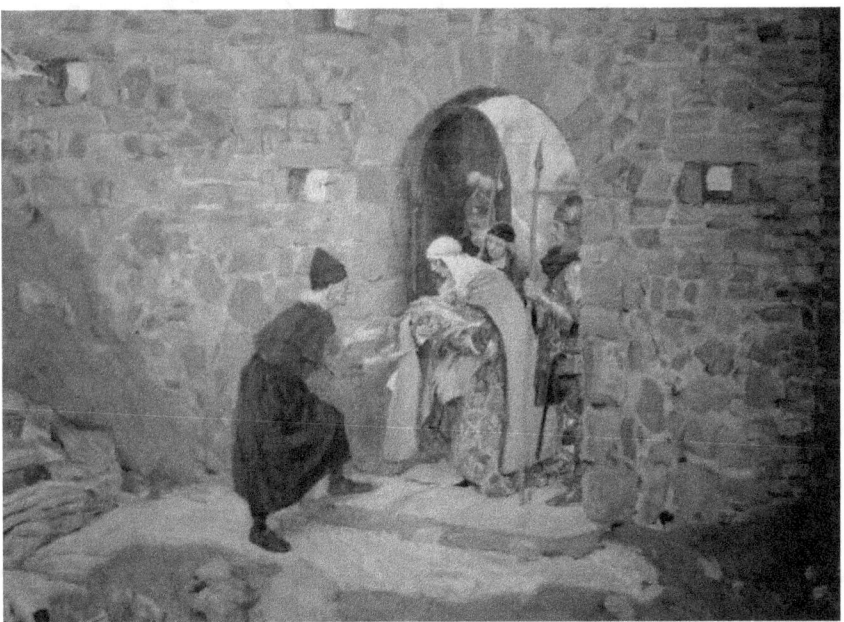

The baby Arthur is given to Merlin: detail of a painting by William Hatherell in King Arthur's Halls.

Tennyson was ready to believe that he was viewing Arthur's castle itself, though now, of course, it is accepted that the ruins on the headland date from the 13th century. Some days later he visited the site of the battle of Camlan: *June 7th: Slaughter bridge, clear brook among alders. Sought for King Arthur's stone, found it at last by a rock under two or three sycamores…*[20]

Tennyson's poem boosted Tintagel's reputation as a centre of Arthuriana, and in 1899 King Arthur's Castle Hotel (now Camelot Castle) was constructed in roughly the same spot that Tennyson and Hawker would have sat together. Designed by Cornish architect Silvanus Trevail from his office at the bottom of Lemon Street in Truro, it was one of a series of similar grand hotels then built in the Duchy (Great Western Hotel, Newquay, 1879, Carbis Bay Hotel, 1894, Headland Hotel Newquay 1900).

---

[20] An association of Arthur with Slaughterbridge, and its inscribed stone, had been known for many years. Borlase (1754) describes a garden created with the stone as a centre-piece: *"This inscrib'd Stone, nine feet nine inches long and two feet three inches wide, was formerly a foot bridge near the late Lord Falmouth's seat of Worthyvale. It was called Slaughter Bridge, and, as tradition says, from a bloody battle fought on this ground, fatal to the great King Arthur. A few years since, the present Lady Dowager Falmouth, shaping a rough kind of hill, about 100 yards off, with spiral walks, remov'd this stone from the place where it served as a bridge, and building a low piece of masonry for it's support, plac'd it at the foot of her improvements, where it still lyes in one of the natural grotts of the hill.'*

3. Legend-land: the folklorists

The revival of interest in King Arthur emerged as part of a wider interest in British folklore and Celticism, and in the years either side of the opening of Brunel's railway in 1859[21], several collections of Cornish folklore were published.

Shortly before publishing 'The Quest of the Sangraal', Revd Hawker had collaborated with a young artist from Penzance called J.T. Blight on the book 'Ancient Crosses of East Cornwall'[22]. Blight was born in 1835, and was a beneficiary of the Penzance Library, which opened in 1818 amidst the magnolia trees of Morrab Gardens. In 1857, at the age of 21, Blight published the companion volume 'Ancient Crosses and Other Antiquities in the West of Cornwall', and in the introduction describes his motivation for doing so: *The destruction of many monuments of remote antiquity which formerly existed in the West of Cornwall, and the mutilation which several others have sustained by mischievous and ignorant persons, have induced the author to attempt the present work, in order to preserve the forms of those remains which are so valuable to the Antiquary and the Historian.*

Blight explains that some of the ancient crosses he depicted would have been erected as long ago as AD 500, at a time when Christianity had completely died out in most other parts of Britain, but had very recently been brought to Cornwall by Irish saints, like St Piran. At the time, the early church did not have stone buildings as we know them now, but merely *'small huts made of wattles'*.

---

[21] The first tramway in Cornwall is thought to have been built between Redruth and Chacewater in 1809. The wagons were horse-drawn. Hayle Railway, which was partly steam-powered, first carried passengers in 1841, having opened in 1837. This became part of West Cornwall Railway which in 1852 linked Truro to Penzance. After the Saltash Bridge was completed in 1859, Brunel's railway then linked Truro to London.
[22] The relationship between the two men, which at times was strained, is described in 'A Short Life at The Land's End' by Earth Mysteries writer, John Michell (Michell, 1977).

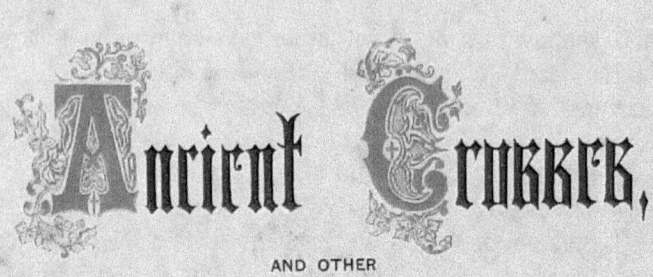

Ancient Crosses,

AND OTHER

ANTIQUITIES

IN THE EAST OF CORNWALL.

BY

J. T. BLIGHT.

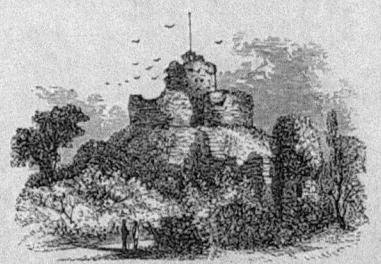

Launceston Castle.

LONDON: SIMPKIN, MARSHALL, AND CO.   DUBLIN: HODGES AND SMITH.

PENZANCE: F. T. VIBERT.

1858.

Both Blight's books were important early additions to the burgeoning literature on Celtic Cornwall, and are copiously illustrated with the author's own delicate line drawings. They complement William Borlase's 'Antiquities of Cornwall', and related historical works by poet and historian Richard Polwhele. Indeed there are frequent references to the former, especially in explaining the superstitions attached to the holy wells of East and West Cornwall: *The spread of Christianity occasioned the dedication of many of the springs to which miraculous virtues had been ascribed to Patron Saints... and over these, small edifices were set up which were used as Oratories and Baptistries, or for other religious purposes...Dr Borlase says that the Druids pretended from the several waves and eddyes which the river water exhibited to foretell with great certainty the event of battles; a way of Divining still usual amongst the vulgar in Cornwall...Faith in the efficacy of the water at St Madron's Well is not yet lost for on the first Sunday in May a great number of persons take their children there, that by immersion in the spring water, they may be strengthened if weak and cured if diseased. After the visitation small pieces of rags and bandages will be found fastened on the surrounding bushes...*

J.T. Blight's later works include the more informal guidebook 'A Week at The Lands End' (1861) together with 'A list of the Antiquities in the hundreds of Kirrier and Penwith' (1862), and 'Churches of West Cornwall' (1865).

Blight went on to illustrate William Bottrell's 'Traditions and Hearthside Stories of West Cornwall' (Vol 2. 1873) and is known to have approached folklorist Robert Hunt requesting that he also provide illustrations for the major work 'Romances of the West of England (or The Drolls, Traditions and Superstitions of Old Cornwall)' published in 1865. However Blight ultimately struggled to make ends meet and he ended up penniless in Bodmin Lunatic Asylum.

Robert Hunt, the folklorist, was one of the most interesting members of the Royal Cornwall Polytechnic Society (RCPS) in Falmouth. Born in 1807, he was a polymath, who trained in medicine in London, and ultimately worked as a chemist (pharmacist).

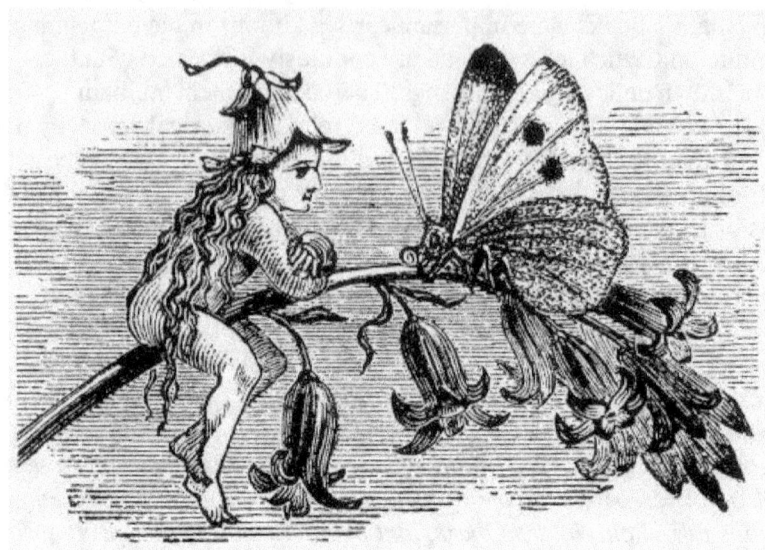
An illustration from Bottrell's 'Traditions and Hearthside Stories' by J.T.Blight

He invented some of the first photographic paper, and after taking up a post as secretary to the RCPS wrote the first manual of photography in 1841[23]. He also developed the actinograph, a device used to measure the chemical intensity of light.

Hunt is, however, now best remembered for his book of folklore. It is hugely ironic that this catalogue of superstition and magic should have been produced alongside his scientific work, as it is very much a record and celebration of an older, pre-scientific world.

Hunt himself acknowledges the subversive qualities of the work in the preface to the third volume: *While correcting the pages for a new edition, a scientific friend, who was deep in the cold thrall of positivism, called upon me. He noticed the work upon which I was engaged and remarked 'I suppose you invented most of these stories'. In these days when our most sacred things are being sneered at, and the poetry of life*

---

[23] Photography was an endeavour strongly nurtured by a number of the scientifically curious members of the Polytechnic, and in fact Charles Lemon was closely related to Fox Talbot who is known to have taken some very early photos at Carclew, Lemon's stately home outside Falmouth.

is being repressed by the prose of a cold infidelity, this remark appears to render it a necessity to assure my readers that none of the legends in this volume have been invented...

Importantly, he is also conscious of the impact of the arrival of the railway in Cornwall. He mentions the 'wild savage beauty' of Dartmoor and the moorlands of Cornwall, and says: *The railways give great facilities for visiting those scenes of which the public readily avail themselves. But they have robbed the West of England of half its interest, by dispelling the spectres of romance which were in hoar antiquity, the ruling spirits of the place.*

Robert Hunt was one of the first folklorists active in England (Dorson, 1968). He collected stories over a period of around 35 years, also continuing to do so whilst in post with the RCPS: *As its secretary my duties took me often into the mining and agricultural districts...Away from the towns at a period when the means of communication were few, and those few tedious primitive manners still lingered. Education was then not as now the fashion.*

He clearly viewed the folktales of Cornwall, including the belief in fairies and giants, to be residual traces of a more ancient Celtic world-view: *When our Celtic ancestors – in the very darkness of their ignorance – were taught through their fears a Pantheistic religion, and saw a god in every grand phenomenon: then was moulded the Celtic mind, and the early impressions have never been completely obliterated....These wild dreams which swayed with irresistible force the skin-clad Briton of the Cornish hills, have not yet entirely lost their power where even the British schools and Mechanics Institutions are diffusing the truths of science...*

It was a world view preserved in Cornwall especially, because of its inaccessibility: *It must not be forgotten that Cornwall has until a recent period maintained a somewhat singular isolation. England with many persons appeared to terminate on the shores of the River Tamar...The difficulties of travelling in Cornwall were great. Within my own memory the ordinary means of travelling from Penzance to Plymouth was by a van called a 'kitterine' and three days were occupied in the journey...The difficulty of transit explains the seclusion of the people...and to it we certainly owe the preservation of their primitive character...*

Hunt also comments on the fact that newspapers were also not available, and so communication was by other means: *They were informed of the active life of the world beyond them by the traveling historian only who as he also sought to amuse the people, was called the 'droll-teller'...In 1829 there still existed two of those droll-tellers, and from them were obtained a few of the stories here preserved.*

His folklore book incorporates stories taken from a number of sources including other collectors like William Bottrell, T.Q. Couch, and C. Taylor Stephens[24] all of whom he thanks before concluding: *Romances such as these have floated down to use as wreck upon the ocean. We gather a fragment here and a fragment there, and at length it may be we learn something of the name and character of the vessel when it was freighted with life, and obtain a shadowy image of the people who have perished...*

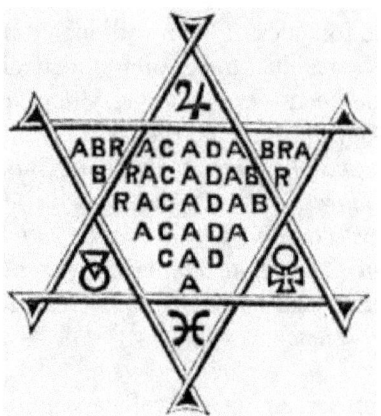

Drawing of charm from Bottrell's 'Traditions...'

---

[24] Hunt acknowledges the earlier efforts of other folklorists, like Mrs Bray of Tavistock (author of Legends, Superstitions and Sketches of Devonshire (1836) written in the form of letters to the Poet Laureate Robert Southey), and J.O. Halliwell (who published 'Rambles in Western Cornwall, by the Footsteps of Giants' in 1861; an early tourist guide partly inspired by Borlase).

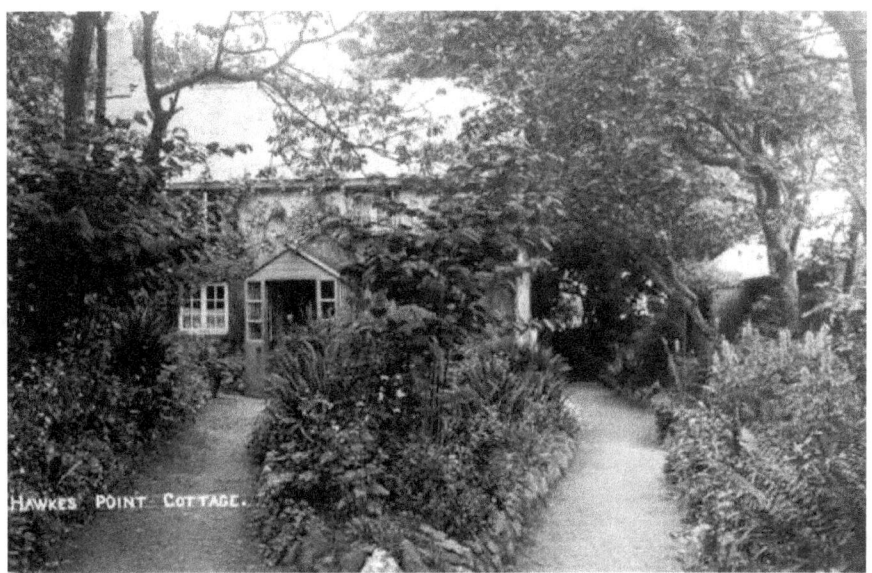

Bottrell's house near St Ives.

Bottrell's own collection was published in three volumes in 1870, 1873 and 1880. It overlaps with Hunt's in many respects but is remarkable for including many more examples of charmers, folk healers and witchcraft: *According to ancient usage, the folks from many parts of the west country make their annual pilgrimage to some white witch of repute, for the sake of having what they call 'their protection renewed.' ....There used to be rare fun among the folks in going to the conjuror in the spring, when they were sure to meet, at the wise man's abode, persons of all ages and conditions, many from a great distance. Then the inhabitants of the Scilly Isles came over in crowds for the purpose of consulting the white witches of Cornwall, and that they might obtain their protection, charms, spells, and counter-spells. Many of the captains of vessels, belonging to Hayle, St. Ives, and Swansea, often visited the Pellar before they undertook a voyage, so that, with seaman and tinners, there was sure to be great variety in the company...*

...The conjuror received the people and their offerings, singly, in the room by courtesy styled the hale (hall). Few remained closeted with him more than half-an-hour, during which time some were provided with little bags of earth, teeth, or bones taken from a grave. These precious

relics were to be worn, suspended from the neck, for the cure of prevention of fits, and other mysterious complaints supposed to be brought on by witchcraft. Others were furnished with a scrap of parchment, on which was written the ABRACADABRA or the following charm:—

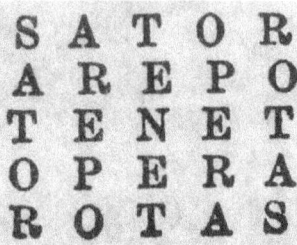

Bottrell's tales are also sprinkled with fascinating references to the 'Bucca' or 'Bucka-boo', most notably in the story of 'Duffy and the Devil' - a version of 'Rumpelstiltskin' - in which a young woman makes a pact with a devil *'in the shape of a black man, with half-cocked, squinting eyes, and the barbed or forked tip of his tail just seen below his coat-skirts'*.

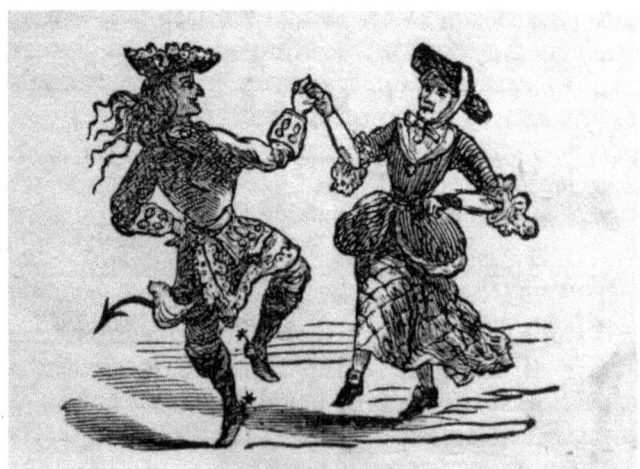

Joseph Blight's drawing of Duffy and the Devil in Bottrell's 'Traditions…'(1873)

T.Q. Couch, who like Bottrell also assisted Robert Hunt, had his own research published (alongside that of other family members) in 'A History of Polperro' (1871), and 'Ancient and Holy Wells of Cornwall' (1894). Other relevant books of folklore and folk music produced around the turn of the century include 'Songs of the West' (1889) Sabine Baring-Gould, 'Cornish Feasts and Folklore' by Margaret Courtney (1890)[25], 'The Piskey-Purse' and 'North Cornwall Fairies and Legends by Enys Tregarthen (1905 & 1906 respectively), and 'The Fairy-Faith in Celtic Countries', by W.Y. Evans-Wentz (1911).

The latter is important for a number of reasons, most notably because it attempts to test Hunt's assertion that the belief in giants and fairies dates back to pre-Christian Celtic societies. As late as 1910 Evans-Wentz also forcibly states the case for the rural-dweller having a distinct world-outlook: *What is there, for example, in London, or Paris, or Berlin, or New York to awaken the intuitive power of man, that subconsciousness deep-hidden in him, equal to the solitude of those magical environments of Nature which the Celts enjoy and love? The great majority of men in cities are apt to pride themselves on their own exemption from 'superstition' and to smile pityingly at the poor countrymen and countrywomen who believe in fairies. But when they do so they forget that, with all their own admirable progress in material invention, with all the far-reaching data of their acquired science, with all the vast extent of their commercial and economic conquests, they themselves have ceased to be natural. Are city-dwellers like these, Nature's unnatural children, who grind out their lives in an unceasing struggle for wealth and power, social position, and even for bread, fit to judge Nature's natural children who believe in fairies?*

Evans Wentz's descriptions of Cornwall and its spiritual heritage are also highly provocative: *On Dinsul (Michael's Mount), 'Hill dedicated to the Sun', pagan priests and priestesses kept kindled the Eternal Fire, and daily watched eastward for the rising of the God of Light and Life, to greet his coming with paeans of thanksgiving and praise. Then after the sixth century the new religion had come proclaiming a more mystic Light of the World in the Son of God, and to the pious half-pagan monks who*

---

[25] Courtney's collection was originally written for the Folklore Society, which formed in 1878.

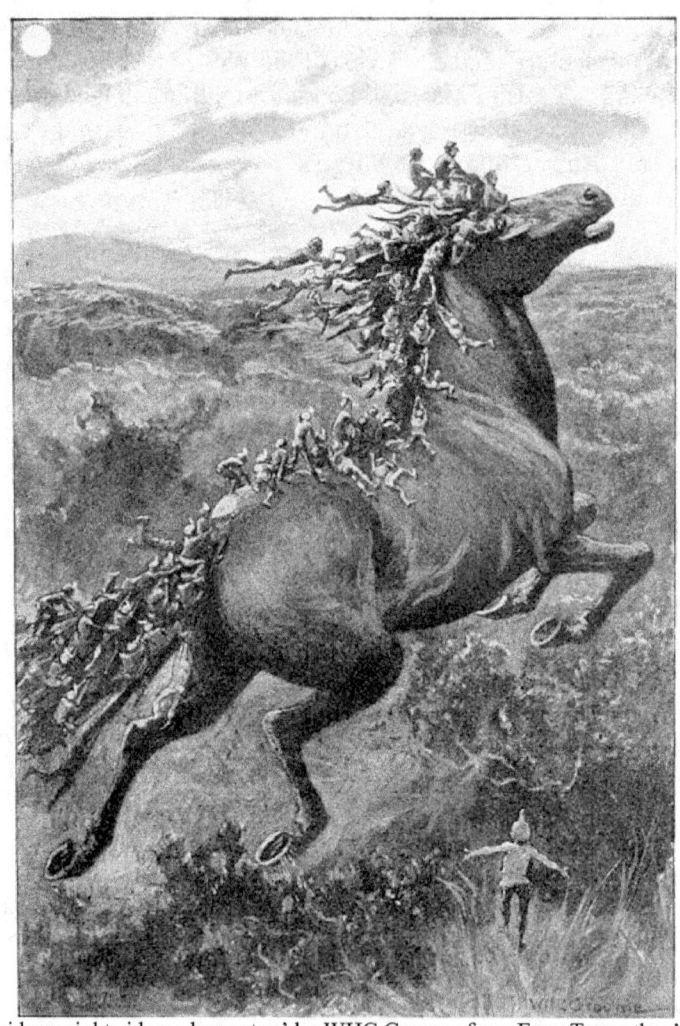

'Night-riders, night-riders please stop' by WHC Groome from Enys Tregarthen's 'North Cornwall Fairies and Legends' (1906). Enys Tregarthen was the pen name of Nellie Sloggett (1851-1923) who lived in Padstow.

succeeded the Druids the Archangel St. Michael appeared in vision on the Sacred Mount. And before St. Augustine came to Britain the Celts of Cornwall had already combined in their own mystical way the spiritual message of primitive Christianity with the pure nature-worship of their ancestors...[26]

'Songs of the West: Folk Songs of Devon and Cornwall'[27] (1889) by writer and parson Sabine Baring-Gould of Lew Trenchard on Dartmoor is another book of particular interest because it is one of the first folk-song collections in the British Isles: preceding better known efforts by Cecil Sharp and Ralph Vaughan Williams by several years. Baring-Gould amassed over 100 tunes (or 'airs') using the same painstaking method as Hunt: *Nowadays, domestic servants sing nothing but hymns, and the use of ballads and folksongs has died out among farm girls...But the old men sing their ditties, or did so till within the last fifty years. Now they are no longer called on for them, but they remember them, and with a little persuasion can be induced to render them up...*

Baring-Gould was a Tractarian Anglican: *One of my old singers was the son of very strict Wesleyans. When he was a boy, he was allowed to hear no music save psalm and hymn tunes. But he was wont to creep out of his window at night, and start away to the tavern where the miners congregated, and listen to and heap up in his memory the songs he there heard. As these were forbidden fruit they were all the more dearly prized and surely remembered and, when he was a white-haired old man he poured them out to us.*

---

[26] Evans Wentz's book includes contributions by others who he had chosen for their local knowledge. Cornwall language expert Henry Jenner demonstrates his knowledge of esoteric traditions in his essay for the book: *There seems to have been always and everywhere (or nearly so) a belief in a race, neither divine nor human, but very like to human beings, who existed on a 'plane' different from that of humans, though occupying the same space...These beings are held to be normally imperceptible to human senses, but conditions may arise in which the 'astral' plane' of the elementals and that part of the 'physical plane' in which, if one may so express it, some human being happens to be, may be in such a relation to one another that these and other spirits may be seen and heard.*

[27] Baring-Gould was not alone in including parts of Devonshire, especially Dartmoor, in his collection. Robert Hunt acknowledged that up until 927 AD, when King Athelstan of Wessex is supposed to have driven the Cornish out of Exeter, Cornwall was, with Devon, part of the kingdom of Dumnonia.

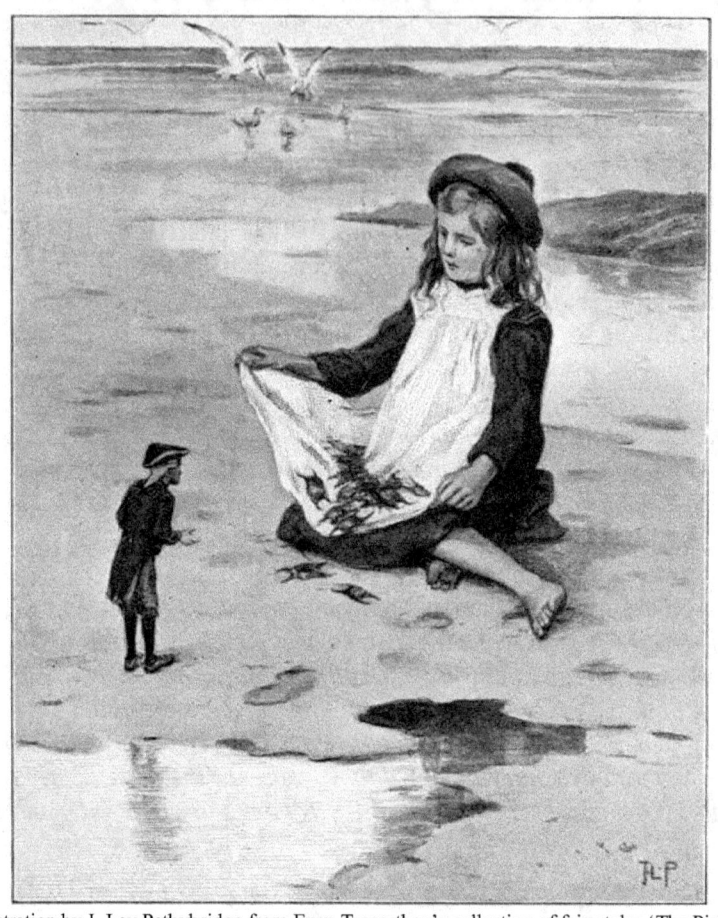

Illustration by J. Ley Pethybridge from Enys Tregarthen's collection of fairy tales 'The Piskey-Purse' (1905). Pethybridge (1865-1905), who was from Launceston, provided grisaille illustrations for a number of other books of local interest, including publications with folkloric content by Robert Hawker, Mark Guy Pearse and Eden Phillpotts.

It has been suggested that, for the Cornish themselves, folk-tales and folk-songs provided a reassuring sense of continuity with the past, at a time of great cultural change (McMahon, 2015). Certainly by 1870

Cornwall was fast becoming the first post-industrial region of Britain. As the price of minerals collapsed (in 1866 there was a sudden crash in the price of copper, and the price of tin was also falling) much of the region's workforce dispersed and moved to collieries in the North, or emigrated to Australia and the US[28].

As its mines and mine-stacks were abandoned, much of Cornwall's industrial past was forgotten. However, with the coming of the railway in 1859 it was possible to get from London to Cornwall in less than a day, and Cornwall's folklore started to be used to sell the Duchy as a unique, magical tourist destination. This was blatantly so in the case of the beautifully illustrated Great Western Railway Legend-land books and leaflets of 1922, which read: *The western parts of our country are richer in legend than any other part…perhaps this is because life is, and always was, quieter there, and people have more time to remember the tales of other days that in busier more prosaic districts…*[29]

But folklore, with its evocation of a timeless pre-industrial past, was only a part of the appeal to the many artists and writers from around the world who, after the railway, started to live and work in Cornwall.

---

[28] It was partly because its industry was in sharp decline, that no discernable labour movement developed in Cornwall as it did in more industrial areas, like the North East. By coincidence, however, the People's Charter of 1838 was written by a Cornishman, William Lovett who was then living in London. The Charter looked to improve the predicament of the working man, and called for universal suffrage.

[29] Many of the Legend Land illustrations are signed 'Cooper'. This is likely to be Austin Cooper who was employed by GWR for many years as an artist.

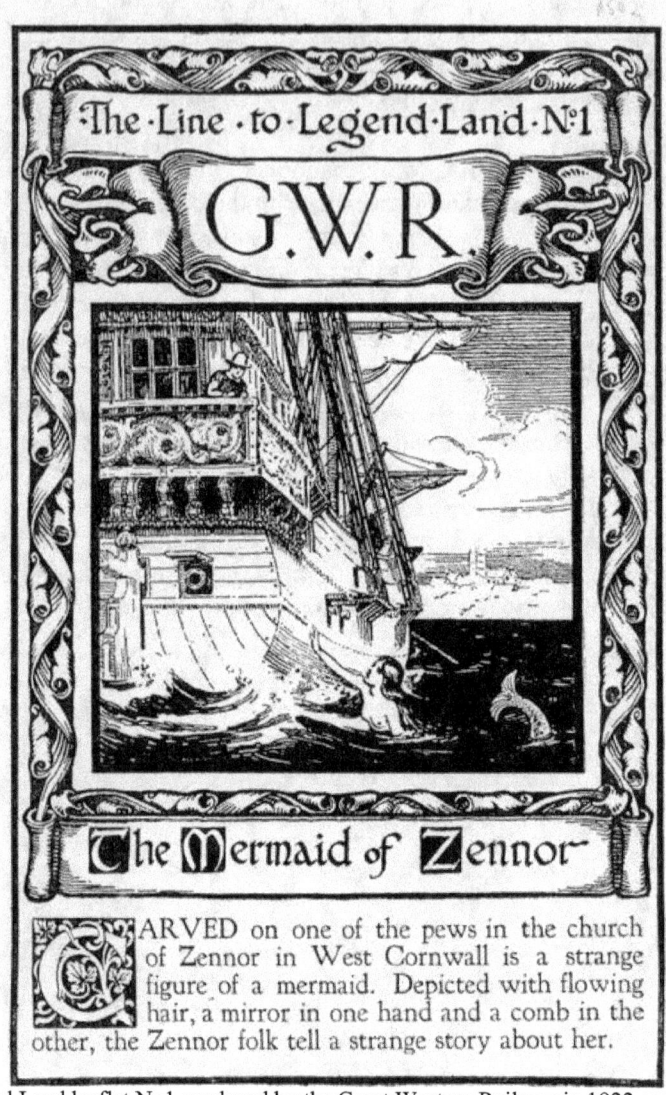

Legend Land leaflet No1 produced by the Great Western Railway in 1922 and sold at Paddington Station. Many such leaflets were produced and were later compiled into four 'Legend Land' books.

4. The Art-colonies form

'Fish Sale on a Cornish Beach' was first exhibited at the Royal Academy in London in the summer of 1885. It was the first painting to bring national recognition to the artist's colony of Newlyn, and in its realism and its portrayal of rural life in West Cornwall, it can be seen as the blueprint for all subsequent Newlyn School painting.

Stanhope Forbes, its creator, had arrived in Cornwall in 1884, and spent most of that year working on the canvas outdoors in all weathers. He had previously studied at the Royal Academy Schools, but like many younger European and American artists in the 1870s, had fallen under the spell of progressive French art much of which, rather than being painted in the artificial light of the studio, was now executed 'en plein-air'.

Forbes had gone on to study in Paris in 1880, but found that, during the warmer months there was an exodus of painters to the countryside, and particularly to Brittany where a number of colonies had sprung up. The most influential of the French artists, like Millet and, later, Bastien Lepage, preferred to depict remote, unspoilt locations in their work: *In almost all the places where colonies were established, the artists fancifully saw their surroundings in terms of a primitive world far removed from modern civilization…And it was essential that such areas should be populated by old fashioned peasant and fishing communities* (Jacobs, 1985).

They were figure painters rather than landscape painters, but their interest in rural communities was not simply voyeuristic or sentimental; it also had a strong political dimension[30]. The rise of socialism across

---

[30] Millet, based in Barbizon, was himself from a peasant family, and was keen to depict the simple reality of the rural poor whilst also giving them a heroic aspect. Perhaps too overtly political, he initially struggled for critical recognition, however painters like Bastien Lepage who were active a decade or so later, achieved considerable success by

Europe - in the UK associated with Charterists, the Fabian Society, and artists like Ruskin and Morris - had led to a reconsideration of the value of traditional work. In 1853 Ruskin described the plight of the factory worker thus: *It is not that men are ill fed, but that they have no pleasure in the work by which they make their bread... they feel that the kind of labour to which they are condemned is verily a degrading one, and makes them less than men...To feel their souls withering within them, unthanked, to find their whole being sunk into an unrecognized abyss, to be counted off into a heap of mechanism numbered with its wheels, and weighed with its hammer strokes, this nature bade not; this God blesses not* (Ruskin, 1853).

Tolstoy argued that now, even the rich viewed their own work as odious: *'I say odious because I have never yet met with a person of this class who was contented with his work, or took as much satisfaction in it as the man who shovels the snow from his doorstep...* (Tolstoy, 1882).

Both men, influential as they were, saw a return to the land as the solution to modern man's ills. Tolstoy, who took to wearing a simple peasant costume, started a community based on the principles of self-sufficiency and the simple life, whilst in the 1870's Ruskin set up the 'Guild of St George', which included rural communities and farms based on the principle of medieval craft guilds that could provide alternatives to mass production. His example was later emulated all over Europe and America (Marsh, 1982).

The peasant communities of Brittany unchanged for centuries, uncorrupted by industrialisation and apparently contented in their work, must have therefore exemplified a similar ideal, as highlighted by Jacobs: *Almost all the visitors to Brittany in the nineteenth century viewed the region in a similar way; and to many the experience of coming here was like travelling back to the Middle Ages, or even further back in time, to a primeval era. This fanciful image ...had an obvious appeal to artists who...isolated themselves more and more from their own period, whose preoccupations with industrialisation disgusted them.* (Jacobs, 1985)

---

combining the picturesque qualities of the peasant with recognition of the moral worth of their labours.

Jacobs also asserts that the artists were interested in the Celticism of Brittany: *It was not only the Breton environment which so fascinated artists, but also the people themselves...first they were not French but Celts who had come over to France from England to escape the Anglo-Saxon invasion...there were other aspects of the Bretons which interested foreign observers, such as their strong folklore tradition and intense Catholicism...*

The Bretons also still wore their national costume, which is much in evidence in all the paintings completed in the main colonies of Pont-Aven and Concarneau, not least in those produced by Post-impressionist Paul Gauguin during the last decades of the century. Gauguin arrived in Pont-Aven in 1886, and in 1888 wrote: *'I love Brittany. I find there the savage, the primitive. When my clogs resound on the granite soil I hear the muffled dull powerful tone that I seek in my painting'*.

Stanhope Forbes, whose boyhood home was in London, had two summers and autumns painting in Brittany before travelling to Penzance. When he reached Newlyn, he discovered other painters that had also recently arrived: Ralph Todd, who had stayed with him in the same hotel in Quimperlé, and Walter Langley and Edwin Harris, both originally from Birmingham, who had also painted in Brittany before coming to Cornwall.

The residents of Newlyn did not have had the same 'picturesque' costumes as the Bretons, and Forbes' first impressions suggest they had other less endearing qualities: *All the men, or nearly all, are teetotalers and every one of them goes to church or chapel and keeps the seventh day holy, and the effect of this abstinence from strong drink and indulgence in strong prayers is to make them a most disagreeable set of people, full of hypocrisy and cant.*

But by 1898 Forbes was able to look back on his first impressions of Newlyn with more fondness: *The little port was active and picturesque, and the commerce of the place, carried on under more primitive conditions, was none the less attractive to an artists eye....from the first I was fascinated by those wet sands with those groups of figures reflected on the shiny surface which the auctioneers bell would gather around him for the barter of his wares...Yes those were the days of unflinching realism, of the cult of Bastien Lepage. It was part of our artistic creed to paint our pictures directly from Nature, and not merely to rely upon sketches and studies which we could afterwards amplify in the comfort of a studio* (Forbes, 1898).

He was already regretting the fact that the village was being modernised: *Alas again many an old house, which made the irregular line along that uneven cliff still more interesting, has been pulled down and its place filled by some terribly commonplace modern structure devoid of character and charm. One cannot help foreseeing a time soon approaching when the unfortunate painters must needs forsake their native land and seek refuge in countries where age and beauty are thought worthy of respect* (Forbes, 1898).

Given these views, one can only guess at the way in which the Newlyn painters were regarded by the fishermen, and there is always that nagging sense that the locals were exploited for the entertainment of the metropolitan bourgeoisie. In one of his first letters from Newlyn (1884) Forbes referred to the availability of local models, who were paid for their time: *The girls are quite pretty in spite of their rather ugly costume – sixpence an hour is the tariff – higher than France of course* (in Cross, 1994)

However, the villagers were always depicted sympathetically. It is this that Tolstoy himself recognised in singling out Walter Langley's 'Charity' for praise in his book 'What is Art?' (1897): *The boy, pitifully drawing his bare feet under the bench is eating; the woman is looking on, probably considering whether he will not want some more; and a girl of about seven, leaning on her arm, is carefully and seriously looking on, not taking her eyes from the hungry boy and is evidently understanding for the first time what poverty is and what inequality among people is, and asking herself why she has everything provided for her while this boy goes barefoot and hungry?...One feels that the artist loved this girl and that she too loves. And this picture, by an artist who, I think, is not very widely known, is an admirable and true work of art.*

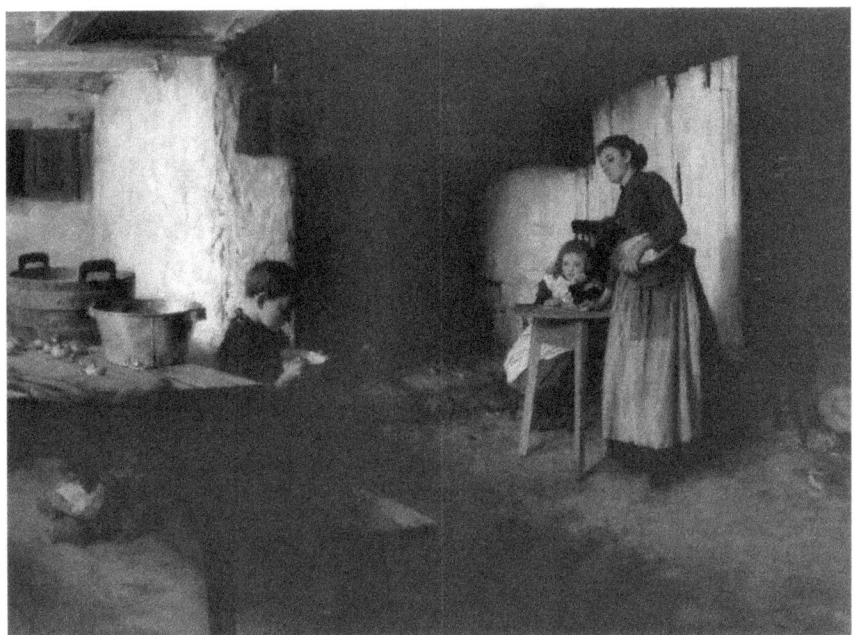

'In Faith and Hope the World will Disagree But all Mankind's concern is Charity'. Called 'Charity' for short and painted in 1897, by Walter Langley, this painting was singled out for praise by Leo Tolstoy. Photo The Haddock Center.

Undoubtedly influenced by its reputation as being a colony like those in Brittany, more artists arrived in Newlyn in the 1880s. This included Frank Brambley, who would paint one of the most celebrated and moving paintings of the Victorian era: 'A Hopeless Dawn' (1888), and Elizabeth Armstrong who, as well as being an accomplished painter would later marry Forbes.

Armstrong was a Canadian who, in 1882, had stayed in Pont-Aven where she had met another future 'Newlyner', Edwin Harris. She arrived in Newlyn late in 1885, and in the summer of 1886 went to stay, temporarily, in the more salubrious surroundings of St Ives, about ten miles north of Newlyn. St Ives, as well as having white, sandy beaches and crystalline waters, also had two hotels (The White Hart and The Tregenna Castle), and since the branch-line had opened in 1877 was rapidly metamorphosing into a popular holiday resort.

By the mid-1880s artists from all over Europe and America had started to settle in St Ives. Like the Newlyn painters they were nearly all veterans of Pont Aven and Concarneau, and saw in St Ives similar 'picturesque' qualities. These early St Ives artists, like Émile Vernier, Edward Simmons, Edith Lees, Adrian and Marianne Stokes, the Swede Anders Zorn and the Finn, Helene Scherjbeck, tended to be maritime or landscape painters rather than figurative painters; many of them taking spectacular studios in the old fishing (sail) lofts in 'Downalong' overlooking Porthmeor Beach, but living in larger houses at the top of the town.

In 1888, the first meeting of St Ives Arts Club took place in a studio belonging to Australian artist, Louis Grier, and in 1890 a permanent home was found for the club on Westcott's Quay close to the sea-shore.

By the end of the decade it was the Newlyn painters that were receiving the greatest accolades, however, and after success at the Royal Academy, in 1889 Stanhope Forbes' 'The Health of the Bride' was bought by Henry Tate (of the Tate Gallery). Appropriately enough Forbes married Elizabeth Armstrong the same year. Ten years later the couple, who were among the few original settlers still living there, started a school of painting.

In 1895 the Passmore Edward's Gallery opened specifically to show the work of Newlyn artists. Stanhope Forbes commented: *It was a kind and generous thought of the giver to bestow this admirable little gallery upon us, and not the less gratifying for being so entirely spontaneous and unsought for. The success it has met with so far, not only from the support which the public of West Cornwall has given it but also from the valuable assistance of many eminent artists who have lent us interesting works, augurs well for its future prosperity* (Forbes, 1898).

Writing in 'The Studio' at around the same time, Norman Garstin was much less upbeat and optimistic: *It has all come too late, the colony in Newlyn is dispersing and some share of the blame must be taken by the new gallery...It has seemingly led to a disintegration of the Newlyners...This is only a coincidence, but certainly we cannot shut our eyes to the fact that Newlyn has thinned lately – leaner by many good men and good painters* (Cross, 1994).

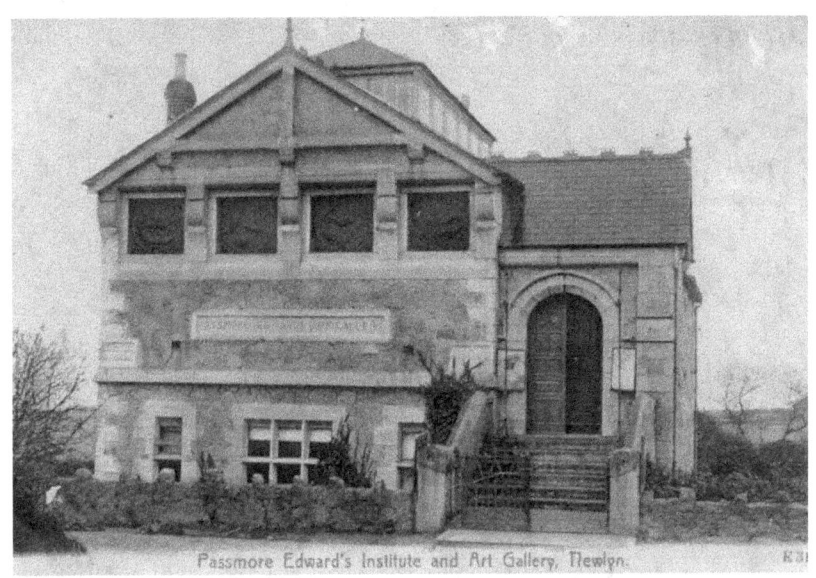

Passmore Edward's Institute and Art Gallery, Newlyn.

In fact Newlyn, and as we shall see the adjacent smaller colony of Lamorna, remained a centre for painting in Cornwall for many decades. Indeed Newlyn, for a while, also became known for its repoussé copperwork: hand-crafted copper domestic-ware which was produced from the early 1890s onwards. As Stanhope Forbes describes: *In the narrowest part of the little lane there hangs a curiously fashioned sign, indicating that here an industrial class is held. A terrible din assails your ears, and curious to find what occasions it you enter a courtyard and climbing a steep ladder into an old net loft find a room full of lads all busy hammering away at curiously shaped pieces of brass or copper. Originally started by that good friend of Newlyn, Mr Bolitho, with the co-operation of the artists, and chief amongst them Messrs. Gotch and Percy Craft, the idea was to find employment for the spare moments of fisher-lads and certainly a more admirable safety valve for their superfluous energy could not have been devised.....*

But it has served another and very different purpose, and has been the means of giving his opportunity to an artist of rare and very individual talent. Mr J.D. Mackenzie has displayed a perfect wealth of imagination in executing a whole series of designs for the multitude of objects which the class and his able lieutenant Philip Hodder have wrought in repousse work; and so the name of Newlyn has become linked with an art other than that of painting pictures (Forbes, 1898).

West Cornwall, therefore, acquired its own distinctive crafts guild, comparable to others being set up elsewhere in Britain. Due to failing health Ruskin's own 'Guild of St George' had been only partially successful, and instead it was William Morris, poet, designer and socialist, who became the figurehead for the new movement. It eventually acquired a name after 'The Arts and Crafts Exhibition Society' formed in 1887. The Society, for which Morris served as president, reflected the activity of a wide number of guilds, village industries and crafts societies[31].

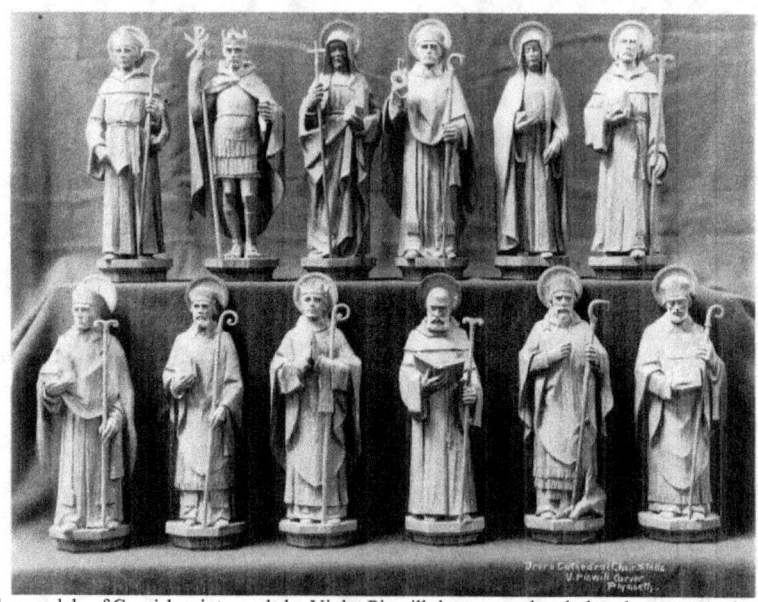

Clay models of Cornish saints made by Violet Pinwill, later carved and placed, over a number of years, in the quire of Truro Cathedral. Pinwill, based in Plymouth, was a prolific wood-carver, commissioned to decorate many churches in the Duchy. Photo Plymouth Archives.

---

[31] Morris later acknowledged his debt to Ruskin in the preface to the Kelmscott Press edition of 'The Nature of Gothic' in 1892.

The Arts and Craft movement, and the revival of handicrafts, left its mark in Cornwall in numerous other ways. For example, after a fire at Lanhydrock House in 1881 Lord Robartes, its owner, arranged for a large section of the house to be rebuilt. Gothic and Pre-Raphaelite elements - including Pugin wallpaper - were introduced.

It is also worth noting here the extraordinary contribution of the Pinwill sisters who, although based in Plymouth, created multiple carvings in wood for churches all over Cornwall. These include, for example, the images of saints they created for Truro Cathedral.

5. Visiting writers and the fin-de-siècle
I am very religious but Huxley and Darwin had done away with the simple religion of my youth (Yeats, 1921)

In the late 1800s Cornwall started to become a holiday destination popular in progressive, literary and bohemian circles. Typically travelling by train, the new visitors appreciated the same 'unspoilt' qualities that appealed to the artists, and some bought second homes, or moved more permanently.

From 1881, a few months before their daughter Virginia (later Virginia Woolf) was born, the historian and biographer Leslie Stephens and his wife Julia, started to lease Talland House in St Ives. The family, including Virginia's younger sister, the Bloomsbury painter Vanessa (later Vanessa Bell), had idyllic summer holidays there every year up until the death of Julia Stephens in 1895, following which Leslie could not bear to return.

Virginia and her siblings, retained strongly nostalgic feelings about Cornwall, and did make several return visits, including one in 1905, recorded in Virginia's diary, in which the magic of the railway is very much evident: *It was with some feeling of enchantment that we took our places yesterday in the Great Western train. This was the wizard who was to transport us into another world, almost into another age. We would fain have believed that this little corner of England had slept under some enchanters spell since we last set eyes on it ten years ago, & that no breath of change had stirred its leaves, or troubled its waters. There too, we should find our past preserved, as though through all this time it had been guarded & treasured for us to come back to one day — it mattered not how far distant. Many were the summers we had spent in St Ives; was it not reasonable to believe that as far away we cherished the memory of them, so here on the spot where we left them we should be able to recover something tangible of their substance? Ah, how strange it was, then, to watch the familiar shapes of land & sea unroll themselves once more, as though a magicians hand had raised the curtain that hung between us, & to see once more the silent but palpable forms, which for more than ten years we had seen only in dreams, or in the visions of waking hours.*

Yesterday…we followed foot paths to Trencrom, which was, 11 years ago, our punctual Sunday walk….On the top of Tren Crom indeed, I was considerably surprised to see how large a view of the surrounding country was unfolded; moreover I had no notion that from this point you can see both sides of the coast at once; Hayle Harbour on the North, St Michael's Mount on the South, & all the long stretch of bay which ends in the Lizard point. But as these features of the landscape have not changed in eleven years, or in eleven hundred, the change must be in my point of view & not in the outlines of the earth.

Other visiting writers saw the income-generating potential of more modest dwellings in the area - many left derelict by emigrating miners - and as early as 1890, writer Edith Lees acquired 'The Cot' in Carbis Bay, which was the first of several properties that she would buy to let during the summer, and live and write in during the winter.

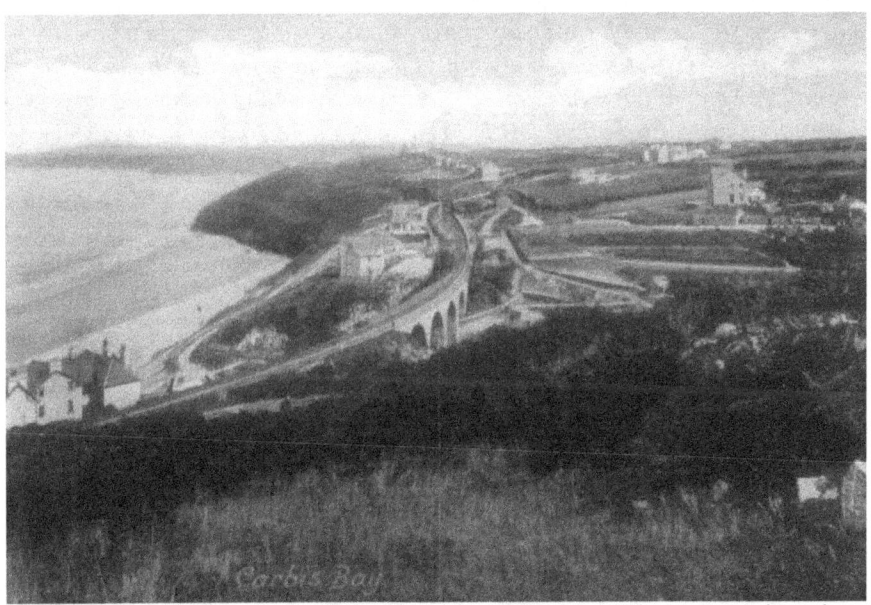

Carbis Bay circa 1910. The branch line from St Erth is unchanged, but the houses are much, much fewer than now.

That same year she became acquainted with her husband-to-be, the sexual and social reformer Henry Havelock Ellis who, having recently completed medical training, worked as a locum doctor in Probus in mid-Cornwall before taking a holiday with a friend in Lamorna. Edith and Havelock met, both there and in St Ives. In his biography he recalls: *Concerning the economic basis of the relations between men and women we had, I think, already begun to speak as we walked along the beach at Porthmear (St Ives). Our opinions on that point were from the first identical. We both alike firmly believed that the social equality of men and women should involve an economic equality in marriage, each partner thus preserving independence* (Ellis, 1939).

Theirs was not simply a marriage of economic convenience however, and Cornwall provided the backdrop for their burgeoning romance, with Havelock asking Edith to join him in Lamorna again the following summer (1891): *Its very lovely here - so delicious to lie in the sun and hear nothing except an occasional insect or bird, and to know that our dear brother men are at a safe distance…I've taken a-little house (rent free) made of granite and bracken and honeysuckle. It's a lovely little house, hidden away from the world; the pillars of it are two huge foxglove stems which tower up above you against the sky when you lie down in it. I've got room in my house for a little wife - but she must be small - I've also got a nest in the rock right over the sea - and a very, very tiny sweet bird might nestle in close beside me there - I've also got an ordinary rock, the same I had last year, where I lie and bask in the sun and read or dream.*

Whilst training at St Thomas's Hospital, Havelock Ellis had developed an eclectic knowledge-base and an interest in literature and social justice, and in 1883 he became one of a handful of founding members of 'The Fellowship of The New Life'[32].

The Fellowship was a group of radical social reformers, inspired by Leo Tolstoy, that included champion of vegetarianism Henry Salt, school reformer Cecil Reddie, future Labour Prime Minister Ramsay MacDonald, and gay rights pioneer Edward Carpenter. All became close friends and colleagues.

---

[32] He also corresponded widely, and in this way became intimate with Olive Schreiner, author of 'The Story of an African Farm'.

Edward Carpenter's description of the fellowship, written for the preface of a book by Edith, explains its relation to the Fabian Society, and to the ideas of Tolstoy and Ruskin: *There was a general urge towards Socialism—though more from the ethical and humanitarian than from the political side; there was a great determination to simplify life as much as possible; servants were to be dispensed with or adopted as friends; manual work to be cultivated side by side with intellectual; education to be greatly reformed. There were schemes for settlement on the land; and schemes for co-operation or community in household life. And always these schemes and reforms were to be carried out as far as possible personally and by the personal effort of the members. They were not to be merely philosophical propaganda applicable in a distant and general way to society at large.*

I think I am right in saying that it was on this point of personal effort that in the quite early days (in 1884) a split occurred in the society, which led to a certain group breaking away and becoming the founders of the Fabian Society. These latter concentrated their energies on general socialist and economic propaganda, apart from the question of individual and personal reform.[33]

Carpenter, like Havelock Ellis, remained focused on the latter and set up the self-sufficient Millthorpe community in rural Derbyshire, thereby influencing a generation of Cambridge graduates and dons, especially EM Forster and Rupert Brooke[34]. As well as being openly gay, Carpenter became a vociferous advocate of the 'nature movement' with its denial of machinery: *We find ourselves today in the midst of a somewhat peculiar state of society, which we call Civilisation, but which even to the most optimistic among us does not seem altogether desirable. Some of us, indeed, are inclined to think that it is a kind of disease which the various races of man have to pass through - as children pass through measles or whooping cough... a move towards Nature and Savagery is*

---

[33] The Fabian Society was so named because rather than Marxist revolution, it favoured a gradual evolution towards a fairer and more equal society. Later it joined with the Trade Union Movement to form the Labour Party. As Carpenter indicates, The Fellowship remained committed to personal rather than societal transformation, however, and many of its concerns were later debated in print on the pages of the journal 'The New Age'.

[34] Rupert Brooke was engaged to Ka Cox. Both were friendly with Virginia Woolf and all three nominally part of a group who called themselves the 'Neo-pagans'. Ka Cox later moved to live in Zennor, near Higher Tregerthen.

for the first time taking place from within, instead of being forced on society from without. The nature movement begun years ago in literature and art is now, among the more advanced sections of the civilised world, rapidly realising itself in actual life, going so far even as a denial, among some, of machinery and the complex products of Civilisation, and developing among others into a gospel of salvation by sandals and sunbaths! (Carpenter, 1891)[35].

At the time that Edith and Havelock Ellis married (in 1891 - at 32 Havelock was reputedly still a virgin), Edith was acting as The Fellowship's secretary, working alongside Ramsay MacDonald, and living in the 'commune' 'Fellowship House'. Though their deep emotional bond survived intact, her marriage to Havelock was far from conventional, and whilst in Cornwall in 1892 Edith had a lesbian affair with a woman called Claire (Brome, 1979). It was the first of several such romances, including one later with Lily Kirkpatrick, a local painter from St Ives[36]. As explained in his autobiography, and reflecting the openness of their marriage, Edith and Havelock then settled into a pattern of living together in Cornwall during the winter months, then living apart during the summer.

---

[35] In the same essay, whilst there is little discussion of sexuality, Edward Carpenter advocates vegetarianism, and interestingly seems to predict the rise of Wicca and Druidry: *And when the Civilisation-period has passed away, the old nature-religion - perhaps greatly grown - will come back. On the high-tops once more gathering Man will celebrate with naked dances the glory of the human form and the great processions of the stars, or greet the bright horn of the young moon which now after a hundred centuries comes back laden with such wondrous associations - all the yearnings and the dreams and the wonderment of the generations of mankind - the worship of Astarte and of Diana, of Isis or the Virgin Mary; once more in sacred groves will he reunite the passion and the delight of human love with his deepest feelings of the sanctity and beauty of Nature; or in the open, standing uncovered to the Sun, will adore the emblem of the everlasting splendor which shines within. The same sense of vital perfection and exaltation which can be traced in the early and pre-civilisation peoples - only a thousand times intensified, defined, illustrated and purified - will return to irradiate the redeemed and delivered Man.*

[36] Havelock Ellis appeared to tolerate her infidelities with equanimity, possibly because although physically attractive to others, he 'lacked virility'- probably a euphemism for impotence.

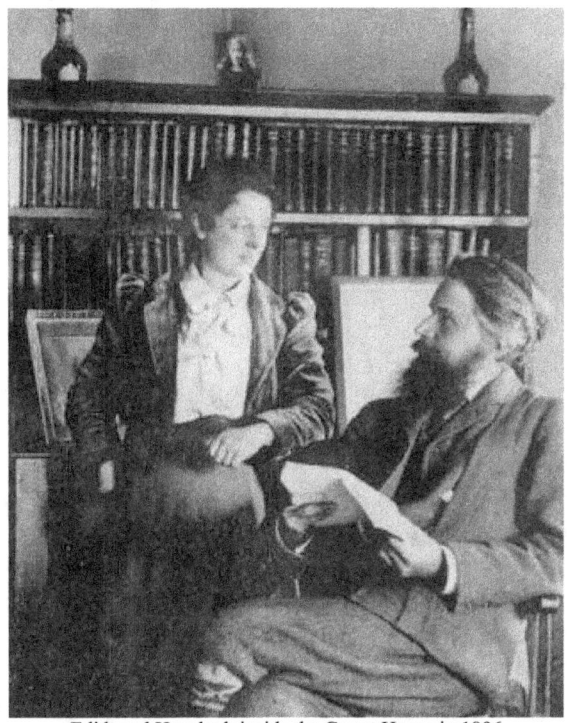
Edith and Havelock inside the Count House in 1896

In 1894 Edith bought Havelock a stone hut at Hawkes Point in Carbis Bay, which overlooked Godrevy Bay and at the time was quiet and isolated. Edward Carpenter, on one of his visits, assured Ellis it had the 'finest prospect in England' (Grosskurth, 1980).

Edith also started renting The Count House in Carbis Bay, a bigger property. It came with land attached, and it allowed her to keep a range of farm animals including a scattering of cows, horses, chickens and pigs. This development is treated with contempt by some biographers, however her interest in farming was partly ideological and inspired by Carpenter's example. She also invested in other cottages in the Carbis Bay area, which she rented out to London friends including e.g. Somerset Maugham.

Havelock, meanwhile, would walk to Hawkes Point every morning and - no doubt between bouts of nude sunbathing - would write in solitude whilst sitting in the shelter of a dinghy turned on its end. During a highly productive career he completed more than fifty books, as well as numerous other papers. This included glowing tributes to Whitman, Millet and Tolstoy amongst others (The New Spirit, 1890) and the first known description of a future National Health Service (The Nationalisation of Health, 1892).

In Carbis Bay in 1897 he wrote a ground-breaking article for The Lancet describing his experience of taking mescaline, the LSD-like hallucinogen derived from the peyote cactus for which he is later credited in Aldous Huxley's 'Doors of Perception'.

It was the first such account outside the US: *MESCAL buttons are eaten by the Kiowa and other Indians of New Mexico and their use is connected with religious ceremonial...On Good Friday, I made an infusion of three buttons (a full dose) and took it in three portions at intervals of an hour between 2.30 and 4.30 P.M...By 7 P.M. visions had begun to appear with closed eyelids, a vague confused mass of kaleidoscopic character. The visual phenomena seen with open eyes now also became more marked, and in addition to the very distinct violet shadows there were faint green shadows. Perhaps the most pleasant moment in the experience occurred at 7.30 P.M., when for the first time the colour visions with closed eyes became vivid and distinct, while at the same time I had an olfactory hallucination, the air seeming filled with vague perfume. Meanwhile the pulse had been rising, and by 8.30 PM had reached its normal level (72 in the sitting posture). At the same time muscular incoordination had so far advanced that it was almost impossible to manipulate a pen, and I had to write with a pencil; this also I could soon only use for a few minutes at a time, and as I wrote a golden tone now lay over the paper, and the pencil seemed to write in gold, while my hand, seen in indirect vision as I wrote, looked bronzed, scaled, and flushed with red. Except for slight nausea I continued to feel well, and there was no loss of mental coolness or alertness.* (Lancet June5th 1897)

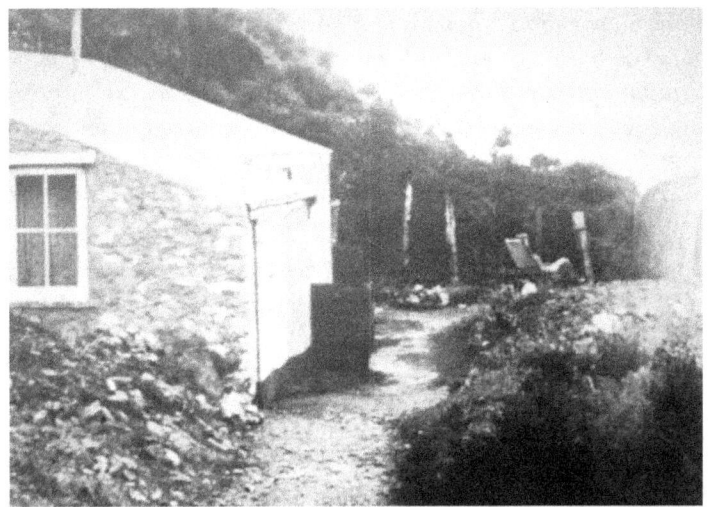

The stone hut at Hawkes Point between Carbis Bay and Lelant, surrounded by gorse and mine waste. Havelock Ellis can be seen sitting on a chair overlooking the sea, near the hull of an upturned boat.

However Havelock Ellis is best remembered now for his pioneering work on sex. His 'Studies in the Psychology of Sexuality' ran to seven volumes published between 1896 and 1928. This monumental work, which was quoted extensively by his contemporary Freud, and which inspired many who advocated for freer and more liberal attitudes to sexuality and the family (including Modernist writers like Woolf, Lawrence and Joyce), was, for the most part, also written in the little studio at Hawkes Point.

The first volume was published originally as 'Sexual Inversion'[37]. It draws on gay literary and historical precedents, and was the first book in English to treat homosexuality as neither a crime nor a disease. Foremost amongst his collaborators was Edward Carpenter, who provided Ellis with much 'case-material', including the following account: *For myself, I may say that since my earliest boyhood (eight or nine) it was always one of my own sex, that I thought or dreamed of - generally one of the same age, tho' when young I often felt also a strong passion and worship for*

---

[37] Later listed as the second volume after it was withdrawn and republished later.

some older boy or man. This passion has always been very strong with me, and perpetually present, making a possible romance in each new male acquaintance, and sometimes causing me the keenest anguish and suffering. It was quite congenital, for nothing occurred in my early life to encourage it, everything to discourage it...Home life was in an atmosphere of entire reserve on matters of love. I only knew that my feelings were entirely different from anything I ever heard mentioned at home or at school, and I looked upon myself as an outcast and a monstrosity. I dreamed of friends but I had none.

Published only months after Oscar Wilde was sent to Reading Gaol (in 1897), it was probably the most controversial and important of Ellis' books, and it lead to the arrest and prosecution of the bookseller George Bedborough. Ellis' prose style within is serene and detached. It was this moral neutrality that his supporters valued most, but it also made him enemies. Many years later Ellis commented: *When only one volume of these Studies had been written and published in England, a prosecution instigated by the Government put an end to the sale of that volume in England, and led me to resolve that the subsequent volumes should not be published in my own country. I do not complain. I am grateful for the early and generous sympathy with which my work was received in Germany and the United States, and I recognize that it has had a wider circulation, both in English and the other chief languages of the world, than would have been possible by the modest method of issue which the government of my own country induced me to abandon. Nor has the effort to crush my work resulted in any change in that work by so much as a single word. With help, or without it, I have followed my own path to the end...Men die, but the ideas they seek to kill live. Our books may be thrown to the flames, but in the next generation those flames become human souls.*

As a respected polymath, Havelock Ellis' influence reached in many directions. For several years he leased rooms in the Temple area of London, and sublet some to Arthur Symons. Symons (a Cornishman) was editor of 'The Savoy' literary magazine and author of 'The Symbolist Movement in Literature' (1899), a book that introduced

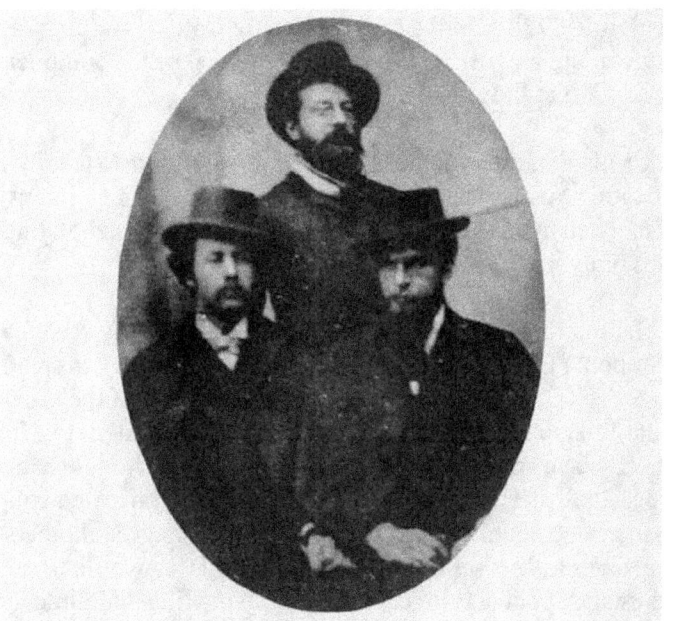

Havelock Ellis was well connected in literary circles. Here he is pictured (right) with Arthur Symons (editor of the Savoy Magazine) and Remy De Gourmont (French Symbolist poet who collaborated with Alfred Jarry, and was an influence on George Bataille). Ellis travelled to Paris with Symons in 1889 and this photo may have been taken on that trip, or on one the following year.

Rimbaud and other French poets to English speakers. One year, whilst Havelock was away in Cornwall (winter 1895-1896) Irish poet and occultist WB Yeats also used the flat. It has been noted that, at the time, Yeats was impressed by Ellis's writing on Nietzsche in the Savoy.

Before the close of the century Edith herself wrote a novel, 'Seaweed: a Cornish Idyll' (1898 – also known as Kit's Woman), and later published a selection of short stories ('My Cornish Neighbours' (1906)), and a number of plays (e.g. 'The Subjection of Kezia' (1908). She also collaborated with Havelock on 'Three Modern Seers' (1910): a study of the life and works of James Hinton, Fredreich Nietzsche and Edward Carpenter.

In 1906, with the farm proving too much for Edith's then failing health, the couple moved out of the Count House to Moor Cottages near Carbis

Bay. Then in 1909 they moved again to Rose Cottage Carbis Water. After a drawn out and difficult illness, Edith died of the complications of diabetes in 1916 at the age of 55.

Havelock Ellis's international stature continued to grow steadily after Edith's death, however, and publication of his works in Germany resulted in extensive correspondence with Sigmund Freud, dating from 1907 until both men's death 30 years later.

Though sharing many of Freud's concerns (including his sceptical views of 'civilisation') Ellis never developed the same armoury of treatment techniques. To his enduring credit, he remained wary of the scientific claims that Freud and his followers made, and was content to offer commonsense sympathy and advice - free of charge - to those that came to him for help instead. These included heterosexual married couples wanting marriage counselling, as well as homosexuals and others who saw themselves as 'perverted' in some way. This, as we shall see, included imagist poet and lover of Ezra Pound, Hilda Doolittle, (who in fact had the distinction of having received treatment from both Ellis and Freud).

Manifestations of Havelock Ellis's undying affection for Cornwall are scattered throughout his work, particularly in the three volumes of his diaristic 'Impressions and Comments'. In 1913, for example, he wrote: *February 5, 1913. Dirt remains the note of London, brown dirt all over the streets, black dirt all over the buildings, yellow dirt all over the sky, and those who live in it become subdued to what they live in, "like the dyer's hand," even literally. So the sight of the Cornish coast, the prospect of seeing it, the very thought of its existence, has the exhilaration of a rapturous prayer. There—sometimes, at all events—the earth is exquisitely clean, the bright sea bubbles like champagne, and its mere mists are rainbow-hued dreams; the sky has flung off its dingy robe and is naked, beautiful, alive. Profoundly alien to me as I always feel this land of Cornwall to be, it is much to feel there something of that elemental reality of which men count God the symbol. Here the city-stained soul may become the sacramental agent of a Divine Transubstantiation of the elements of earth, of air, of water, of fire.*

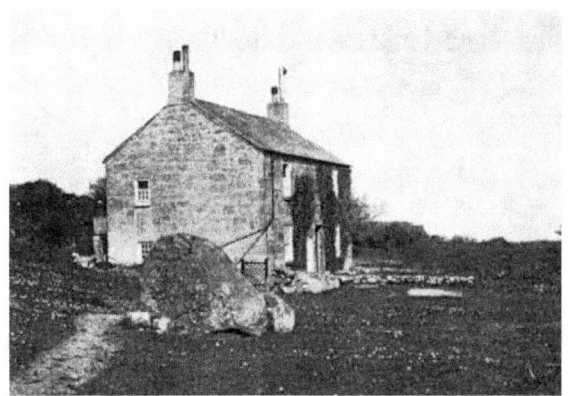

Moor Cottages near St Ives. Havelock and Edith Ellis bought the two adjacent houses in 1894, and moved into them in 1906. They had one cottage each.

Whilst there is evidence of his wife Edith visiting the Arts Club in St Ives, and having a degree of involvement with the arts community there, Havelock appears to have rather kept himself to himself. This characteristic reticence did not prevent him from writing perceptively about Cornwall in 1897 for New Century Review, however: *THE River Tamar divides from the rest of Great Britain an ancient land, small in extent but strong in its individuality. The first impression which Cornwall makes on the traveller who enters it by rail is that of a semi-French country; he passes stations with names of totally foreign complexion, St. Germans, Menheniot, Doublebois; and when he reaches his destination the names of the streets confirm this suggestion—thus, Street-an-Pol indicates a French rather than an English method of denomination. The language the people speak also scarcely sounds English to the stranger. I know a lady who immediately after arriving in Cornwall was addressed by a Cornishwoman in words that were unintelligible, but in tones that sounded so French that before realising where she was she spoke in French...*

For the sake of convenience I have called the Cornish Kelts. There is no doubt whatever that the language was purely Keltic, but the modern ethnologist is inclined to demur when the race is called Keltic...

6. Piper at the Gates of Dawn: 'Q' and the CKK

Havelock Ellis' comments about Cornwall and its 'Keltic' language were very timely. For the generation after Ellis, Celticism, spirituality and politics became closely intertwined, and they would soon combine, explosively, to bring about the 'Cornish revival'.

Arthur Quiller-Couch, writer and critic, was the son of folklorist and doctor Thomas Quiller-Couch, one of the sources for Hunt's 'Popular Romances'. Having attended Oxford University and worked there as a lecturer Arthur, or Q as he became known, returned to live in Fowey in 1891.

Q was a friend to J.M. Barrie and Kenneth Grahame (known for 'Peter Pan' and 'Wind in the Willows' respectively), both of whom spent time with him in Cornwall. Q himself became best known as the editor of the Oxford Book of English Verse, first published in 1900. However, during the two years prior to this, he was engaged in a more purely local endeavour.

Launched in 1898, with Q as its editor, The Cornish Magazine was a first attempt to publish together in a single volume original literature and articles related to Cornwall[38]. Notable in some of the earliest editions, are comments from 'eminent Cornishmen and others' on 'how to develop Cornwall as a holiday resort'. Q's contribution included the following: *I see Cornwall impoverished by the evil days on which mining and to a lesser degree agriculture have fallen…In the presence of destitution and actual famine (for in the mining district it came even to this a little while ago) one is bound, if he care for his countrymen, to consider any cure thoughtfully suggested … It is for us to provide amenities (for visitors) only we should do so with decent respect for our country and its past. I*

---

[38] Many years later Denys Val Baker's Cornish Review would follow an almost identical format.

do not, for example, look forward to seeing Dozmare turned into a sheet of ornamental water, or a casino in full swing of business amid the ruins of King Arthur's Castle...

Q's outward-looking, cosmopolitan magazine represented the first stirrings of the 20th century Cornish revival. Then, in 1901, Q became one of the founding members of Cowethas Kelto-Kernuak (CKK), or the Cornish Celtic Society, which was the brainchild of an intriguing figure by the name of L.C.R. Duncombe Jewell.

Born in Liskeard (1866), but living in London (writing for the Pall Mall Gazette in 1894, his address is given as 4, Park Place, St James's), Duncombe Jewell became friendly with another key figure of the CKK, Cornish language expert Henry Jenner, through their mutual involvement with legitimist politics in the 1890's. Both men were monarchists and members of the Order of the White Rose, a secret society of Jacobites loyal to the House of Stuart and supportive of its claims to the British throne[39].

Duncombe Jewell became editor of the order's magazine 'The Royalist' after joining it in 1890. Jenner, as Chancellor of the order, presided over the elaborate initiation ceremonies of the 'Companions-elect' and had been instrumental in organising The Stuart Exhibition which opened at the New Gallery in December 1888[40] (Lowenna, 2005).

It is not known if Aleister Crowley, the infamous occultist, was a member of the order but he is likely to have been, as he became involved in a conspiracy involving Jenner and some of the other members. He was also a close friend of Duncombe Jewell, both men having lived in strict Plymouth Brethren households in Streatham when they were younger (Kaczynski, 2010).

Like Jenner and Duncombe Jewell, Crowley had, in the period before he became immersed in the occult, been seduced by Celticism. Crowley explains it thus: *My reactionary conservatism came into conflict with my*

---

[39] Just as most Cornishmen had supported King Charles I in the Civil War, many Jacobites, and members of the Order had links to the Celtic nations. (Sharon Lowenna, 2004)

[40] The Order of the White Rose had religious, fraternal and political elements. Jenner, for example, saw parliamentary democracy as the regrettable product of a more rational and secular society. His loyalty to the monarchy could largely be explained by his religious faith and belief in the divine right of kings (ie that the authority of kings is ordained by God.

anti-Catholicism. A reconciliation was effected by means of what they called the Celtic Church. Here was a romantic and mystical idea which suited my political and religious notions down to the ground. It lived and moved in an atmosphere of fairies, seal-women and magical operations. Sacramentalism was kept in the foreground and sin was regarded without abhorrence. Chivalry and mystery were its pillars. It was free from priestcraft and tyranny, for the simple reason that it did not really exist! My innate transcendentalism leapt out towards it. The Morte d'Arthur, Lohengrin and Parsifal were my world. I not only wanted to go out on the quest of the Holy Grail, I intended to do it.

The subversive spirituality of the Celt was also linked to Crowley's Jacobitism: something, as a callow 23 year old, he was seemingly willing to fight for: *Scott, Burns and my cousin Gregor had made me a romantic Jacobite. I regarded the Houses of Hanover and Coburg as German usurpers; and I wished to place "Mary III and IV" on the throne. I was a bigoted legitimist. I actually joined a conspiracy on behalf of Don Carlos, obtained a commission to work a machine gun, took pains to make myself a first-class rifle shot and studied drill, tactics and strategy.* (Crowley, 1989).

The conspiracy in question was conceived by members of The Order of the White Rose at the instigation of Lord Ashburnham, who had acquired a boat 'The Firefly'. In summer 1899 it was intercepted by Spanish authorities, and found to be carrying 4000 rifles intended for Carlist insurgents. Henry Jenner, using his expertise as a linguist honed during many years working in the library of the British Museum, is known for his part to have helped send coded messages to the Carlists in Spain.

At around the same time (November 1898) Crowley, famously, joined The Hermetic Order of the Golden Dawn, a magical secret society then presided over by another extremist Jacobite: Samuel Liddell MacGregor Mathers from his base in Paris. Some authors have claimed that Mathers too was a member of the Order of the White Rose.

Certainly many members of the Golden Dawn, including Mathers, had been involved with Madame Blavatsky's Theosophical Society, which introduced Buddhism, yoga, meditation and other oriental religious practices to Western audiences for the first time. The Golden Dawn, in contrast, drew more on Western occult and esoteric traditions and was established as a direct offshoot of the Freemasons.

> **SEIZURE OF A BRITISH YACHT.**
> MADRID, JUNE 17.
> The Spanish Consul at Arcachon officially confirms the report of the seizure at that port of the British yacht Firefly, 138 tons, having on board 4,000 rifles, supposed to be intended for the Carlists. It is alleged that the yacht belongs to an Englishman representing Don Carlos in England. There were 15 men on board, and the name of her commander is given as Mr. Vincent English. The vessel is stated to have come from Dartmouth. The rifles seized are described as being of the chassepot pattern.—*Reuter.*

Visionary Irish poet and Celtic Revivalist WB Yeats, who lived in Havelock Ellis's flat and contributed poetry to Q's Cornish Magazine, joined The Golden Dawn in 1890, some years before Crowley. He is another who was drawn to both Celticism and the occult. Their mutual appeal seems, for Yeats, clearly linked to the crisis of faith brought about by the rise of evolutionary theory. Two scientists who had done much to popularise the work of Charles Darwin, and thereby promote the cause of Scientific Naturalism, were considered especially blameworthy in this regard: *I am very religious, and deprived by Huxley and Tyndall, whom I detested, of the simple-minded religion of my childhood, I had made a new religion, almost an infallible Church of poetic tradition, of a fardel of stories, and of personages, and of emotions, inseparable from their first expression, passed on from generation to generation by poets and painters with some help from philosophers and theologians. I wished for a world where I could discover this tradition perpetually, and not in pictures and in poems only, but in tiles around the chimney-piece and in the hangings that kept out the draught* (Yeats, 1921)

The situation in Ireland, which was still seeking Home Rule, meant that for the Irish the notion of Celticity had become strongly politicised. Like Evans-Wentz (author of 'Fairy-Faith in Celtic Countries') who had been inspired by him, Yeats saw a stark dichotomy between the Celt and the Anglo-Saxon, and referred to the Celtic revival as 'the revolt of the soul against the intellect'. Here he is responding to Matthew Arnold's own theories on the Celtic sensibility: *Literature dwindles to a mere chronicle of circumstance, or passionless phantasies, and passionless meditations, unless it is constantly flooded with the passions and beliefs of ancient times, and that of all the fountains of the passions and beliefs of ancient times in Europe, the Slavonic, the Finnish, the Scandinavian, and the Celtic, the Celtic alone has been for centuries close to the main river of European literature. It has again and again brought 'the vivifying spirit' 'of excess' into the arts of Europe.* (Yeats, 1897)

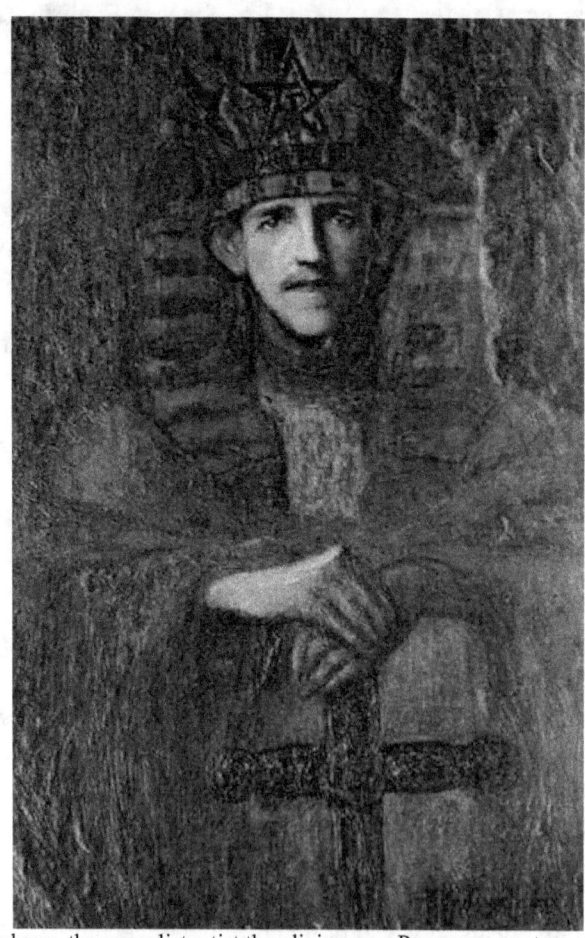

Ithell Colquhoun, the surrealist artist then living near Penzance, wrote a very personal account of the history of the Golden Dawn (Sword of Wisdom 1975). She had, in her house in Paul near Newlyn, an oil painting of Mathers that his wife Moina had painted. It remains the most important image of the most important modern occultist.

In August 1901 Yeats attended the Celtic Congress in Dublin, and would have heard a paper written by Duncombe-Jewell on behalf of the Cornish Celtic Society, famously arguing that Cornwall be recognised as a sixth Celtic nation.

> in Ireland at the earliest opportunity, in 1904 if possible. The next question that came on for consideration was as to whether Cornwall should be recognized as a Celtic nation. Mr. Fournier read a paper written by Mr. L. C. R. Duncombe Jewell, M.A., giving reasons in favour of the recognition of Cornwall. The writer of the paper, who was unable to attend the congress, stated that the objection that the Cornish language was dead could readily be disposed of. It was not dead, and there was a growing movement in the country to learn more about it. A resolution having been formally moved by Mr. Le Fuster, and seconded by the Hon. Stuart Erskine, in favour of the recognition of Cornwall, Lord Castletown said one of their great points was that the nations who joined them should have a living language, and they had no evidence that Cornish was spoken as a living language. He proposed as an amendment that the question should be postponed to the next pan-Celtic congress. The amendment on a division was carried by 34 votes to 22. On

Duncombe Jewell's attempt to have Cornwall recognised by the Celtic Congress. The Times August 1901. This paper was published in its entirety in Celtia journal October 1901.

The paper in question was later published in Celtia (October, 1901) and its impassioned prose restates some of the themes so beloved of Duncombe Jewell and his circle: *That Cornwall, for lack of spoken word or written paper, should be allowed to slip from the charmed circle of Celtia, with all its enormous treasures of Celtic antiquities, its literature, its language, its fascinating folklore, its historical struggles against the encroachments of the Saxon, its still strong and vivid belief in the ultimate re-incarnation of its hopes, and dreams, and aspirations in the person of King Arthur—whose soul, according to Cornish tradition, passed into the body of the sacred chough, the Tshauha of our tongue, from the Pool of Dosmare, until the time of the re-union of Celtdom under one Arluth, one Ard-righ,— is something not to be thought.*

Duncombe Jewell's paper also includes an intriguing reference to WB Yeats' Golden Dawn-infused 'The Tables of the Law' which was published in 'The Savoy' by Havelock-Ellis's friend Arthur Symons: *The Cornishman is a dreamer of the sort to which Mr. W. B. Yeats, in The Tables of the Law, gives definitive words. He has "the nature that is half monk, half soldier of fortune, and must needs turn action into dreaming, and dreaming into action."*

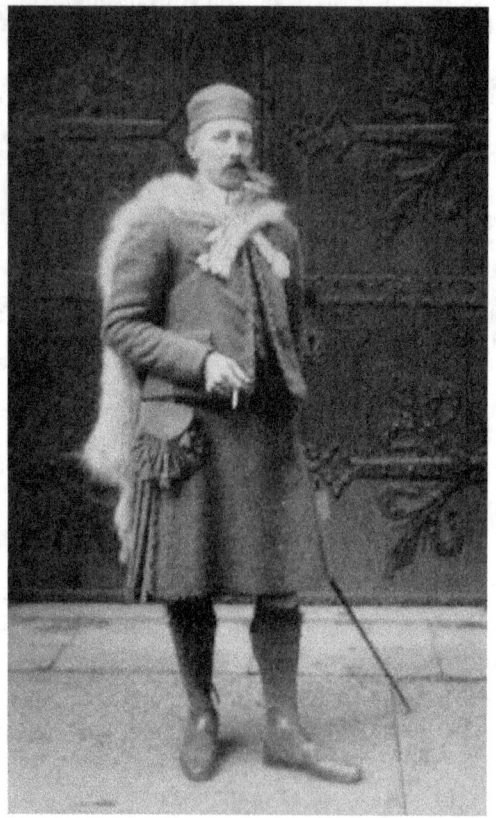

Duncombe Jewell

The folklore of Cornwall, one of exceptional richness, will be found curiously like that of Ireland on the one hand and of Brittany on the other. Those interested in this so fascinating subject may be advised to take and compare Lady Wilde's Legends of Ireland with Robert Hunt's Popular Romances of Cornwall. They will find there the fairy legends of Ireland and Brittany, the same belief in witchcraft, in mermaids, in demons and spectres...We have the Arthurian legend, the Tregeagle legend, the tales of the giants; and although we cannot boast of the great inheritance of epic heroes like Oisin and Fingal, we have at least one tale of like calibre in the legend of Tamara.[41]

Duncombe Jewell can be regarded as the unsung hero of the Cornish Celtic revival. He is the first to have suggested that Cornwall could have its own Gorsedd, and he appears to have been crucial in galvanising Henry Jenner to write up his Cornish language research, and produce the influential 'Handbook of the Cornish Language' of 1904.

But his activities remain somewhat shadowy, particularly as regards the extent of his involvement with the occult. He clearly had a number of contacts in the Golden Dawn. After publishing several more times in Celtia, late in 1902 he went to Ireland, to visit WB Yeats, ostensibly to have his tarot read by Annie Horniman. In a letter to Yeats subsequently he referred obliquely to a thwarted ambition to stage a Cornish miracle play: *I came back from Ireland on Wednesday. I have not slept since then with the exception of a few hours today. I have been in great trouble. My conscience has been going here and there like a weather cock. I could not find out what I had to do – I wanted to do right. She has held my conscience still. I know now where it is pointing. But there may be no*

---

[41] The legend of Tamara – as told by Duncombe Jewell: *Tavy and Tawrage, sons of Dartmoor giants, loved Tamara, the beautiful daughter of earth spirits, who, glorying in the light of the sun, left her cavern and was pursued long time by her admirers over moor and heath and fen; until caught by them under a bush, in Moorwinstow, they attempted to compel her to a choice between them. Here they were surprised by Tamara's father, and the gnome cast over the giants the spell of slumber and endeavoured to persuade his daughter to return to him to his cavern. Enraged at her refusal, he put upon her a terrible curse and Tamara, dissolving in tears changed into a river which should flow on for ever to the ocean. When Tavy awoke and found Tamara gone, his father, at his request, transformed him likewise into a stream, and rushing down from the hills, he still goes seeking his Tamara; his only joy that he runs by her side, and that mingling at length their waters, they glide together to the eternal sea. Tawrage, too, found an enchanter, who, at his prayer, changed him likewise into a river; but, mistaking the road by which Tamara travelled, he fares northward on the hopeless, never-ending quest, his bitter fate that, still sorrowing he must continue to flow on, ever getting farther and farther from his lost Tamara.*

miracle play now. This may be social extinction for me (Kaczynski, 2010).

Here he is also referring to his marriage, which appears to have been failing, as early in spring 1903 he went to live in Scotland with Aleister Crowley, who had recently bought Boleskine House near Loch Ness - later owned by Jimmy Page of Led Zeppelin - with the express intention of performing the elaborate ritual of Abramelin the Mage.

A SONNET IN CORNISH.
By L. C. Duncombe-Jewell.

Mychternes, Mychternes a'n eleth dhus!
Pan us 'gan beunans moel wherow vre,
  Hag an treys skith war an fordh difygans,
  Luen ef a beryl; sellys 'gan guelvans
Dre'n armor mear; agan skovornow, gwae,
Bodhar a gwrys gans lef a gwyns adre:
  Pan lowen cellys demythas tristans,
  A neb a flehes 'gan pesadow gens:
Pan an gelvinak ole war an bre:

Dus, a Varia, steyr y'th vlew, a dhus!
  Ha syns dhe lau, par del an loer gwen,
  Avan war agan pennow'n agan ken.
    Del welon, dres tubbanow dybyta,
    Dew, ar tir dagrow a welas adrus,
      Ha Cryst a marow auch war crows-an-wra.

which may be translated:—

When our life is a bare bitter hill, and our tired feet upon the way of peril full are failing; salted our lips by the great surge...

Possibly the first modern poem written and published in Cornish appeared on the pages of the October 1901 edition of Celtia.

Crowley, in his highly amusing 'autohagiography', describes Duncombe Jewell and his influence on his writing at the time: *There is a touch of the influence of a man named L.C.R. Duncombe Jewell, the eldest son of a Plymouth Brother at Streatham, who had "gone to the bad" by becoming a Roman Catholic. I had asked him to spend a week at Boleskine and he had managed somehow or other to settle down there as my factor. I suppose he saved me trouble in one way or another, and was some sort of companion. He called himself Ludovic Cameron, being a passionate Jacobite and having a Cameron somewhere in his family tree. He was very keen on the Celtic revival and wanted to unite the five Celtic nations in an empire. In this political project he had not wholly succeeded: but he had got as far as designing a flag. And, oh so ugly!*

Duncombe Jewell was at Crowley's wedding in Scotland, as Crowley recalls: *We repaired to the sheriff's and were induced to swear the most formidable oaths; about nothing in particular, but they apparently gratified the official instinct and filled the official coffer. Duncombe Jewell excelled himself. The ordinary oath was not for him. He produced a formula the majesty of which literally inhibited the normal functions of our minds. It was the finest piece of ritualistic rigmarole that I have ever heard in my life.*

There are several other mentions of Duncombe Jewell in Crowley's account of his colourful life: *On July 28th my wife (Rose) gave birth to a girl, called Nuit Ma Ahathoor Hecate Sappho Jezebel Lilith. Nuit was given in homage to our Lady of the Stars; Ma, goddess of Justice, because the sign of Libra was rising; Ahathoor, goddess of Love and Beauty, because Venus rules Libra; I'm not sure about the name Hecate, but it may have been as a compliment to the infernal gods; a poet could hardly do less than commemorate the only lady who ever wrote poetry, Sappho; Jezebel still held her place as my favourite character in Scripture; and Lilith, of course, holds undisputed possession of my affections in the realm of demons. Duncombe Jewell remarked later on that she had died of acute nomenclature.*

Duncombe Jewell seemed to lose his close involvement with the Cornish revival after disappearing to Boleskine[42]. Parenthetically, in 1903 he

---

[42] Duncombe Jewell saw active service with the Cameron Highlanders during 1915 but otherwise spent most of the rest of his life in quiet part-time administrative jobs, managing sports clubs in Hendon and Gloucester and working as Road Transport Officer in Hereford, whilst trying to maintain his career as a writer. In this latter capacity he published books on field sports and fox hunting, (eg 'The Hunting Horn: What to blow and how to blow it' (1908), 'Otters and Otter-hunting' (1908)) and another on wild-foods and foraging ('The Wild Foods of Great Britain' (1917) and also contributed several articles to The Occult Review. But it was a precarious existence, and in November 1918

published two poems ('Mermaid of Zennor' and 'Kyn Vyttyn (Before Morning)' in Pamela 'Pixie' Coleman Smith's magazine 'The Green Sheaf'. Coleman Smith was another member of the Golden Dawn, and an artist who designed AE Waite's definitive tarot card deck (the Waite-Smith deck). After converting to Catholicism, Smith moved to Parc Garland on The Lizard in West Cornwall in 1918, eventually dying in Bude, where she is buried.

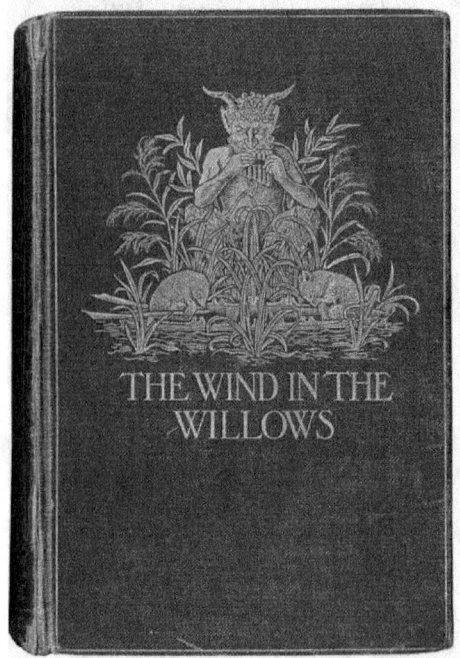 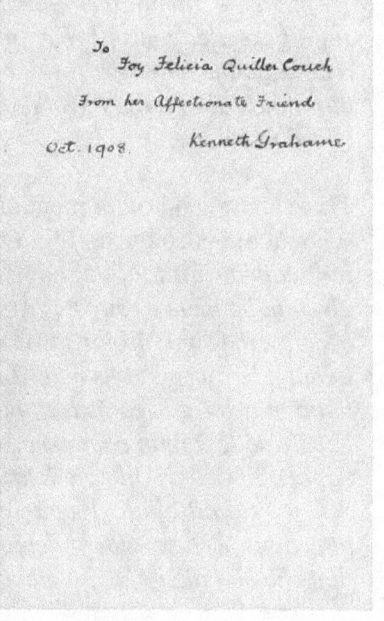

The first edition of The Wind in the Willows, depicting Rat and Mole bowing in worship of Pan. The book is dedicated to Quiller-Couch's daughter.

---

the Gloucester Chronicle reported on his appearance in the local Bankruptcy Court. More newspaper articles in 1929 (eg Western Daily Press) reported that he had paid his debts in full.

If Edward Carpenter and Havelock Ellis were Victorian social reformers who emphasised sexual freedom, and linked it to healthy, natural living, others, particularly the romantic poets (and lesser occultist-poets like Crowley who were inspired by them) extolled the virtues of nature and the English landscape symbolically, by invoking the Greek god 'Pan'.

Depicted peacefully reclining in groves of dappled light, Pan had, increasingly, been seen as the guardian of all that was beautiful and good about the natural world and in this sense was at his most popular in the twenty years leading up to WW1. It has been argued that, for many, Christianity had become tainted by its complicity with civilisation and industrialisation, hence the decisive emergence of this pagan god, who was seen, increasingly, as a benign protector (Hutton, 1999)

Crowley's own fondness for Pan was such that his controversial 'Hymn to Pan' was read at his funeral. Pan is also seen as the obvious precursor of the post-war Neo-pagan horned god of Wicca (Hutton, 1999).

But Pan's most notable appearance in the literature of this period is in the chapter entitled 'The Piper at the Gates of Dawn' - later an inspiration to Syd Barrett's Pink Floyd - in 'The Wind in the Willows' by Kenneth Grahame (1908). It is a book that was partly written in, and inspired by, Cornwall.

In this extract, Pan is here referred to as 'the Friend and Helper'. It is the early hours of the morning: ......*Trembling (Mole) raised his humble head; and then, in that utter clearness of the imminent dawn, while Nature, flushed with fullness of incredible colour, seemed to hold her breath for the event, he looked in the very eyes of the Friend and Helper; saw the backward sweep of the curved horns, gleaming in the growing daylight; saw the stern, hooked nose between the kindly eyes that were looking down on them humorously, while the bearded mouth broke into a half-smile at the corners; saw the rippling muscles on the arm that lay across the broad chest, the long supple hand still holding the pan-pipes only just fallen away from the parted lips; saw the splendid curves of the shaggy limbs disposed in majestic ease on the sward; saw, last of all, nestling between his very hooves, sleeping soundly in entire peace and contentment, the little, round, podgy, childish form of the baby otter. All this he saw, for one moment breathless and intense, vivid on the morning sky; and still, as he looked, he lived; and still, as he lived he wondered.*

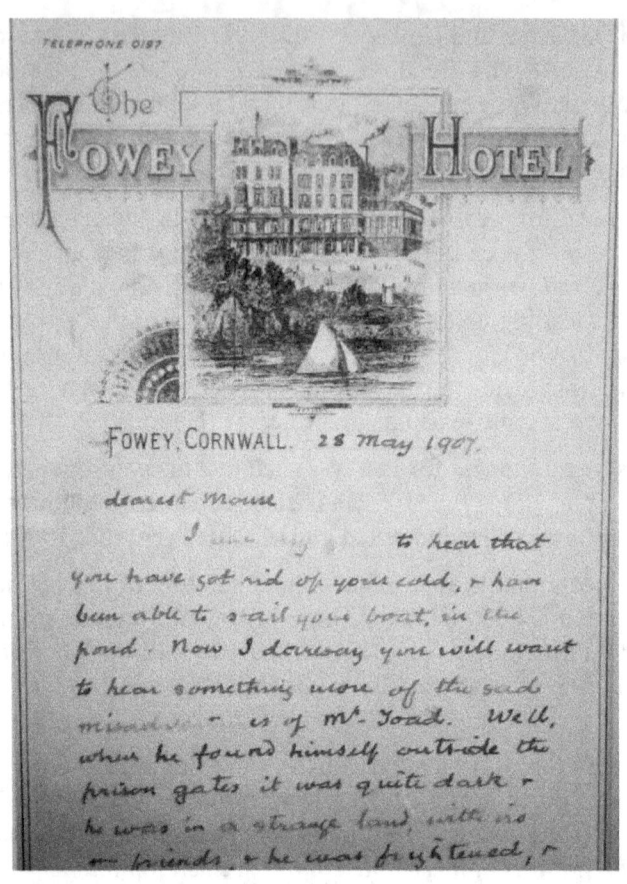

The origin of 'Wind in the Willows': letters home to Kenneth Grahame's 7 year old son 'Mouse', written from Fowey in 1907. Photo the author.

"Rat!" he found breath to whisper, shaking. "Are you afraid?"
"Afraid?" murmured the Rat, his eyes shining with unutterable love.
"Afraid! Of Him? O, never, never! And yet—~and yet—O, Mole, I am afraid!" Then the two animals, crouching to the earth, bowed their heads and did worship.

Friend of 'Q', Kenneth Grahame worked in a senior position in the Bank of England. It was a job which he loathed, but he always took holidays in Cornwall and enjoyed boat trips on the peaceful River Fowey towards

Lerryn[43]. Indeed he was married in Fowey Church in 1899, his bride-to-be having soaked her wedding dress in the morning dew (Hutton, 1999). 'The Wind in the Willows' started as a series of letters written in Cornish hotels, particularly the Greenbank, Falmouth and the Fowey Hotel, to his son who had the nick-name 'Mouse'.

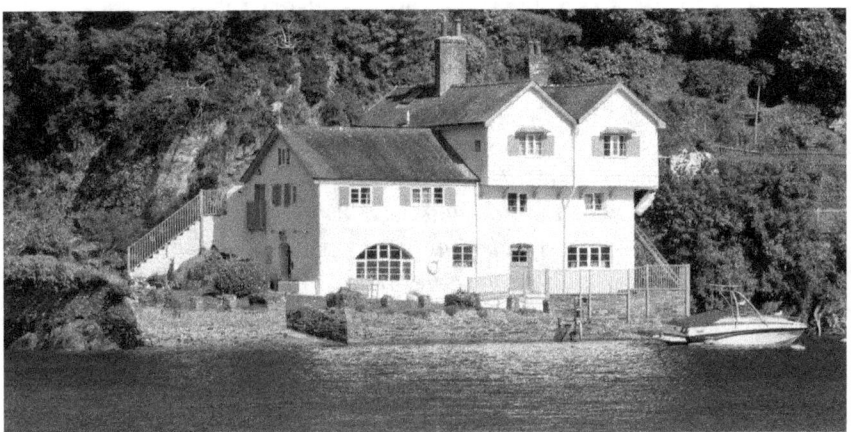

Ferryside in Bodinnick. Owned by the Du Maurier family since 1926.

Fowey itself subsequently became the epicentre of Daphne Du Maurier's Cornwall. It is located between her first house in Cornwall, 'Ferryside' in Bodinnick (a boat-builder's workshop which her family acquired and converted in 1926 when Daphne was 19) and her second, the very grand Rashleigh-owned 'Menabilly', near Par.

---

[43] A few years later, in 1922, the now ruinous Tivoli Gardens opened to the public. They were built by China Clay magnate Frank Parkyn on the banks of the river in Lerryn, and were the site of a popular regatta. Also on the river, nearer Fowey, is Sawmills, where, before it became a recording studio, the Val Baker family lived.

7. Rananim: DH Lawrence and his circle

In his early 20s (during 1908-1909), the novelist DH Lawrence was exposed to the writing of Havelock Ellis, Edward Carpenter and other modernist writers via the pages of 'The New Age', to which he is known to have been a subscriber and, later, a contributor. Like Ellis he became a victim of the censor and the popular press, and like Carpenter he saw great value in 'natural man': *My great religion is a belief in the blood, the flesh, as being wiser than the intellect. We can go wrong in our minds. But what our blood feels and believes and says, is always true. The intellect is only a bit and a bridle. What do I care about knowledge? All I want is to answer to my blood, direct, without fribbling intervention of mind, or moral, or whatnot* (cf Sagar, 1975).

Lawrence lived in Cornwall between December 30th 1915 and October 15th 1917. He and his wife Frieda, like Ben Nicholson and Barbara Hepworth more than twenty years later, were fleeing Hampstead where they had recently witnessed the first big Zeppelin raid on London from a vantage point on the Heath. Feeling alienated from England and English society, Lawrence had for some time been talking about leaving for America to form a community, which in letters at the period he referred to as 'Rananim': *I want to gather together about twenty souls and sail away from this world of war and squalor and find a little colony where there shall be no money but a sort of communism as far as the necessities of life go, and some real decency*[44].

At the time he was struggling to make ends meet, and though he had made some influential friends, including Bertrand Russell and many of the Bloomsbury Group, he felt misunderstood and persecuted by the English establishment. These feelings were compounded when his book 'The Rainbow' (1915) was panned by the critics, and, famously

---

[44] Indeed throughout his life, Lawrence would wistfully refer to 'Rananim', and when he did he had in mind an anti-urban, self-sufficient agrarian community not unlike those promoted by Ruskin, Carpenter, Tolstoy and Kropotkin/Bakunin.

described as 'a monstrous wilderness of phallicism'. And as we shall see, though he failed to create his ideal community, Lawrence was at the centre of a small group of other creative souls in Cornwall.

He and Frieda initially moved into a farmhouse in Porthcothan in North Cornwall loaned to him by science fiction writer JD Beresford (father of Elizabeth Beresford of The Wombles). From there he wrote daily to friends, publishers and benefactors, captivated by the landscape, its Celticism and its perceived 'otherness':

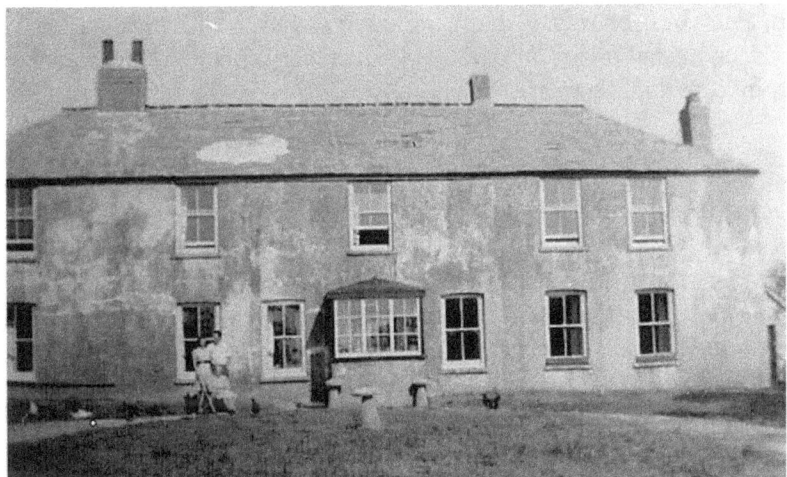

Porthcothan House, Porthcothan in 1949. DH Lawrence and Frieda lived here before moving to Zennor.

To Catherine Carswell 31/12/15
I love being here: such a calm, old, slightly deserted house — a farmhouse; and the country remote and desolate and unconnected: it belongs still to the days before Christianity, the days of Druids, or of desolate Celtic magic and conjuring; and the sea is so grey and shaggy, and the wind so restless, as if it had never found a home since the days of Iseult. Here I think my life begins again — one is free. Here the autumn is gone by, it is pure winter of forgetfulness. I love it. Soon I shall begin to write a story — a mid—winter story of oblivion.

To Bertand Russell 13/1/16
I like being here very much. Cornwall isn't England. It isn't really England, nor Christendom. It has another quality: of King Arthur's days, that flicker of Celtic consciousness before it was swamped under Norman and Teutonic waves. I like it very much. I like the people also. They've got a curious softness, and intimacy. I think they've lived from just the opposite principle to Christianity: self-fulfilment and social destruction, instead of social love and self-sacrifice...That's why they're generally disliked. And that's why they were wreckers and smugglers and all antisocial things...

In fact Lawrence spent much of his time at Porthcothan laid up in bed with a nervous illness but, as spring came and his health improved, he was keen to stay on in Cornwall. Here he records his joyful optimism on first discovering Zennor:

To Lady Ottoline Morrell 25/2/16
Zennor is lovely — 5 miles S. of St. Ives: lovely pale hills all gorse and heather, and a great peacock—iridescent sea. We can have a house at Gurnards Head for 25/- a week. The Murrys will come in April and share it with us: also Heseltine, if he escapes conscription. So all will be well. They will help us to live cheaply. Heseltine is very good, always paying more than his share. We have got nothing coming in, as yet: but perhaps something will turn up. I shall tell you when we are really in need. When we came over the shoulder of the wild hill, above the sea, to Zennor, I felt we were coming into the Promised Land. I know there will a new heaven and a new earth take place now: we have triumphed. I feel like a Columbus who can see a shadowy America before him: only this isn't merely territory, it is a new continent of the soul. We will all be happy yet, doing a new, constructive work, sailing into a new epoch. Don't let us be troubled.

The abovementioned Philip Heseltine (known later as the composer Peter Warlock), who at the time was only 21, stayed with the Lawrences in both Porthcothan and Zennor. Heseltine had been encouraged to become a composer by Frederick Delius, with whom he had corresponded since he was a boy.

In April 1916, Heseltine wrote to Delius describing a failed attempt to raise money by contacting friends and benefactors in order to publish

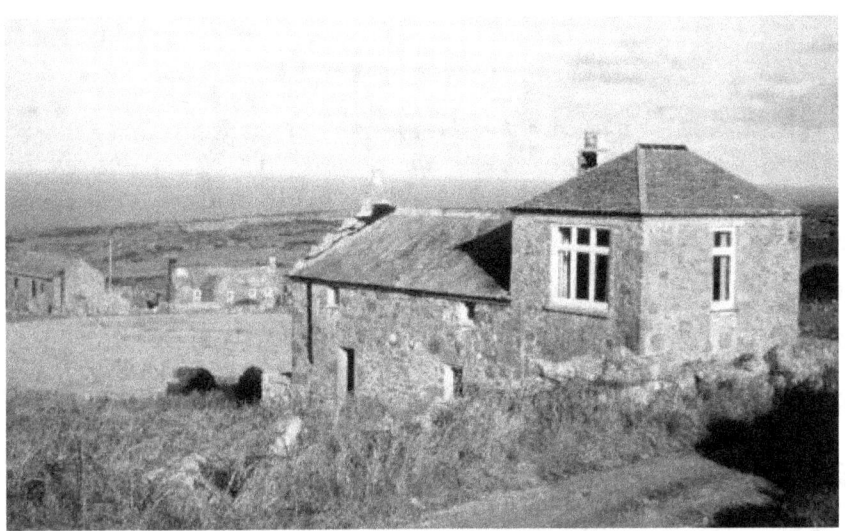

Tower House, Higher Tregerthen: the house where Mansfield and DH Lawrence lived. Later Michael Morpurgo also lived and worked here.

'The Rainbow' on Lawrence's behalf. *The Rainbow scheme fulfilled your prophecy and died the death. I got 30 replies to 600 circulars. But I would gladly lend you my copy of The Rainbow if you are keen to see it...Lawrence is a fine artist and a hard though horribly distorted thinker. But personal relationship with him is impossible – he acts as a subtle and deadly poison.*

John Middleton Murry and Katherine Mansfield, two other modernist writers, also stayed at Tregerthen (Zennor), but within a few months had moved away again to live in Mylor near Falmouth[45]. Like Heseltine, they had found that Lawrence was often not easy company. Certainly Lawrence's letters from Zennor become increasingly infused by anger and hatred towards humanity; feelings largely provoked by the ongoing carnage of the First World War:

---

[45] Katherine Mansfield, acquired a reputation as a short story writer, but died of tuberculosis when she was only 34. Her husband, Middleton Murry, went on to found and edit The Adelphi Magazine and literary journal, rival to TS Eliot's Criterion.

Letter to Barbara Low 1/5/16
My dear Barbara,
I would write to you oftener, but this life of today so disgusts one, it leaves nothing to say. The war, the approaching conscription, the sense of complete paltriness and chaotic nastiness in life, really robs one of speech.
It is very lovely here, with the gorse all yellow and the sea a misty, periwinkle blue, and the flowers coming out on the common. The sense of jeopardy spoils it all — the feeling that one may be flung out into the cess-pool of a world, the danger of being dragged in to the foul conglomerate mess, the utter disgust and nausea one feels for humanity, people smelling like bugs, endless masses of them, and no relief: it is so difficult to bear.

Letter to Catherine Carswell 9/7/16
I never wrote to tell you that they gave me a complete exemption from all military service, thanks be to God. That was a week ago last Thursday. I had to join the Colours in Penzance, be conveyed to Bodmin (60 miles), spend a night in barracks with all the other men, and then be examined. It was experience enough for me, of soldiering. I am sure I should die in a week, if they kept me. It is the annulling of all one stands for, this militarism, the nipping of the very germ of one's being. I was very much upset. The sense of spiritual disaster everywhere was quite terrifying. This is the most terrible madness. And the worst of it all, is, that it is a madness of righteousness. These Cornish are most, most unwarlike, soft, peaceable, ancient. No men could suffer more than they, at being conscripted — at any rate, those that were with me.

Cornwall helped Lawrence's withdrawal from a mad, uncaring world, but it also appears to have heightened his paranoia and sense of rejection by the establishment. In one of his letters he compares himself to a monk:

Letter to Lady Cynthia Asquith 1/9/16
Here in Nitria there is great space, great hollow reverberating silent space, the beauty of all the universe:- nothing more. The few visionary temptations: heather and blackberries on the hills, a foamy pool in the rocks where one bathes, the postman with barbed letters: they are the disordered hallucinations of temporal reality. Saint Anthony is not

deceived by them. In truth there is vast unechoing space where one goes forth and is free....Frieda talks of coming to London for a few days this month. I simply dare not. The thought of the masses of humanity frightens my very soul. I dare not be jostled into them. But before long, when I am stronger than they, I shall come back. Meanwhile, the monk of Nitria fitfully types out his novel, which is a sequel to the Rainbow.

Philip Heseltine wrote from The Tinner's Arms, Zennor early in 1917: *This stupendous spring is going to blow my head clean off, I am sure, and I shall have to go chasing it over the moors like a bit of dandelion fluff from one sea to the other!* (Gray, 1934).

And from Newmill outside Penzance: *I am living now in a little wooden house on the highest point of the moor....all round on all sides nothing but open moorland and rock-strewn hills, mostly crowned with marvelous Druidic temples. The sky never grows dark; the darkness seems rather to come welling out of the earth like a dye, infusing into every shape and form, every twig and every stone, a keen intense blackness...*

It seems Heseltine enticed fellow musician, Cecil Gray to come to the cliffs of West Cornwall later that spring. Regulars at the Café Royal in Piccadilly, the two musicians had shared a studio in Battersea during 1916, and Gray ended up renting Bosigran Castle, with the intention of moving there permanently. The landscape also made a deep impression on him. Talking of Morvah and Bosigran, he wrote in his autobiography: *It is a magical country but the magic is black....It must have been the centre in ancient times - prehistoric no doubt - of sacrificial blood-rites and unspeakable abominations, the exhalations of which still unmistakably hover around, poisoning the air.* (Gray, 1948)

At around the same time, Heseltine introduced DH Lawrence to Meredith Starr and his new wife Lady Mary Stamford who were staying at Treveal, a farm near Bosigran, where they had hoped to start an artist's colony[46]. Like Gray, Starr was part of the circle centered on the Café

---

[46] Meredith Starr was the pen-name of Herbert H. Close, as explained by Ithell Colquhoun in 'Sword of Wisdom' (1975). Later, in the 30s, Close worked as a 'free-lance psychotherapist', and Colquhoun spent an unsatisfactory weekend with him at a therapeutic retreat in Devon.

Royal, and was another close to Aleister Crowley. In 1910 Starr's interest in occultism had led him to join Crowley's A∴A∴ (Order of the Silver Star). He had also become a sub-editor of, and contributor to, Crowley's Equinox Magazine (Newman, 2005).

Starr encouraged Philip Heseltine's burgeoning interest in the occult, and in a letter to poet Robert Nichols, Heseltine indicates that just before leaving Cornwall he had been dabbling with ceremonial magic: *I wrote you an idiotic letter some four months ago – believe it or not as you like, I was suffering from the reaction that inevitably overtakes those who tamper prematurely with the science vulgarly known as Black Magic. But a new environment has I think quite cured me....*

Starr was in Cornwall in August 1917, when he put on a performance of his concert-play 'East and West'. The occasion provoked violent correspondence in the St Ives Times and Echo[47], with the loudest, most disparaging voice that of A G Folliott Stokes, artist turned art-critic, of the Arts Club: *'Mr Starr's attempts were little more than buffoonery...'*

The following week Starr, with extraordinary self-belief, defends himself:
Dear Sir
...I think that a certain amount of buffoonery is both necessary and desirable at the present stage of the people's evolution. Among hundreds of admittedly brilliant men I have not met more than five who are capable of even thinking....I have only come across one supreme genius, an all round, (or practically so), synthetic genius, in fact a Man. This miracle is Aleister Crowley, the Rosicrucean —who possesses more subtlety than Leonardo, more power than Zanoni, more humanity than Mejnour, united to a versatility and perfection of literary and poetic technique that render him by far the greatest living artist in England a Gulliver among mere Lilliputians. The men who have the unenviable reputation of being on the Parnassus of English Art, such as Augustus

---

[47] This is explained in a letter (September 1917) in which Lawrence describes Starr and his wife to Lady Cynthia Asquith: 'a pair of herb-eating occultists: they fast, or eat nettles: they descend naked into old mine-shafts, and there meditate for hours and hours, upon their own transcendent infinitude: they descend on us like a swarm of locusts, and devour all the food on shelf or board: they even gave a concert, and made most dreadful fools of themselves, in St Ives: violent correspondence in the St Ives Times'" (Newman, 2005).

John, the painter, Jacob Epstein the sculptor, D. H. Lawrence, the celebrated Author and other revolutionaries whom I have met are of the opinion that ninety-nine per cent of British- art is worse than buffoonery.

> **A CONCERT-PLAY**
>
> (By Meredith Starr), entitled—
>
> **"EAST AND WEST,"**
>
> Will be given in
>
> **The Pavilion, St. Ives,**
>
> On Wednesday, August 22nd, at 8 p.m.
>
> Artistes—
> LADY MARY STARR
> MR. MEREDITH STARR & others.
> Violin: Mr. H. TREVOR WHITE, A.C.V.
> Piano: MISS PRAHM.
>
> **SONGS AND DANCES**
>
> Will be included in the Programme.
>
> Prices of Admission: 3/3, 2/2 and 1/2, including Tax.
>
> Doors open 7-30 p.m.
>
> One third of the Proceeds will be given to the Local Red Cross Fund.
>
> Plan of Hall and Tickets at the office of the *St. Ives Times.*

From the St Ives Times And Echo 1917

If the artists in St. Ives are willing, I shall be delighted to give an address, not only upon Art, but upon the psychology of the Artist. I have discovered a secret source of energy which enables me to turn on the tap of inspiration whenever and wherever I choose. I have several pupils -all well-known men - whom I am educating along the lines I refer to. But I do not expect the Artists of St. Ives will take my offer seriously (a veiled challenge) which is made, however, in perfect good faith. If any do I shall begin to think that St. Ives is not quite so conservative as it appears to be.

Yours truly,
MEREDITH STARR.

Horace Wooller also jumps to Starr's defence. Wooller, an alumnus of the Royal College of Art in Kensington, was staying with the Starrs and is known to have been a member of the esoteric branch of the Theosophical Society.

Undeterred, the Starrs and Wooller advertised an art exhibition at Treveal the following month evidently aimed, at the 'conservative' art-community in the town: *'The works demonstrate new methods of execution and conception'.*

DH Lawrence viewed Meredith Starr and his activities with a healthy scepticism, but enjoyed the use of his library, for example, becoming first aware of the Hindu concept of the chakras through reading Pryse's 'The Apocalypse Unsealed' and becoming more interested in Theosophy.

During this period Philip Heseltine changed his name to Peter Warlock, and became more engaged in occult research, something which his biographer describes as having been all-consuming later in 1917 when he moved to live in Ireland to avoid conscription. Whilst in Ireland Heseltine also started to teach himself the Cornish language, and using it to write songs, as he describes in a letter to Cecil Gray: *All neo-Celtic nationalism is in effect anti-national, in the sense in which we detest nationality…What more effective protest against imperialism could you or I make than by adopting, as a pure ritual, a speech, a nationality, that no longer exists – the rebirth of a something that never was born?*

And in another: *I am writing with great enthusiasm, two Cornish hymns: it is probably the first time the old language has ever been musicked deliberately (assuming that the folk-songs – of which Cornwall seems to possess practically none – generated spontaneously).*

Cecil Gray describes the incident that lead to DH Lawrence and his wife being ejected from Cornwall in October 1917, under the terms of the Defense of the Realm Act: *The Lawrence's were spending the night at my house, and after supper, when it was already dark, we were sitting around the fire amusing ourselves by singing German folk-songs when suddenly there came a peremptory hammering at the front door. I went to open it, but even without waiting for me to do so the door was flung open and in marched half a dozen or so men with loaded rifles who proceeded to search the house saying that lights had been noticed flashing out to sea from my windows....Actually all that had happened was that a strong westerly gale was blowing that night and one of the drawing pins fastening the curtains of one of the windows had worked loose and allowed a flicker of light to escape at irregular intervals in such a way as to suggest a signalling code to those suspiciously inclined...At the very time that the light had been seen shining out to sea, a German submarine had been located in the vicinity. This coupled with Frieda's German nationality and Lawrences reputation as an immoral and subversive writer, was more than enough to create a thoroughly unpleasant, not to say dangerous, situation for us all* (Grey, 1948).

The St. Ives Times, September 7th, 1917.

ARTISTS

Living in or near St. Ives are cordially invited to a

Small Exhibition

(Drawings and Paintings chiefly) held at

THE COTTAGE, TREVEAL.

The Works demonstrate new methods of execution and conception.

Tuesday and Friday Afternoon.
Sept. 11—Sept. 14.

MEREDITH STARR
HORACE J. WOOLLER,
LADY MARY STARR.

Lawrence wrote 'Women in Love' in Cornwall. His stay left its mark on some of his later writing too, especially the novel 'Kangaroo' and the short stories 'Samson and Delilah' and 'The Fox'. The phoenix that first appeared as a drawing in one of his letters to Koteliansky, and would later form the headstone of his grave, can also be thought of as part of the legacy of his stay in Cornwall.

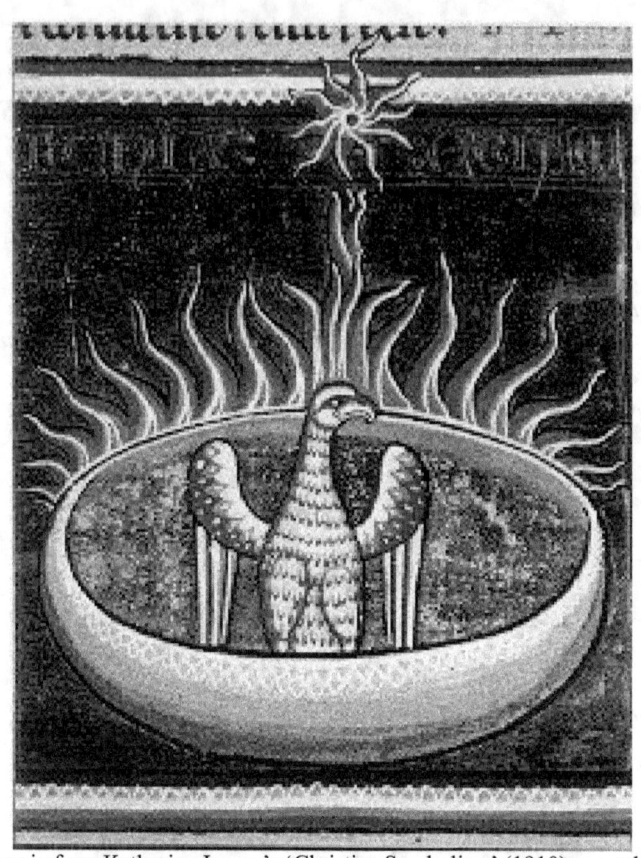

The phoenix from Katherine Jenner's 'Christian Symbolism' (1910), a symbol later adopted by DH Lawrence. Katherine, who moved to Hayle in 1909, published a number of novels in the 1890's, and went on to write 'Christ in Art' (1906), and 'Our Lady in Art' (1907).

Viewed by Lawrence as a symbol of Rananim and of hope rising from the ashes of the war, it must have been much on his mind. In 1967 an American writer visiting Cornwall discovered a handmade tapestry of the phoenix that Lawrence had painstakingly made on the clifftop of Tregerthen, and given as akeepsake to the Hocking family, his neighbours in Zennor (Payton, 2009)[48]

---

[48] The symbol of the phoenix was, incidentally, taken from the book 'Christian Symbolism' (1910) by Katherine Jenner, younger wife of Henry Jenner who had moved

After DH Lawrence left he and Frieda stayed with the leading Imagist[49] poets, husband and wife Hilda Doolittle (or 'H.D.') and Richard Adlington[50]. At the time, however, the Aldingtons' were becoming estranged, and after Lawrence introduced HD to Cecil Gray, HD moved to live with him in Bosigran, West Cornwall for nearly six months. Here in the farm on the cliffs, Gray and HD conceived their daughter Perdita, who was born in March 1919.

Whilst in Cornwall H.D. met Winnifred Ellerman, a young heiress and aspiring poet known as Bryher. Bryher, who deliberately took her nom-de-plume from the Scilly Island of the same name, had sought out HD in Bosigran having obtained her address from a mutual friend.
She nursed HD through a mental breakdown during the summer of 1919 which was spent in Cornwall and the Isles of Scilly. Indeed in the Scillies HD wrote the short book 'Notes on Thought and Vision', which describes the breakdown, and her related notion of 'jellyfish vision'.

In 1920, Havelock Ellis, who had become a mentor and therapist to many moneyed bohemians, subsequently traveled to Greece with H.D. and Bryher, whom he had met the previous year when they came to him for psychological help. He returned alone, however, after deciding that they were too 'indecisive' for him. H.D. later brought Ellis the message that Freud wanted to meet him, but Ellis, apparently, demurred.

---

to live in Hayle near St Ives after retiring from his work at the British Museum in 1909. Lawrence read and enthused about the book in 1914. The phoenix image came to represent Rananim, and later adorned both the front cover of 'Lady Chatterley's Lover' and the headstone of Lawrence's grave (see image).

[49]Imagism constituted the first and most influential English-language literary movement of the modernist era, and it had its origins in discussions on poetry in the correspondence pages of The New Age journal. These debates then continued at the tables of the Eiffel Tower Restaurant, and in 1909 came to include Ezra Pound, who is thought to have first coined the name. HD was at one stage, engaged to poet Ezra Pound who helped to launch her writing career.

[50] HD travelled, in 1911, with close friend Frances Gregg, who later had an affair with John Cooper Powys, before moving to Cornwall (St Columb) during the war, only to die in Plymouth during an air raid. Gregg's memoirs, together with letters from Pound, HD and others was rescued from the rubble.

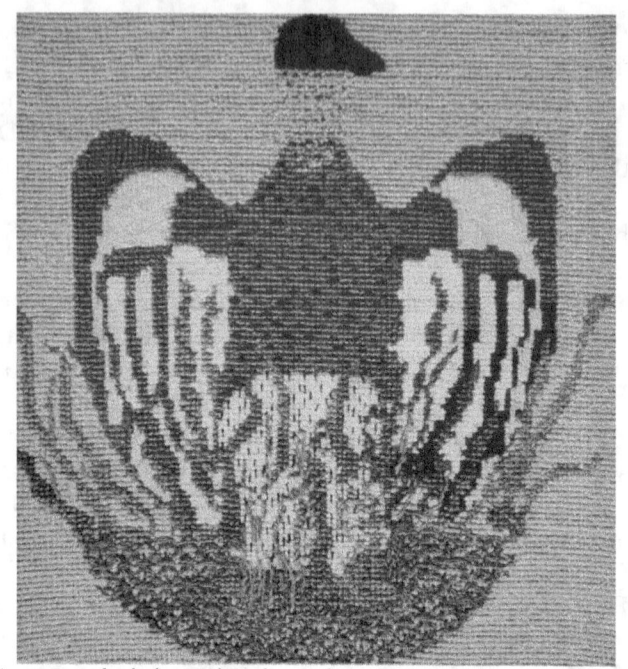

A tapestry depicting a phoenix, made by D H Lawrence in Cornwall.

DH Lawrence, meanwhile, spent the rest of his life restless and itinerant, living frugally with little money. In a sense he continued his search for a place and a people unspoilt by civilization. In this regard he was particularly taken with New Mexico, where he lived for a couple of years from 1924, and found in the American Indian a wholeness and a reverence for life that he admired immensely.

8. Primitivism and a new generation of artists

Taking their cue from Ruskin, Morris, Carpenter and Havelock Ellis, and journals like The New Age, by the early 20th century it became commonplace amongst a younger generation of British modernist artists and writers to believe that there was a malaise at the heart of civilization[51]. Though not all shared the same intense, visceral disgust as DH Lawrence, this belief was confirmed beyond all doubt by the mechanised carnage of the First World War.

In 1910, the exhibition 'Manet and The Post-Impressionists' had opened at The Grafton Galleries in London. Gauguin, who had rubbed shoulders with Newlyn artists in Pont-Aven, was given the largest amount of wall-space, contributing 46 works. Cezanne and Van Gogh were also prominent.

The exhibition organizer, Roger Fry, was a respected British art critic with close connections to the Bloomsbury group. The essay he wrote for the catalogue seemed to consign Impressionism, and with it the impressionistic realism of Newlyn and early St Ives School, to the scrapheap. The French avant-garde had replaced naturalism with primitivism, as Fry reiterates at least four times: *the Post-Impressionists consider the Impressionists too naturalistic.....They said in effect to the Impressionists: "You have explored nature in every direction, and all honour to you; but your methods and principles have hindered artists from exploring and expressing that emotional significance which lies in things, and is the most important subject matter of art.*

Cezanne, when rendering the novel aspects of nature to which Impressionism was drawing attention, aimed first at a design which

---

[51] Anecdotally, Jacob Epstein's celebrated futuristic sculpture 'Rock Drill' (1913-16), a study for which was featured in The New Age, is thought to have been constructed using a drill on a tripod originally manufactured by Holman's in Pool, West Cornwall.

should produce the coherent, architectural effect of the masterpieces of primitive art.

In his (Gauguin's) Tahitian pictures by extreme simplification he endeavoured to bring back into modern painting the significance of gesture and movement characteristic of primitive art. In the work of Matisse, especially, this search for an abstract harmony of line, for rhythm, has been carried to lengths which often deprive the figure of all appearance of nature. The general effect of his pictures is that of a return to primitive, even perhaps of a return to barbaric, art.

The value placed on 'primitivism' would affect new British art for decades. Embracing the new credo required a decisive leap of faith that many were not willing to take, however. One of the main consequences was that there was no longer the same emphasis on the craft or skill of the artist, and in fact being over-trained was seen as a disadvantage.

Matthew Smith, who was born in Manchester in 1879, visited Pont Aven in the early 1900s. He was, though, a generation older than Stanhope Forbes and the other Newlyners, so was better placed to respond to the influence of Gauguin and Post-Impressionists like Matisse[52]. He did so by exploiting the emotionality of extreme colour.

After a holiday with his young family in Porthcothan in the summer of 1920, Smith stayed on in Cornwall, renting a room in an imposing gothic building called Bank House in the centre of St Columb Major several miles inland (Yorke, 1997). Originally attracted to the area because of its similarity to Brittany, Smith painted around twenty views of St Columb during that wet autumn. Career-defining works, many were views from his room in Bank House, and some include the church clock tower nearby. All are extraordinary and highly original: roughly painted landscapes devoid of people, but pulsating with intense hallucinatory colour, apocalyptic black skies and burning red stone.

The 'primitivist' credo became even more perfectly embodied in the work produced slightly later by the most influential art society of the 20's 'The Seven and Five' which formed in 1919 and included several artists with strong connections to Cornwall.

---

[52] Smith met Matisse briefly in Paris in 1911.

It is not known whether one future member, Frances Hodgkins, met DH Lawrence and his circle in Cornwall, but she is likely to have done, as she was in St Ives throughout the duration of the First World War at a time of austerity for the colony when sketching and painting outdoors was banned.

Born in New Zealand in 1869, Hodgkins had first come to Europe in the early 1900s. It is thought that first generation Newlyn painter Norman Garstin introduced her to Cornwall as they had become friendly whilst both were painting in Normandy. In St Ives Hodgkins rented one of the Porthmeor Studios, and became acquainted with a younger artist called Cedric Morris who painted her portrait in 1917.

Like Hodgkins, Morris came to Cornwall on the recommendation of one of the Newlyn School painters, in this case Alfred Munnings, and spent two years (1917-18) living in Zennor, before moving to Newlyn in 1919 with the man that would become his life-partner Arthur Lett-Haines (known as Lett) (Hepburn, 2012). During this period in Newlyn Cedric Morris made his first oil painting, and met Cordelia and Frank Dobson[53]. Cordelia's sister, known by her married name of Mary Jewells, whilst having no connection to the 7&5 also painted in a naïve style, having been encouraged to do so by Cedric Morris.

At the end of October 1920 Hodgkins left Cornwall for Paris. Then, at Christmas, Morris and Lett-Haines followed her. Many artists and writers were drawn to the French capital in the early 20s by the heavily devalued French currency and more liberal attitudes, particularly to homosexuality, which was still illegal in Britain.

The painter Christopher Wood, who created some of the most memorable images of the coast and people of Cornwall arrived into this Parisian milieu in 1921. Wood was born in Liverpool in 1901, and like the other Post-Impressionists he was much taken with primitive art. In a letter from Paris of 1923 he invoked the naïveté of child art to explain Post-Impressionism to his mother: *Do you know that all the great modern painters who we may not quite understand through their pictures, are not trying to see things and paint them through the eyes and experience of a*

---

[53] Frank Dobson (1868-1963) was a sculptor loosely associated with Wyndham Lewis and the Vorticists. His first one-man show in 1914 was organised with the help of Augustus John who he had met in Newlyn. He married Cordelia Tregurtha in 1918, and for a while, lived in the Tregurtha family home.

man of forty or fifty...but rather through the eyes of the smallest child who sees nothing except those things which would strike him as being the most important? To the childish drawing they add the beauty and refinement of their own experience – this is the explanation of modern painting.

His charm and good looks had, at the tender age of 19, given him entry into the decadent beau-monde of Parisian society and he came to know Picasso, Diaghilev and Cocteau, the latter of whom - despite being 10 years older - shared his studio for a while. Cocteau also introduced him to opium, to which, like numerous writers of the Romantic era, he rapidly became addicted.

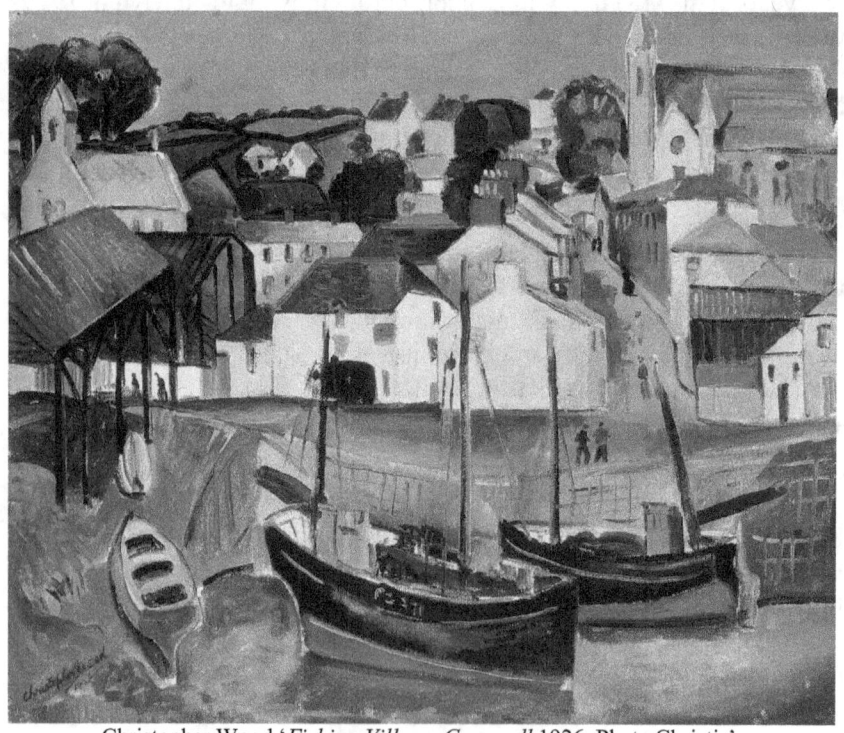

Christopher Wood '*Fishing Village, Cornwall* 1926. Photo Christie's.

As a painter, his biggest influences were Van Gogh, Gauguin, Picasso and the fashionable naïve artist, Henri Le Douanier Rousseau, but Wood only managed to develop his own original voice in 1926 when he reconnected with his roots (his mother was Cornish) by visiting Cornwall, and St Ives, for the first time (Button, 2000). He had probably done so on the recommendation of his friend Cedric Morris.

During this first visit to Cornwall, Wood quickly developed the iconography of fishermen, boats and water that came to distinguish his best-loved later work. There are obviously echoes of Newlyn School painters in its subject matter, and the same concern with depicting an uncorrupted, picturesque, traditional way of life, but the paint is applied quickly and loosely, and the effect is indisputably more childlike and mystical. Arguably, therefore, there is in Wood's work a more natural fit between the meaning and subject of the painting. By comparison, his portraits and Parisian paintings seem airless and claustrophobic.

Towards the end of 1926 Cedric Morris introduced Wood to Ben and Winifred Nicholson, who visited him in Chelsea and immediately recognised the value of his work. Winifred Nicholson responded thus: *Crowded together in his small bedroom were an amazing array of canvases. He produced masterpiece upon masterpiece... here was England's first painter. His vision is true his grasp is real, his power is life itself...*

The Nicholsons, both born in the mid-1890s into artistic families, met and married each other in 1920. They spent many of the next few years abroad, in Switzerland, or in Cumbria developing their own brand of naïve Post-Impressionist landscape painting. Though Ben's art benefitted greatly from his relationship with Winifred, his career, largely through his association with Barbara Hepworth and St Ives, would overshadow hers by some way.

Charles Harrison has noted that Nicholson was, consistently, an exemplary exponent of 'art for arts sake'. His art always tended to seem strangely detached: *Unlike many of his contemporaries who had attracted attention before the war, Nicholson had probably never considered the possibility of an art that was anything but asocial...It is as much to this that Nicholson owes his status as the paradigm modernist painter...*

This was largely the basis of Ruskin's argument with Whistler, when he accused him of 'flinging a pot of paint in the fact of the public': modern art was becoming increasingly abstract, and detached from social reality or morality (Harrison, 1983).

In 1926 Ben Nicholson was elected chairman of the Seven and Five society, which became the most progressive art society of the interwar period, later mounting the first all-abstract art show in 1935 at Zwemmers.

In 1927 Christopher Wood was invited to join the society, alongside Cedric Morris, potter William Staite Murray, poet David Jones and other emerging British modernists. In 1929 Frances Hodgkins became another member of the society with links to the Cornwall colonies, after being recommended as a member by Morris just over ten years after painting her portrait in Cornwall.

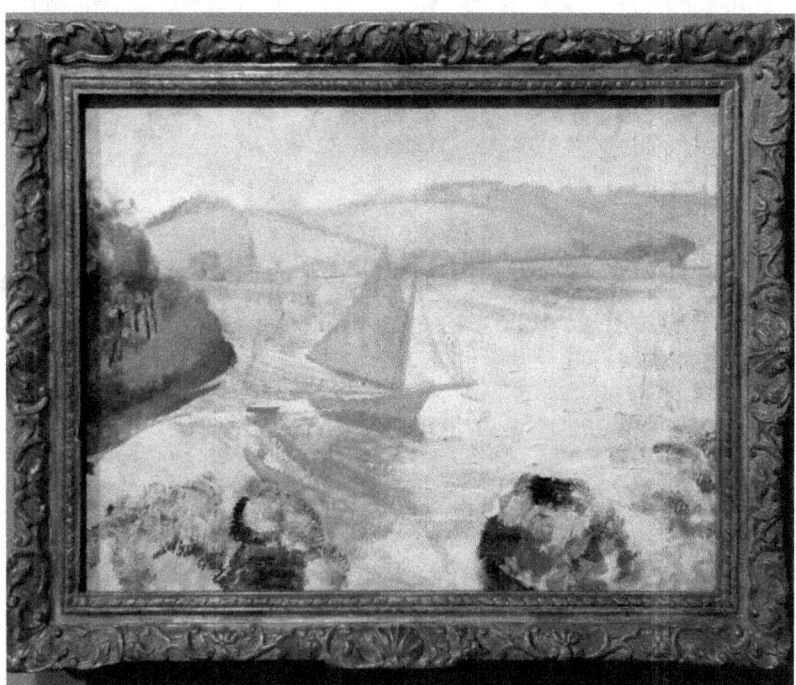

Winifred Nicholson *Estuary 1928* at *Liberation of Colour* Falmouth Art Gallery 2017 Photo the author. One of several paintings completed during the visit to Pill Creek, Feock.

In the spring of 1928, Wood stayed with the Nicholsons in Cumbria. Then in the summer, in search again of unspoilt rustic subject matter, the three of them travelled to Cornwall staying initially in Pill Creek, Feock near the house of their friend from Hampstead, advertising executive, Marcus Brumwell. Whilst several exemplary canvasses were painted in Feock, the trip to Cornwall in 1928 is remembered now for the encounter between Ben Nicholson, Christopher Wood and Alfred Wallis.

On a day trip to St Ives, the two younger men, having left Winifred behind, famously noticed Wallis's paintings through the open doorway to his tiny terraced house. With their visual intensity and radical use of pictoral space, they seemed to confirm everything Wood and Nicholson believed about painting at the time. The diminutive, bible-reading Wallis, then already into his 70s, was not a faux-naif painter, however, he was the 'real thing', and he became a talisman both for them, and for all the St Ives Modernists who came after.

Then, as now, there were naïve, untutored artists all over the country. The fact that Nicholson and Wood found and singled out Wallis in St Ives that summer is a testament to the fact that, as late as 1928, there was still an enduring notion of Cornwall as a place apart, a place untouched by modernisation, where the genuinely primitive could still be found.

In 1930 Wood returned to Cornwall, having spent time in Brittany: *I won't write more as I am working at an enormous pace and absolutely deliriously happy painting. Never have I had such a delicious sensation from life before....Its wonderful to be able to not consider anything but ones want to work and to work and not to sleep and eat just when one wants.*

But on 21st August, probably deranged by the effects of opiate withdrawal, he threw himself in front of a train at Salisbury station, having stopped off there to visit his mother.

Nicholson continued to buy Wallis's paintings, and showed his work in London. Jim Ede, a curator at the Tate, also bought Wallis's work which later formed the basis of the collection at Kettle's Yard in Cambridge. Before he died, in 1942, however, Wallis developed a paranoid psychosis, believing that Satan lived in a room in his house, and he spent his last years in the workhouse in Madron.

Wallis's grave incorporating twenty-one ceramic tiles in Porthmeor cemetery, is possibly Bernard Leach's most poignant artwork. At its centre is the lighthouse that often features in Wallis's paintings. A figure, which we take to be Wallis himself, is seen climbing the stairs as if about to ascend to heaven, and the light above. But it wasn't just Wallis that had died. In a way, Wallis's death marked the end point of a

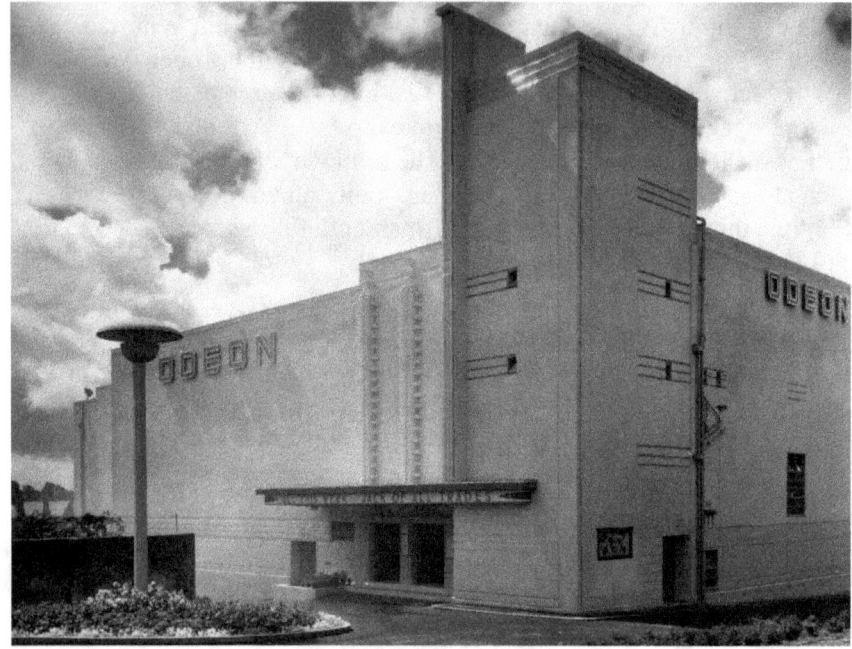
St Austell Odeon in 1936

trajectory that had begun with Ruskin's rejection of Classicism and the academy.

Paris, as a centre of art and design, remained pre-eminent in the lead-up to WW2. The international style now known as Art Deco, which was influenced by the art just discussed, originated there, and in Vienna. Its clean, geometric lines - so starkly different to those of the Gothic revival - became a marker of modern, technological progress, and they are as much in evidence in Cornwall as they are elsewhere in Britain.

The Capitol in St Austell, a purpose-built Art Deco cinema, opened in 1926 with a screening of 'Goldrush' by Charlie Chaplin. It went on to show 'talkies', the first being Al Jolson in 'The Singing Fool', as early as 1930. In 1936 St Austell managed to acquire a second cinema: an Odeon, complete with a dramatic 'fin-tower', which was one of scores designed for the cinema chain by architect Harold William Weedon.

Sadly the Capitol's façade has since changed beyond recognition, and the Odeon was demolished in 2007, but the cinemas in Truro, Redruth and Camborne which were built in 1936 - during the Golden Age of Hollywood - by Bristol architect William Henry Watkins have remained largely intact. Grand and imposing inside, each have also retained their own unique facades[54].

---

[54] The Capitol is now a bingo hall, as is King's Cinema in Camborne. The Royal Cinema in St Ives, which opened in 1939, is another example of a purpose-built Art Deco cinema, whilst the Jubilee Pool in Penzance, which opened in 1935, is an Art Deco structure of a different kind. 'Polventon' is an Art Deco house near Padstow that has featured in Rick Stein's cookery programmes, and in a video of the same name by his artist niece, Lucy Stein.

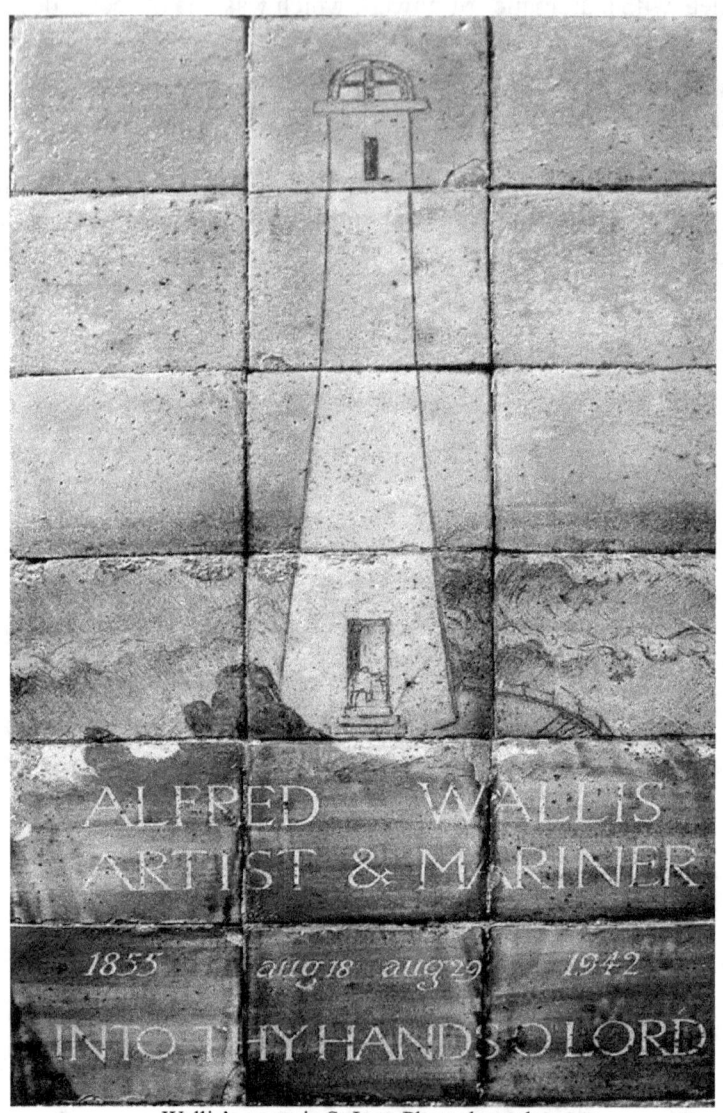

Wallis's grave in St Ives. Photo the author.

9. Robert Morton Nance

The pages of Q's Cornish Magazine were, from its first edition to its last, enlivened by illustrations by a certain Robert Morton Nance. Nance, then, was a 25 year old artist-craftsman who, unlike the Post-Impressionists and the Art Deco designers, retained a strong affinity with William Morris and the Arts and Crafts movement. This, as we shall see, will help explain both his friendship with potter Bernard Leach and his role, later, as the chief instigator of the Cornish Gorsedh and Cornish Revival[55].

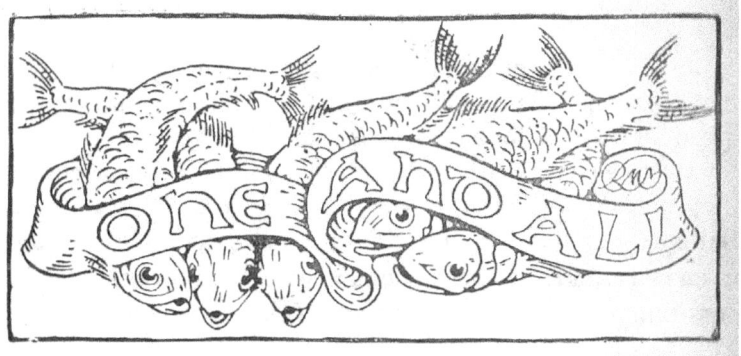

A page banner by R Morton Nance for The Cornish Magazine (1898 & 1899)

Though Nance's parents were Cornish, he was born - in 1873 - in Cardiff, his father originally travelling there by boat from Padstow to find work. (Indeed many from Cornwall emigrated in this way to Wales in the 1800s). His childhood home in Cardiff commanded a view of the Bristol Channel, but there were seafarers and boatbuilders on both sides of the family, and regular holiday visits to his grandfather at 4, The

---

[55] Deacon (1993) suggests however that, in terms of the wider Cornish culture, Nance's medievalism was problematic as it 'lacked continuity with the more immediate past'.

Terrace, St Ives stimulated an interest in boats that would stay with him for the rest of his life[56].

In 1893, at the age of 20 he enrolled at the art school in Bushey, Hertfordshire. Its Principal was Hubert Von Herkhomer who designed the ceremonial robes of the Welsh Gorsedd. Herkhomer's progressive and non-doctrinaire school took a number of students later associated with the St Ives and Newlyn schools (eg Algernon Talmage, Arnesby Brown, W.H.Y. Titcomb, Arthur Meade, and the father of Ben Nicholson, William).

Nance married a fellow student, Beatrice Michell in 1895, aged 22, and they returned to Wales after short spell of 6 months living in St Ives. Before doing so, Nance also took part in the RA summer exhibition for the first and only time, showing three portraits made at Bushey (1895). His address then is recorded as Bourne Hall Road, Bushey (Raymont, 1962).

During 1897 Nance had several mentions in the hugely influential 'Studio' magazine (later Studio International), including the award of first prize for a design for a Christmas card. 'The Watchman', depicting a galleon steering a course between two malevolent sea monsters, was clearly inspired by Japanese woodcuts (like Hokusai's 'Great Wave'): the flattened perspective and bright unmodulated colour of the genre known as ukiyo-e, was important to many Impressionist, Post-Impressionist and Art Nouveau artists (including Gauguin)[57].

In 1897 several of his drawings were also published in The Studio. They were naturalistic charcoal portraits completed at Bushey of villagers described as the 'Bushey Models'. Nance's commentary for them hints at a dissenting attitude to the modern world: *in the talk of these old country people one often catches something suggestive of the primitive life that still lingers on in such old-fashioned places as this, despite the*

---

[56] Many details in this chapter draw from 'Setting Cornwall on its Feet: Robert Morton Nance 1873-1959' (2007) eds Thomas, P. & Williams, D.

[57] Japanese art also included a tradition of decorated screens, which were made up of several tall panels, hinged together, and whilst Nance dropped the overt references to Japanese art, he later painted and exhibited such screens (eg 'Blake and Van Tromp').

modernisation and betterment which are gradually spreading their pall over the majority of rural districts.

In 1898 six of his sketches of St Ives were published, this time without any explanation or commentary. They are similar in their execution to

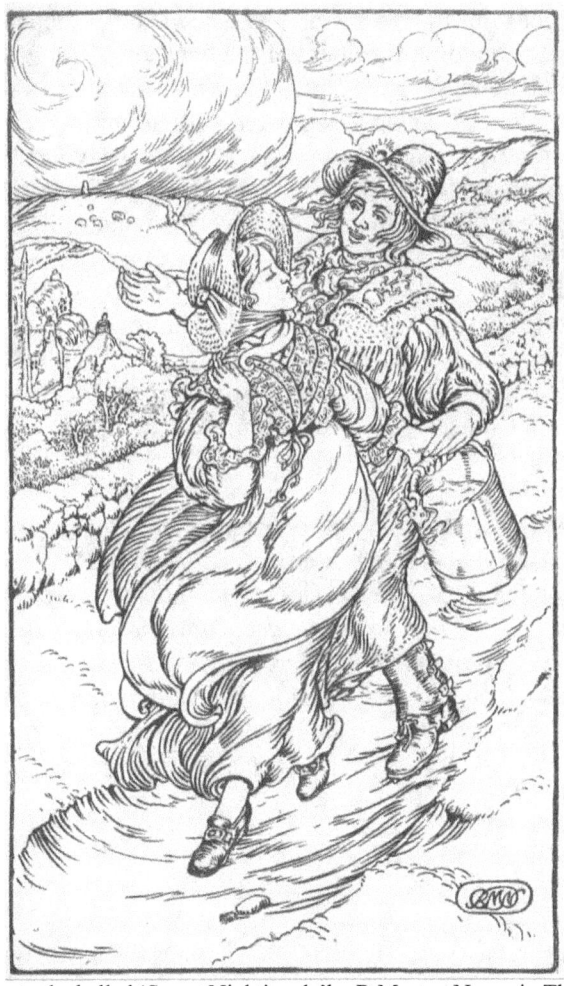

Illustration to the ballad 'Sweet Nightingale' by R Morton Nance in The Cornish Magazine Vol2 (1899).

the six Bushey model portraits. It is possible that Q had seen these works, which led to his commissions for the Cornish Magazine, however the illustrations in Q's magazine are very different in quality, and mainly comprise jocular line drawings of medieval peasants and Jacobean cavaliers.

Nance had attended Herkhomer's with the intention of being a book illustrator, and the illustration work in the Cornish Magazine, which ran to eleven editions during 1898 and 1899, shows the influence of Walter Crane, who was founding President of the Arts and Crafts Exhibition Society, and an active socialist[58]. It is known that Walter Crane's songbook 'Pan Pipes', lavishly populated with its smiling satyrs, coy mermaids and jolly musketeers was one of Nance's favourite childhood books. Nance also had a fondness for John Ruskin's illustrated fantasy book for children 'King of the Golden River'(Raymont, 1962).

Beatrice, sadly, died in 1901. That same year Robert Morton Nance became a member of the Arts and Crafts Exhibition Society[59], and, after a short stint in Paris (in 1902) was selected for inclusion in their 1903, 1906 and 1910 exhibitions. Through his participation he became better acquainted with Crane, whose illustration work he had so enjoyed when he was younger.

In January 1903, for example, he contributed more than one work to the exhibition at The New Gallery. 'Screen', depicting a 17th century naval battle, was painted during the previous year and was reproduced in The Studio VolXXVIII: *Some handsome decorative paintings by Mr Morton Nance may be conveniently noted here; more especially a screen entitled 'Blake and Van Tromp' which if a little turbulent in line at least attracts attention by its breezy strength and buoyancy of composition. An overmantel, entitled 'Westward Ho' is based on the model of a Dutch man of war of about 1730'*

---

[58] Walter Crane gave up his post as president to William Morris in 1891, however, in 1896 William Morris, who had initially been sceptical about the value of the society, died.

[59] Formed originally in 1887, prior to Nance becoming a member, it held exhibitions in 1888, 1889, 1890, 1893, 1896 and 1899.

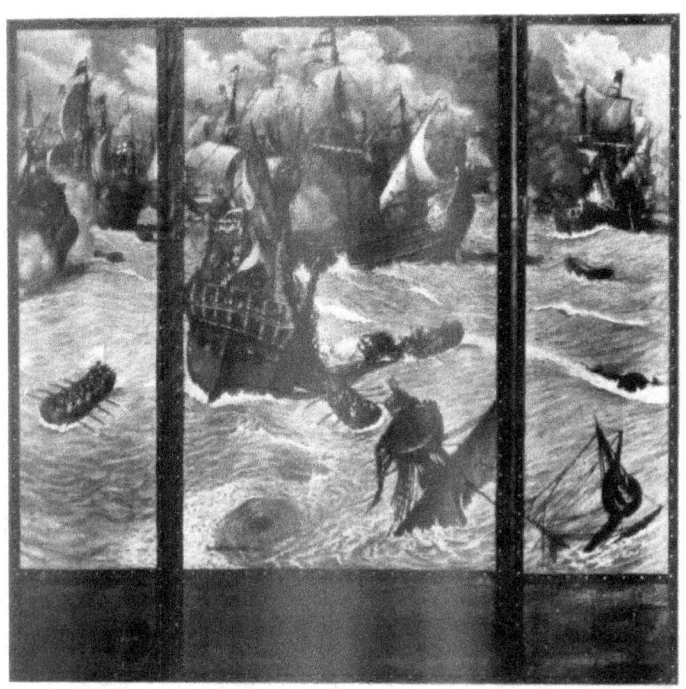

Robert Morton Nance: 'Blake and Van Tromp' from The Studio VolXXVIII 1903

During his period of involvement with the Arts and Crafts Exhibition Society, Nance was also employed as an illustrator for several substantial books on boats and seafaring by E. E. Speight[60]. The books include numerous line drawings, as well as reproductions of oil-painted seascapes. Nance also started making models of Elizabethan sailing ships, and in 1906 he remarried, and moved with his new wife, the weaver Anne Maud Cawker, to Nancledra between Penzance and St Ives.

Already having one daughter by his first wife, Nance had three more children, Robert (known as Robin), Richard (known as Dicon) and Phoebe all of whom would later become involved in some way with the artist community in Cornwall. (His two sons were founding members of

---

[60] 'Hakluyt's English Voyages' (1905), 'Britain's Sea Story' (1905) & 'Romance of the Merchant Venturers' (1906). Coincidentally, E.E. Speight knew Bernard Leach in Japan.

the Penwith Society, with Dicon marrying Bernard Leach's daughter. Phoebe, meanwhile, married Dod and Ernest Procter's son Bill). The family were all vegetarian, and teetotal, and tried to be self-sufficient (Raymont, 1962)

Whilst at Nancledra Nance wrote, and performed, 'The Cledry Plays: Drolls of Old Cornwall for Village Acting and Home reading', which makes extensive use of the Cornish dialect. He also became more widely known as an expert on nautical history, and a founder member of the Society for Nautical Research, writing regularly for its journal 'The Mariner's Mirror'[61].

In 1914, when RMN was 41, the Nance family moved into Chylason in Carbis Bay, a semi-detached house near the church. Charles Thomas recalls visiting it later, in the 1930s: *My brother and I - fed by dear Granny Nance – would stand and gawp in wonder at the magnificent, the truly incredible, models of galleons and frigates and sailing-ships around the dark drawing room. Sometimes the master would explain bits of the riggings; we never touched anything, hardly dared breathe.*

It was Nance's research into dialect that led to his meeting and befriending language expert Henry Jenner in Morrab Library in about 1918. This encouraged Nance's more active engagement in the language revival: *I first met Mr Jenner, and then began a friendship during which he literally told me all that he knew of Cornish, and set me finding out more for myself.*

The aforementioned Henry Jenner (see earlier chapter) had been born in 1848 in St Columb Major, but had moved away from Cornwall as an infant, and spent most of his working life in London, employed in the Department of Manuscripts at the British Museum.

Jenner had had a lifelong interest in the Cornish language and whilst working at the museum in the 1870's attended meetings of the Philological Society at University College. It was not until 1904,

---

[61] He became well known for model ship-building, and in 1924 went on to publish the popular book 'Sailing Ship Models'.

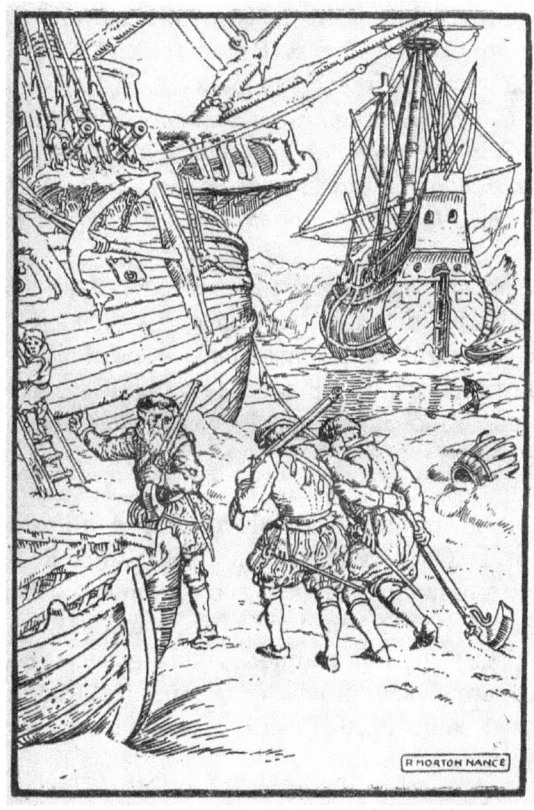

'The Last Days of Willoughby' by R Morton Nance, in Speight's 'Hakluyt's English Voyages'

however, that he published the influential 'Handbook of the Cornish Language'.

Jenner's 'handbook' - which is likely to have been the book that Philip Heseltine (Peter Warlock) used to teach himself Cornish[62] - draws on his own research in West Cornwall, and the work of predecessors like Lluyd, Borlase and others. Jenner became a bard of the Breton Gorsedd in 1903, and significantly, just like the Newlyn painters, he recognized a close affiliation between Cornish and Breton culture.

---

[62] Warlock's 'Cornish Carol' of 1924 was written to words in Cornish by Jenner

In 1904 Jenner successfully made the case for Cornwall to be accepted as member of the Pan Celtic Congress. His address at the time is a fascinating document, and it included the following provocative statement: *The Cornish are mainly of Celtic blood. They are probably of more unmixed Celtic descent than any of the other Celtic nations…There is little or no Scandinavian element among them, as in the Isle of Man, The Highlands and Islands of Scotland, and parts of Ireland.*

He encouraged Nance's existing interest in medievalism, but Jenner was right-leaning in his politics, and endorsed a view of 'Merry England' that was predicated on a rigid - and almost feudal - social hierarchy, where the working classes 'knew their place'. He certainly seemed alarmed by the rise of the labour movement, which he viewed as sowing division in society.

However, in 1920, with Jenner's involvement, and following successful performances of the Cledry Plays, the more egalitarian R. Morton Nance[63] became a founding member - and lynchpin - of the first Old Cornwall Society (OCS). Formed in St Ives, and concerned with collecting and preserving folk traditions and language, it became the template for numerous other groups. (The Truro and Redruth Old Cornwall societies came together in 1922, with other local groups following after).

The Federation of Old Cornwall Societies was created in 1924 with a dedicated magazine - still published now[64]. Nance, as its editor, wrote its first article, which was a powerful statement on behalf of all the societies: *We came together to strengthen one another in our devotion to all those ancient things that make the spirit of Cornwall - its traditions, its old words and ways, and what remains to it of its Celtic language and nationality… (We are) gleaners of the folk-culture of Cornwall, upon which all really Cornish art and literature of the future must be based, and hoping that future generations will arise, Cornish still, to make good use of them…We are as much interested in the holiday, workaday and*

---

[63] Dr Merv Davey's essay on 'Lyver Canow Kernewek' in cornishnationalmusicarchive.co.uk is a useful summary of the two men's politics.
[64] Now known as 'Kernow Goth'

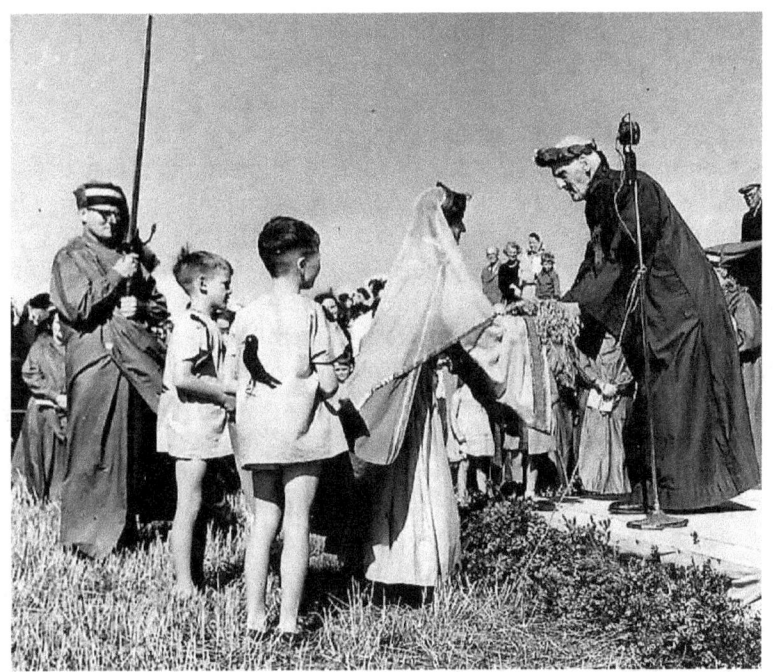

The Gorsedh in Mullion in 1957, Nance, as the Grand Bard, is to the right of the image.

home life of older generations - the festivals, the hearthside tales, the printed dialect literature, and the old songs and words as in any other side of the past of Cornwall...

Nance's democratic instincts are apparent the article, and so too his critique of other learned societies in Cornwall: *For over a century we have had learned societies that deal with Cornish Antiquities, and these have done much to uphold the honour of Cornwall. To them, however, Cornwall's past is a subject for antiquarian discussions; to us it holds a living spirit, and in our unlearned way we aim at spreading knowledge of this past amongst Cornish people of every sort as a thing that is necessary to them if they would remain Cornish.*

Within a few years, Nance's recognition of Cornwall's 'living spirit' would manifest, via the Old Cornwall Societies, as the revival of three local traditions: Guise (or Guize) Dancing (in 1925)[65], Crying the Neck (in 1928) and Midsummer Bonfires (in 1929).

The latter seems to have been particularly successful. Inspired by an account in Bottrell (1873), in the evening of Midsummer's Day the Old Cornwall Societies lit spectacular beacon fires on nineteen different hill-tops, from Chapel Carn Brea in the West to Kit Hill in the East. As reported in newspapers at the time, the societies referred to the bonfires as remnants of a pagan - and specifically druidic - past. William Paynter, known later for his interest in Cornish witchcraft[66], for example, gave a speech which included the following: *It must be remembered that in earliest times these sacrificial fires were kindled to invoke the blessing of the solar deity upon the crops and vegetation. The festival was then observed on a very extensive scale, human sacrifices were offered, and captives, criminals, and animals were confined in cages and were consumed in the flames of the great fire. It was argued that the Bible gave them warranty for that belief. The burning of blood, drawn from a deceased animal, had been a very common mode of appeasing the spirits of disease*[67].

More significantly, however, in early 1928 at a conference of the Old Cornwall Societies, plans were made to create a Cornish Gorsedh. In August ten Cornish bards, wearing light blue robes at the insistence of Morton Nance, were initiated at the Welsh Gorsedd. With Jenner as the Grand Bard, Nance as his deputy, and the support of the Old Cornwall Societies, in September the first Cornish Gorsedh subsequently took place at Boscawen-Un[68].

Then, when Jenner died in 1934, Nance took over as the Grand Bard, and continued in this role for 25 years. Indeed, during the war years he

---

[65] Previously popular, in 1900 guising in St Ives was banned by Mayor Edward Hain. However, the tradition of guise dancing continued unchanged in other Cornish towns and villages (eg Mousehole) until much later.
[66] His Bardic name was 'Whyler Pystri' or 'Searcher out of Witchcraft'. See White, 2017.
[67] James Frazer's 'Golden Bough' seems to have been an influence on the Old Cornwall revivalists and, in his Cornish books, is cited several times by A K Hamilton Jenkin.
[68] Ancient Welsh triads name a 'Beisgawen Yn Dumnonia' as one of three principle gorsedhs or bardic meeting places in Britain.

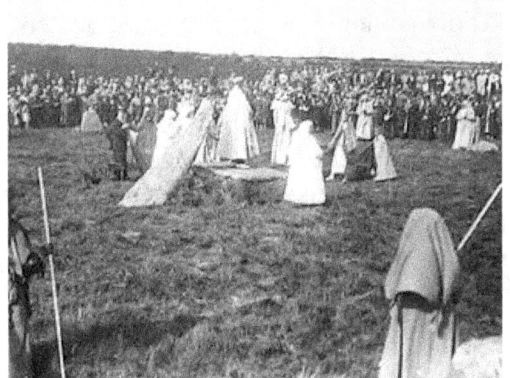

The Gorsedh at Boscawen-Un stone circle. Michael Cardew was initiated as a bard here.

ensured the ceremony continued, and on one occasion it even took place in his little garden at Chylason in Carbis Bay[69].

The extent of Morton Nance's involvement with the arts community in St Ives is deserving of further study. It is known that, as part of his attempt to reach out to others, in 1920 he started running Cornish language classes in St Ives, using Jenner's Handbook. Bernard Leach and Michael Cardew, who would later become two of the world's most celebrated ceramicists, were amongst his first pupils. Both potters also took part in Nance's 'Christmas Play of St George and the Turkish Knight' in 1924 (Kent, 2000).

Nance, Leach and Cardew would have had much in common. Significantly, as artists, all were sympathetic to the principles of the Arts and Crafts movement, and with equal messianic zeal, were concerned to revive lost or threatened medieval traditions.

Bernard Leach was several years younger than Nance but was already 33 years of age when he first came to St Ives in 1920. Born in Hong Kong, he had attended secondary school in Windsor, and art school at the Slade. He learnt etching under Frank Brangwyn at the London School of Art before, in 1909, he moved to Japan, intending to teach there. Instead,

---

[69] Cf gorsedhkernow.org.uk/history/

after attending a raku party in 1911, he became interested in ceramics and went on to learn traditional pottery techniques under Ogata Kenzan[70].

He came to St Ives at the invitation of the wealthy benefactor Frances Horne, who helped him buy the site where his pottery - together with its unique three-chambered climbing kiln - was built at the top of the town. Here, along with Shoji Hamada, he started to take on students and employ assistants, such that, when he was away (eg visiting Japan or teaching at Dartington as he did in the 1930s), the pottery could run by others in his absence.

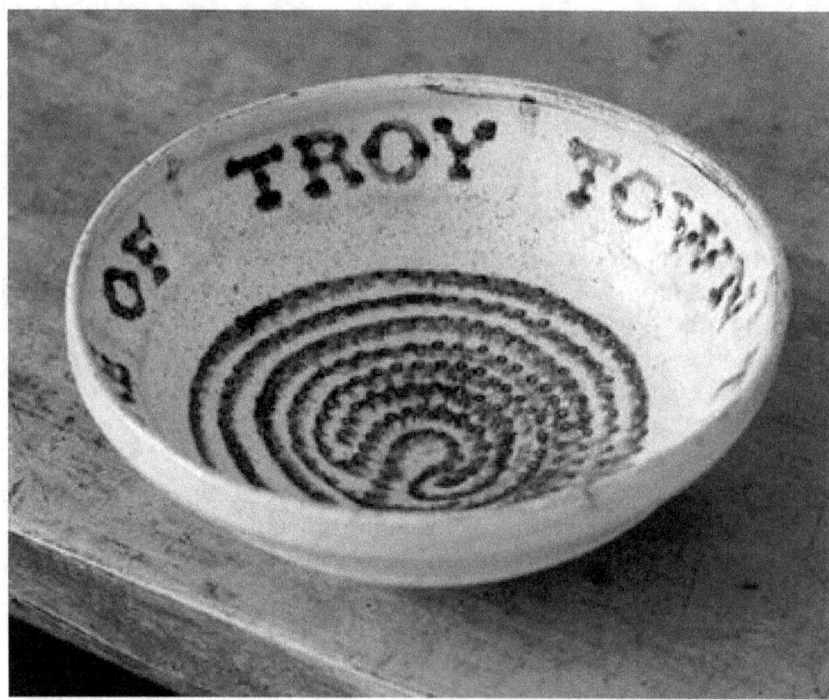

Auctioned by Christies in 2014: a pot thrown by Hamada, but decorated by Robert Morton Nance, and bearing his 'hand incised cursive monogram'. Nance is thought to have given lessons in Cornish to Michael Cardew and Bernard Leach in return for using their pottery.

---

[70] Cf St Ives 1939 -1964 Tate Catalogue.

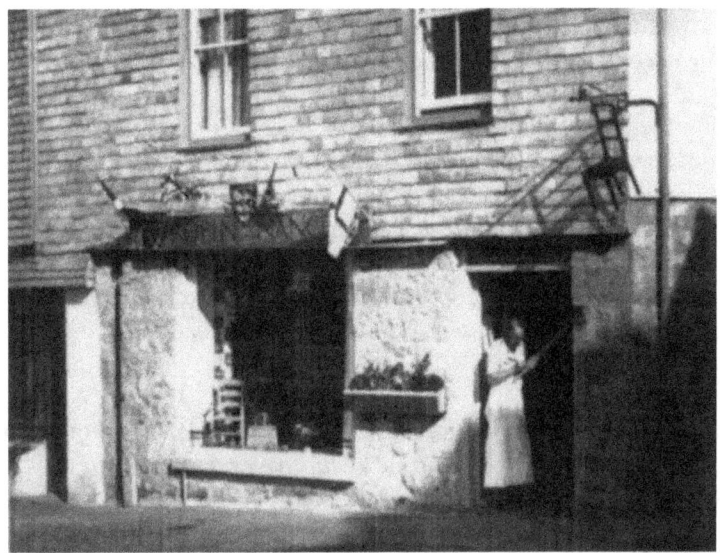
Robin Nance's furniture shop in St Ives

During the 20s Leach and his family - he had five young children - lived in Havelock Ellis' old house, the Count House in Carbis Bay, some distance from the pottery but not far from Robert Morton Nance. Indeed the families saw a lot of each other and Eleanor, Leach's eldest daughter, ended up marrying Nance's son Dicon, who, with his brother Robin, became well known as a furniture-maker[71].

Bernard Leach was insightful and articulate as a writer. In the opening pages of 'A Potters Book' (1940) he makes a very clear statement of his own indebtedness to Ruskin and the Arts and Crafts movement. He is clearly referring to Cornwall when he says: *Factories have practically driven folk-art out of England; it only survives in out of the way corners even in Europe, and the artist-craftsman, since the day of William*

---

[71] The Nance brothers, Dicon and Robin were founding members of the Penwith Society when it formed in 1949. Along with Bernard Leach and Guido Morris they were categorised as 'craftsmen'. Dicon, who also lived in The Counthouse, was later in a long-term relationship with Jessamine, Bernard Leach's youngest daughter.

Morris, has been the chief means of defence against the materialism of industry and its insensibility to beauty.

He also reveals an antipathy to the clean lines of modernist design: *The reaction started by William Morris.....culminated in what I have called the individual craftsman.... Beginning in protest against the irresponsible use of power, it came to an end in pseudo-medieval crafts little related to national work and life. Thence has arisen an affirmation of the mechanical age in art – functionalism (Le Corbusier, Picasso and the Bauhaus)....which tends to an over-intellectual effort to discover norms of orderliness and utility.*

Leach sees intellect and intuition as opposite poles, and denigrates the former: *The art of the craftsman....is intuitive and humanistic...that of the designer rational, abstract and tectonic...We meet everywhere with bad forms and banal, debased, pretentious decoration and tawdriness of form that must be seen to be believed.*

Michael Cardew is, after Leach, the best known of British studio potters. He was an undergraduate studying Classics at Oxford when he first visited Leach in St Ives, and in his autobiography (Cardew, 1988) he describes the day in January 1923 when they first met. He had originally cycled nearly 30 miles from St Breward where he was staying on holiday, to visit Lake's pottery in Truro: *I started early in the morning and found the pottery at Chapel Hill in Truro and met Mr Collins who managed the kiln. He showed me how he dipped the pitchers in galena glaze and set them in the open kiln, and told me about the faggot (dried gorse) firing* (Cardew 1988).

The station in Truro was only a short walk away and it appears that on the spur-of-the-moment Cardew decided to catch a train down to St Ives to visit the Leach Pottery that he had read about in the 'Pottery Gazette'.

Arriving in St Ives at sunset he found the pottery and met the 25 year old, bespectacled Hamada Shoji, who at the time slept in a tiny bedroom at the far end of the workshop. Together they walked two miles to Leach's house in Carbis Bay, and after an informal interview, Leach agreed in principle to Cardew coming to work in St Ives after he had finished his degree. Cardew went on to spend 3 years working as an apprentice to Bernard Leach, absorbing many of Leach's values during this time.

Here Cardew gives his view on the Cornish language, and the lessons provided by Nance: *I had been wanting to learn the language for a long time, chiefly I think because it fed two of my ruling emotions – romanticism and a passion for words. The idea of it tantalized me; there was this ancient language, idiomatic and idiosyncratic, which yet possessed an almost Roman dignity. It seemed as if it had only just appeared over the western horizon, taking with it all sorts of echoes of our ancient British and Romano-British ancestors …Much of its vocabulary and many of its idioms seemed in a way already familiar: to learn one only had to remember.*

In fact Cardew left St Ives in 1926, partly because he had become part of a difficult love triangle involving a girl called Luned Jacobs from Sussex, and influential Cornish historian A K Hamilton-Jenkin, who was another heavily involved in the St Ives Old Cornwall Society[72].

However Cardew was aware, and proud, of his family's Cornish links. His great-grandfather was Cornelius Cardew (1748 – 1831), another Oxford graduate who became headmaster of Truro Grammar School[73], Mayor of Truro and chaplain to the Prince of Wales.

It is not surprising then, that despite moving away to establish his own pottery in Winchcombe (and later Wenford Bridge near Bodmin), Cardew was one of the first intake of bards to be initiated in the first Cornish Gorsedh in 1928 at Boscawen-Un.

He also took part, whenever possible, in subsequent meetings of the bards: *During the thirties when he was living in Gloucestershire, he would boat-hitch his way down to Cornwall to attend the Gorsedh, and visit friends in St Ives, hanging about in Bristol docks until he found a free passage.* (Harrod, 2013)

---

[72] Actually Cardew later acknowledged that he was 'three-quarters homosexual' (Harrod, 2013), which would account for his unusual domestic arrangements, that, during the forties and fifties, would see him separate from his wife for years at a time.
[73] Cornelius Cardew was teacher to aforementioned poet and historian Richard Polwhele.

His love of Cornwall also found its way into his pottery. One of the most striking works of his career is a tall black earthenware pot made in 1936-1938 at Winchcombe. Bearing sgraffito images of Adam and Eve and the Serpent, and inscriptions from the medieval Cornish play *'Ordinale de Origine Mundi',* it toured USA and Canada as part of a British Council exhibition between 1942 and 1945.

10. The Blue Tiger: Lamorna, St Hilary & Mary Butts

Immediately prior to the First World War, the Newlyn colony grew an offshoot as, drawn to the area by the reputation of the Newlyn School, a new generation of artists settled in Lamorna, a hamlet set in a tranquil, leafy valley a few miles down the coast.

Samuel John Birch arrived from Manchester in 1902, having visited West Cornwall in 1889. Inspired by Stanhope Forbes, he went on to adopt the name 'Lamorna Birch' at Forbes' suggestion. Over the next decade and more, Birch was joined by others. Harold and Laura Knight, who had spent time in the colony of Staithes in Yorkshire, arrived in 1908. Known for his paintings of horses, Alfred Munnings first visited Cornwall in 1908, and moved to Lamorna in 1911 where he worked in a studio attached to the tiny pub known as 'The Wink'.

Eleanor and Robert Hughes attended Forbes' School, and after travelling on the continent settled in Lamorna, at Chyangwheal, in 1912. Ella and Charles Naper (jeweller and painter respectively) arrived there at about the same time, moving into Trewoofe House[74]. As well as being known for her Art Nouveau jewelry, Ella Naper helped run Lamorna Pottery with the Westrup sisters, and posed as a model for a number of her artist-friends. It is the nude posterior view of Ella that we see in Laura Knight's controversial 1913 painting 'Laura Knight with model Ella Louise Naper (Self-portrait)', for example[75].

---

[74] CAI Cornwall Artists Index (cornwallartists.org).
[75] Also known as 'Self Portrait with Nude', the controversy at the time was due to the fact that women artists had not previously been permitted to paint from live nude models at schools like the Royal Academy.

Such was its reputation that even Augustus John spent time in Newlyn and Lamorna during 1913[76]. Lamorna was also crucial to the career of Gluck, who committed herself to becoming a painter after visiting artists in the valley with her girlfriend Craig in 1915. Born Hannah Gluckstein to a wealthy London family[77] Gluck, a stylish cross-dressing lesbian, spent all her summers in Lamorna, and eventually took over Laura Knight's studio (Souhami, 1988).

Most of the Lamorna painters gained national reputations, and would show regularly at the RA, with Laura Knight having the distinction of being the first ever woman member (and later being made a Dame).

Although Lamorna would later house the studios of Marlow Moss and Ithell Colquhoun (the former of whom first visited Cornwall in 1919) the original Lamorna artists were not really part of a modernist avant garde. Instead they retained an emphasis on realism and on depictions of the simple pleasures of Cornwall and its landscapes. Indeed with the social and moral content of the Newlyners removed, much of the Lamorna artists' work is beautifully executed but ideologically bland, even though Laura Knight's interest in the female nude resulted in some rather racy images for the time.

Either side of the First World War Newlyn itself became home to other artists who had attended Stanhope and Elizabeth Forbes' school. This included Dod (or Doris) and Ernest Proctor, who first met at the school and were married in 1912. Dod's reputation grew and in 1927 her instantly recognisable image of a sleeping girl, entitled 'Morning', won painting of the year at the RA, and was bought for the Tate by the Daily Mail.

Ernest, a conscientious objector, served with an ambulance unit during WW1, and a number of poignant war paintings survive from this time.

---

[76] John, already interested in the Romany way of life, became obsessed with gypsy culture whilst living in Liverpool in 1901 shortly after leaving the Slade School of Art. He befriended a large band of Romany gypsies, and learnt their language and folk-songs. From then on he adopted the 'look' of a gypsy, and would have periods living an itinerant lifestyle from the back of a wagon, or fleet of wagons travelling the country. He thus sought to live the life of a bohemian, in both senses that the word is used.

[77] The Glucksteins set up and owned the Lyons chain of tea-houses.

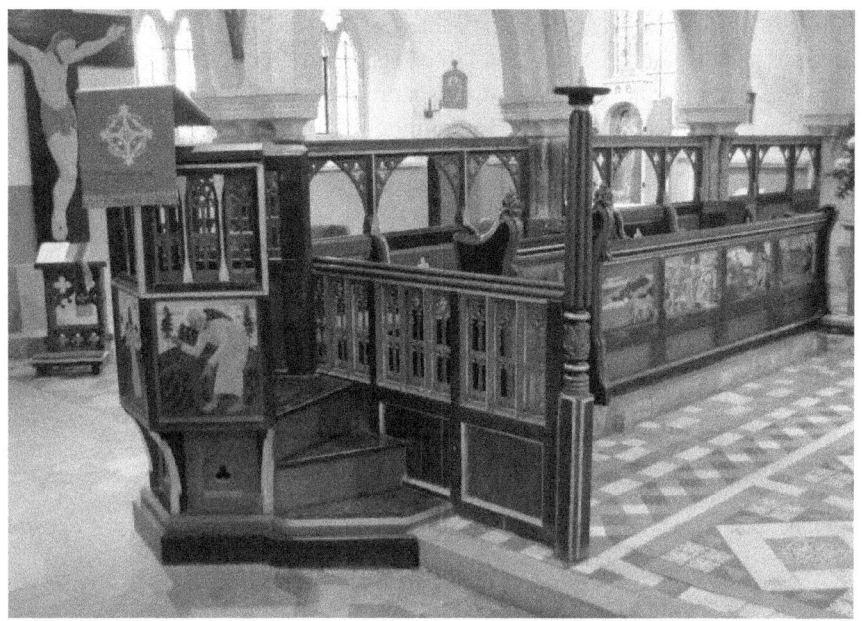

The pulpit and choir stalls at St Hilary. Photo the author.

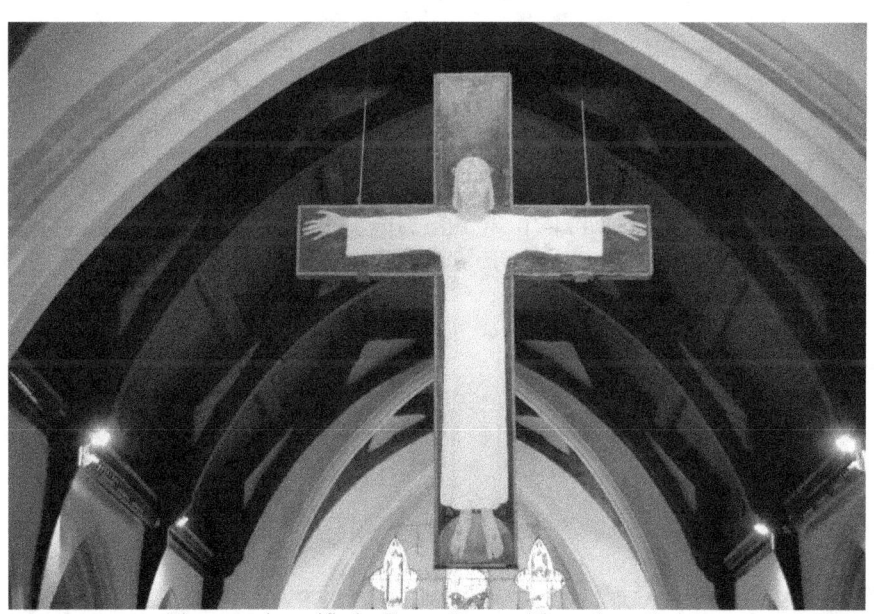

The central crucifix by Ernest Procter. Photo the author.

He is in Cornwall, however, best remembered for his work on the interior of St Hilary's Church, which had been reconstructed after a serious fire in 1853. Artist Annie Walke and husband Bernard commissioned paintings for the church near Marazion after Bernard became the vicar there in 1913.

The first decorations were paintings *'descriptive of the Cornish saints'* on the front of the choir stalls (Walke, 1935). These were by Harold Harvey, Norman Garstin, Harold Knight, Alethea Garstin, Gladys Hynes and the Procters. Then, in 1916, Ernest provided the large imposing crucifix that hangs from the ceiling of the church. He also painted the three panels of the pulpit, using images of St Kevin - with birds and bird's nests on his upturned hands - St Neot and St Mawes, and an extraordinary version of 'The Deposition' on copper.

Much of the art work displays a Post-Impressionist simplicity of form. Appropriately enough, the man who originally introduced Post-Impressionism to London, Roger Fry, even offered a work - a large, faintly menacing, depiction of St Francis of Assisi[78] - after meeting with Walke in London (Walke, 1935).

Walke also arranged for large slabs of granite to be brought from a Newlyn quarry so that, with the help of a local stone mason, he was able to create a total of six altars. He also bought older paintings of St Anne and St Joseph from a favourite antique shop in St John's Wood.

Walke, whose preferred transport was a donkey and trap was, like others in this book, a medievalist (or 'Gothic revivalist') in the sense that he was one of the first Anglicans to reintroduce the Catholic Mass and use it as the basis of his Sunday service[79]. His justification was as follows: *I was persuaded that the religious instinct of the Cornish people would never find satisfaction apart from the teaching and worship of the Catholic Faith: as the last of the English people to forsake the old religion they would be the first to return to the old ways* (Walke, 1935).

---

[78] Fry was an admirer of Giotto who, as he discusses in an essay in 'Vision and Design' (1920), painted a cycle of St Francis frescoes in the basilica in Assisi.

[79] It wasn't until the 1960s that the Eucharist or Communion (which was promoted by the 'Parish Communion Movement') became the norm in Anglican Sunday services.

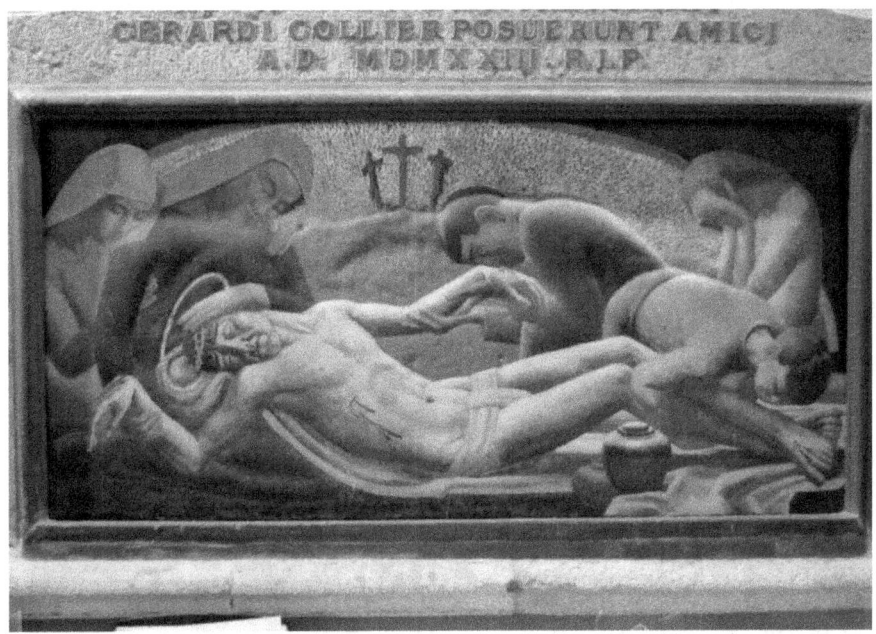

'The Deposition' painted on copper by Ernest Procter. Photo the author.

His efforts to revitalise worship at St Hilary's included the creation of plays which, using local amateur actors, and local dialect, took place in the church. Again he took his inspiration from medieval traditions: *I wanted an act of worship rather than a performance, a return to the old miracle play which was performed either in the church or in some open space, such as the field known as the Plain-an-guarry* (Walke, 1935).

The plays were, from 1926, broadcast live on national radio, and were so successful that they brought praise from the Prime Minister and a certain celebrity to Walke and his church[80]. But they also brought some unwanted attention, such that in 1932 St Hilary's was targeted by two

---

[80] Bernard Walke's plays in St Hilary were not the only local performances to receive acclaim. The first production at the Minack open-air theatre took place in 1932, a mile or two down the coast from Lamorna. The play, The Tempest, with programme and costume designs by the artist-illustrator Hilda Quick, was later reviewed in The Times. The clifftop theatre itself, built by hand into the rocks by Rowena Cade (1893-1983) and her gardener, has been in near continuous use ever since.

coachloads of vandals[81]. In ugly scenes reminiscent of the Reformation itself, they completely destroyed a reredos designed by Ernest Proctor, and damaged other parts of the church.

One of the most interesting members of Walke's congregation at the time was the writer Mary Butts. Butts (1890 - 1937) came with husband Gabriel Aitken to live in Sennen in January 1932, initially staying in a rented bungalow. The night they arrived she wrote: *The sea (is) like a blue tiger lying on its side, stretching out a paw... The first-night's walk, the full moon rising, shining through the wheels of the keltic crosses in St Sennen's churchyard. I think with Montague [M. R.] James that there are things about in Cornwall at night that are better not talked about* (Blondel, 1998).

As well as being a highly regarded modernist writer, Mary Butts was a spiritual 'seeker' whose life intersected with many others in this book. She was friendly with numerous artists, and had her portrait painted by Nina Hamnett (in 1917), Roger Fry (in 1918 - she became besotted with him but he did not reciprocate), Cedric Morris (in 1924), and Jean Cocteau (in 1926).

She also knew composer Philip Heseltine (Peter Warlock), and claimed that, in 1919, *'he induced me into the study of magic'*. This interest was encouraged by the ill-fated Cecil Maitland, with whom Butts subsequently had an affair. Maitland also, it seems, introduced her to opium-smoking.

In Paris, in 1921, Butts and Maitland became acquainted with Alistair Crowley via mutual friend Nina Hamnett. They met on several occasions, with Crowley encouraging Butts' experiments in astral journeying. Then on 11th March Butts was inducted into the A∴A∴, noting in her journal: *Aleister Crowley. 1st degree of initiation.*

In late June 1921 Butts and Maitland went to Cefalù, Sicily, and stayed with Crowley in his infamous Abbey of Thelema. As well as participating in extravagant ceremonies, like the ritual sacrifice of a black cockerel, Butts practiced yoga, meditated, worked on her first novel 'Ashe of Rings' and critiqued Crowley's draft of 'Magick in Theory and

---

[81] These were an organised anti-Catholic mob of 'Kensitites' drawn, mostly, from outside Cornwall.

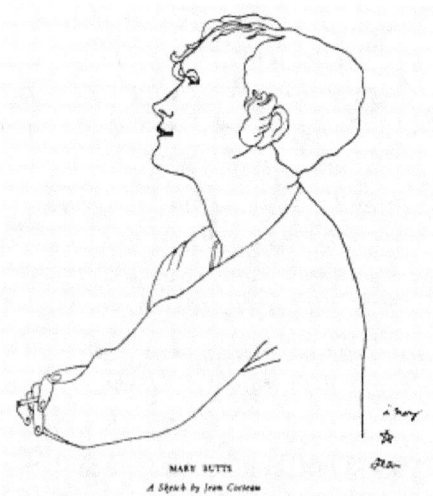

Portrait of Mary Butts by Jean Cocteau used as the cover of 'Imaginary Letters'(1928)

Practice'[82]. At the Abbey various drugs - hashish, cocaine and opium - were in plentiful supply, and Butts returned to England in September more enlightened, but more severely drug-dependent.

Forever courting notoriety, in 1922 Crowley caricatured Butts in his fictional 'Diary of a Drug Fiend'. He based the novel's protagonist, Peter Pendragon, on Maitland, but Butts also appears as a lesser character described as *'a fat, bold, red-headed slut…pompous, pretentious, and stupid. She gave herself out as a great authority on literature; but all her knowledge was parrot, and her own attempts in that direction the most deplorably dreary drivel'*.

Butts retaliated by going to the Sunday Express. Though she is not named, much in the article of November 26th was taken from her testimony: *The story of the bestial orgies conducted by Aleister Crowley in Sicily… was related yesterday to a Sunday Express representative by a woman who has just returned from this place to London.*

---

[82] In her journal Butts refers to this as Crowley's 'biographia mystica'. Her active contribution was later credited in the first single volume edition (Samuel Wieser) of Book 4, where she is referred to as Soror Rhodon of the A∴A∴. and indeed Crowley would later comment 'I am extremely grateful to her for her help, especially in indicating a large number of subjects which I had not discussed. At her suggestion I wrote essay upon essay to cover every phase of the subject'.

The orgies are carried on as mystic religious rites in an old farmhouse near the village of Cefalu, in Sicily. The main room of the house is windowless, with a flagged stone floor. On the floor is painted a great orange circle, lined with pale yellow. Inside the circle are interlaced black triangles. The room is lighted by candles.

A tripod, upheld by three little fauns, burns incense made of burnt goats' blood and honey. In a cupboard are heaps of little cakes, all made of goats' blood, honey, and grain, some raw, and some baked. The raw ones, gone bad, fill the room with their stench.

In this room are carried on unspeakable orgies, impossible of description. Suffice it to say that they are horrible beyond the misgivings of decent people.

In the early 1920s May Butts spent much time in Paris, socialising with HD and her lover Cecil Gray during the summer of 1921, for example. During this period Butts had short stories published, and after initially struggling to find a publisher, 'Ashe of Rings' came out in 1925.

Butts first met Jean Cocteau in January 1926, when staying in Villefranche on the Cote D'Azur. Both were at the Hotel Welcome, and both had a dependency on opium, though at the time saw it as an aid to their creativity. They struck up an easy friendship and Cocteau provided illustrations for her later books 'Imaginary Letters' (1928) and 'The Crystal Cabinet' (1937).

Butts even knew Christopher (Kit) Wood from her time in Paris[83], and was asked to write a tribute to him after his suicide in 1930: *We both came from the same part of England, the short turf & chalk hills which are like nothing else on earth. They sprawl across counties, & our history & the history of man is written on them in flint & bronze & leaf & grey stone. Written on very short grass full of small black & white snail-shells.*

Mary Butts' subsequent years in Cornwall were undoubtedly happy, settled and productive. After six months in rented accommodation, she bought her own bungalow in Sennen and named it 'Tebel Vos' (or 'House of Magic'). Indeed in July 1932, as she was finishing the novel 'The Death of Felicity Taverner' she would say: *These last weeks have*

---

[83] Butts is noted to have attended parties at the flat, owned by Chilean diplomat Tony Gandarillas, where Kit Wood was living (Blondel 1998).

been, no, are being the happiest in my life. A balance of all ways, focused round the new house & the home & in the life we are making.

Part of her contentment in Cornwall can be attributed to her newly found Christianity, and her discovery of the church at St Hilary, half an hour's drive from Sennen. Butt joined the community of souls centred on the church, having probably been introduced to Bernard Walke by her Sennen neighbours Ruth (1888-1988) and George Manning-Sanders (1884-1951)[84].

Mary Butts would attend mass every Sunday, and would quite often have breakfast with the Walkes afterwards. She also became friendly with writer Frank Baker who was employed as the organist at St Hilary's, and later became a successful though now largely forgotten paperback writer (Newman, 2010).

Despite having become - in Sennen - a close neighbour of Angus Davidson, editor at Hogarth Press, in 1936 Butts wrote an essay critical of the Bloomsbury Group. Though she was respectful of their achievements she, like T.S. Eliot, came to dislike their atheism, saying that they had *'a hole in their centre'*.

Butts continued to use opiates in Cornwall, drinking poppy tea and preparing opium using poppies that grew in her garden. She was also partial to a mysterious elixir called 'Champagne Wine Nerve Tonic' which she obtained from a herbalist in Penzance. Sadly, though, she died unexpectedly at the age of 46 of a perforated duodenal ulcer[85].

She remained on good terms with HD and Bryher, and Bryher published her collected essays shortly after her untimely death. Frank Baker and the Walkes subsequently moved to Mevagissey. Here they formed the nucleus of another community of writers and artists which would later include Colin Wilson and Lionel Miskin (Newman, 2010).

---

[84] George had novels published by Faber in the 1930s, whilst Ruth also active as a writer in the 1930s, became best known as a prolific children's author after the war, with a special interest in folklore. Joan Manning-Sanders, Ruth and George's daughter, was only 13 when, in 1926, she was commissioned by the Walkes to make a series of six paintings for the Lady Chapel.

11. This charming man: F.T.Nettleinghame and his piskey empire

Whilst the art colonies of West Cornwall have been well documented, other centres of artistic activity like Mevagissey are less well known. At the turn of the century Polperro, in the east, was another important destination for painters in search of picturesque harbour scenes, and the village attracted artists of various nationalities, including Claus Bergen (German), Auguste Delécluse (French), Edward Ertz (American), Teng Hok Chui (Chinese), and, in the 1930s, Oskar Kokoschka (Austrian). Interestingly, artists like Thomas Gotch, Frank Gascoigne Heath and John Anthony Park, though typically associated with West Cornwall, also lived in Polperro for extended periods[86].

Here, too, a number of craft-based industries flourished, at least transiently. One man, Frederick Nettleinghame, based in Polperro and East Cornwall for most of his life, was the mastermind behind several schemes, which demonstrate a mutually dependent relationship between craft, tourism, folklore and myth-making. Indeed F.T. Nettleinghame seems to have been one of the first and most brazen Cornish entrepreneurs to recognise the value in 'monetising' folklore[87].

Biographical details for Nettleinghame (b.1893-1976) are scanty but, based on various newspaper reports he appears to have served in the Royal Flying Corps during the First World War, and to have been the author of 'Tommy's Tunes', a collection of soldier's songs published in 1918.

In the early 1920's he worked as a 'financial organiser' for two companies run by his father-in-law, but by 1923 he and his young wife Lilian had relocated to Cornwall. With very little money in their pockets,

---

[86] David Tovey has more fully explored this story in his two volume 'Polperro: Cornwall's Forgotten Art Centre' (2021), and in a short 'feature' article on artcornwall.org.
[87] In this case the folklore collections of the Couch family.

they set up a business called 'the Cornish Craft Association', which relied largely on selling locally-made pokerwork (or pyrography) designs: *In 1923 we started off with the Cornish Litany and a half dozen other texts by burning them into wood…There was, we found, a public who cried for more…this resulted in that Exquisite Imaginer, Arthur Wragg, goulieing the Cornish Litany for reproduction as a postcard, to be followed later by St Ives and various other ones.* (Nettlingehame, 1926)[88]

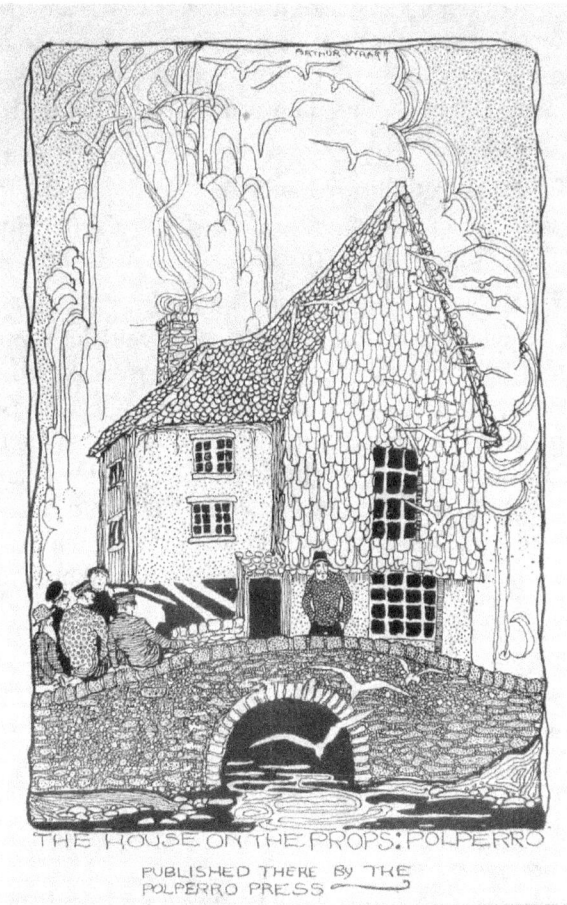

---

[88] As Tovey (2021) has pointed out, Philip Heseltine quotes the Cornish Litany in a letter to artist model, Phyllis Crocker dated 19th April 1917.

The abovementioned Arthur Wragg (1903-1976) was an illustrator from Sheffield. He first visited Polperro in 1924 and, with his artist friend Frederick Roberts Johnson, would work regularly for the Nettleinghames in return for board and lodging. Both men would also, later, provide illustrations and cartoons for the left-wing press, Wragg in particular becoming known for the polemical book 'The Psalms of Modern Life' (1933).

With Wragg's cooperation, multiple postcards were published by Nettleinghame under the name of 'The Polperro Press'. Some were illustrations of Arthurian legends or proverbs or characters from Cornish folklore[89]. The Cornish Litany postcards are particularly striking, however, and were so successful that other versions were produced later by rival companies, even though the words of the litany itself are probably of Scottish origin.

A number of short books followed, with reviews appearing in the press in 1927 for 'Polperro Proverbs', 'Old Cornish Carols' (by Ben Barnicoat), 'Polperro Privateers' (by Q), and a 'Guidebook on Marazion and St Michael's Mount'.

At one point it appears that, with Lilian's help, Nettleinghame was operating out of five separate properties in Polperro: 'Little Laney' (the pokerwork shop); 'The House on the Props'[90] (a gallery, giftshop and tea-room, which was decorated with murals by Arthur Wragg), 'The Noughts and Crosses' (a bakery which, in 1926, Nettleinghame turned into a small hotel), Couch's House (Jonathan Couch's old home, which was from the mid-1920s was marketed as a tourist attraction, library and boarding house), and The Forester's Hall (a shortlived museum near the harbour).

Having bought other properties in Cornwall and Devon (specifically Torquay, where he wanted to set up a mini golf course) Nettleinghame overstretched himself, however, and in February 1931 was declared bankrupt. That same year he was also divorced from Lilian. Writing later Nettleinghame blamed high tides and heavy rain damaging his stock, and forcing him to relocate from Polperro (Nettlingehame, 1948)

---

[89] The Polperro Press also produced postcard versions of the GWR Legend Land leaflets, using the illustrations by Cooper (see earlier chapter).
[90] As Tovey (2021) explains this distinctive building was previously called 'Havenside' and was run as a gallery by a retired schoolteacher called Elizabeth Minards. Minards also produced artist-designed postcards and a guide to Polperro.

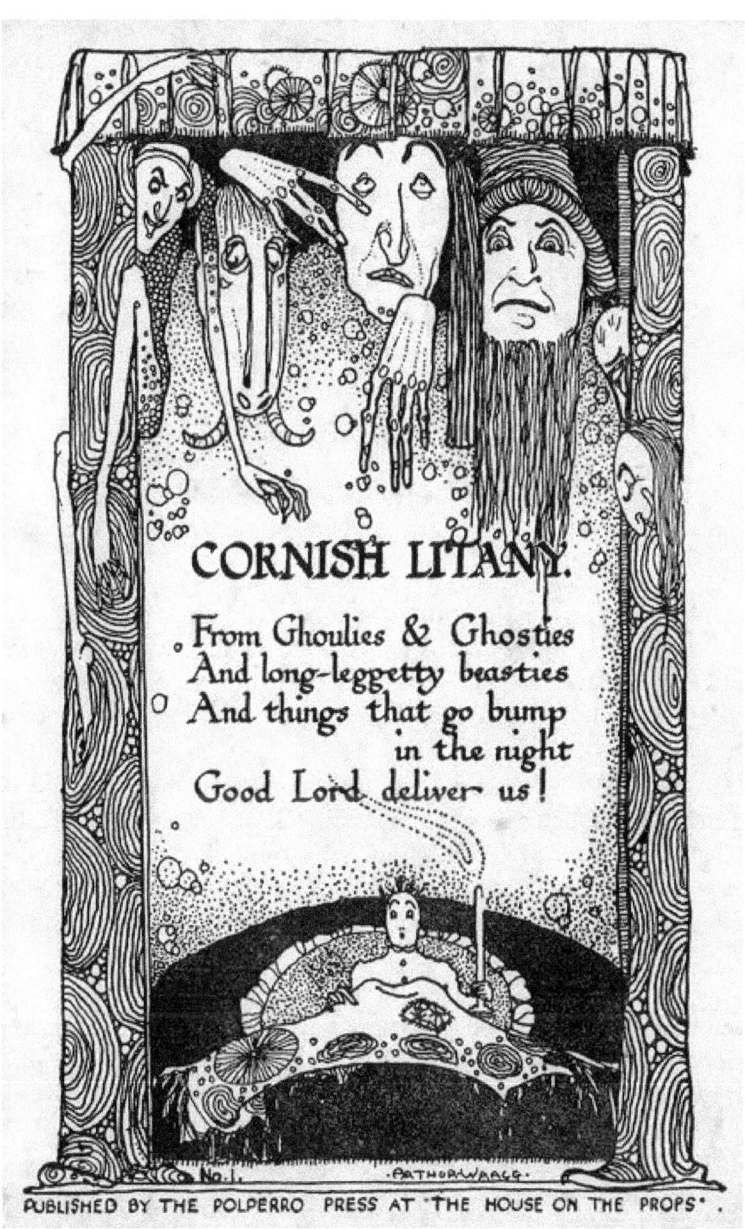

The first Cornish Litany postcard as designed by Arthur Wragg in the early 1920s.

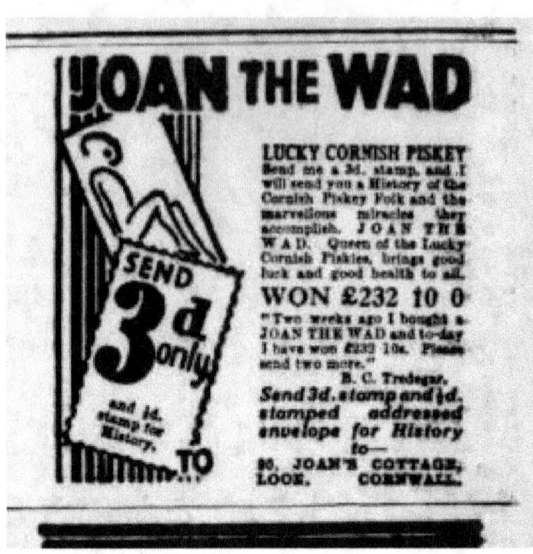

November 1932 Kirkintilloch Herald, Scotland. This is the earliest known newspaper advert.

As an undischarged bankrupt, of course, he could not register a new business or borrow money easily[91]. Probably for this reason, two men called Douglas Sargeant and Harry Alexander became involved with a new business venture already tested in Polperro: selling lucky charms.

On March 2nd 1932, Nettleinghame registered 'Joan the Wad' and 'Jack 'O' Lantern' as trademarks and, operating out of 'Joan's Cottage', Looe, placed an ad in the Daily Express for a cost of £6. By his own account, the response was overwhelming, and as more and more adverts were placed, more and more charms were sold all over the UK and further afield.

Nettleinghame's new business thus grew rapidly into a kind of piskey-kingdom or empire: *I had 80 indoor staff and 40 outworkers. We ran a chain of shops in Devon and Cornwall (sometimes as many as three in one town). By this time we were spending £30,000 per annum in publicity...*(Nettleinghame, 1948).

---

[91] As a result of bankruptcy, Nettleinghame's properties in Polperro were sold off in 1931, but Nettleinghame himself was not released from bankruptcy until 1953 (cf Tovey 2021).

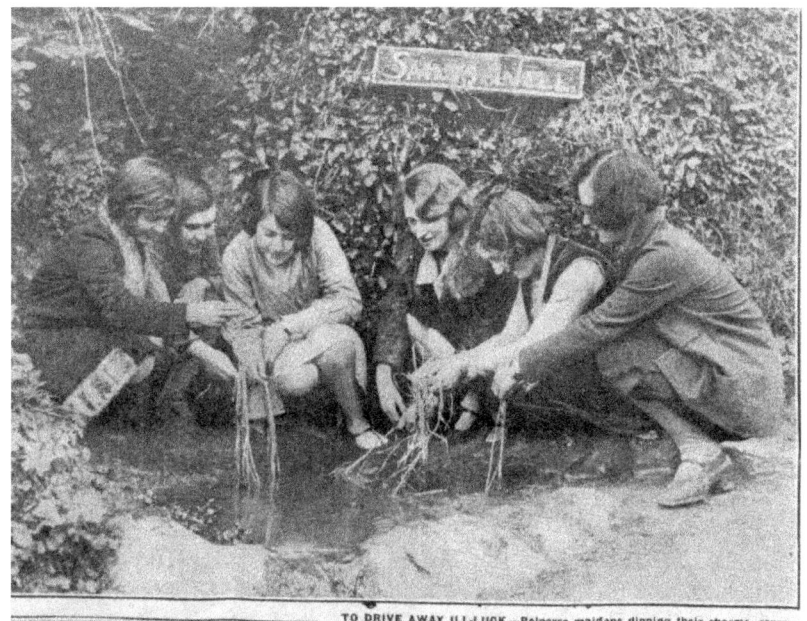

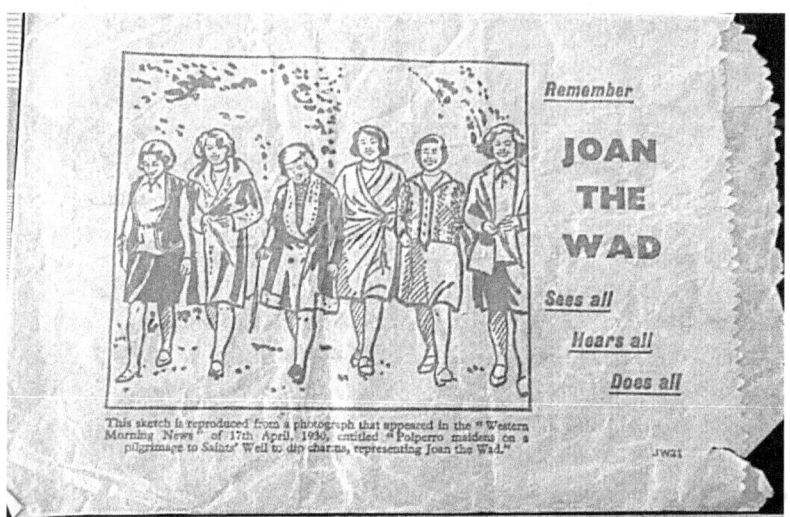

Top: Western Morning News April 17th 1930. The 'Polperro maidens' appear in a photo feature entitled 'Westcountry preparations for Easter holidays'. Behind them is a sign saying 'Saint's Well'. Bottom: a more modern paperbag celebrating the same ritual 'dipping'.

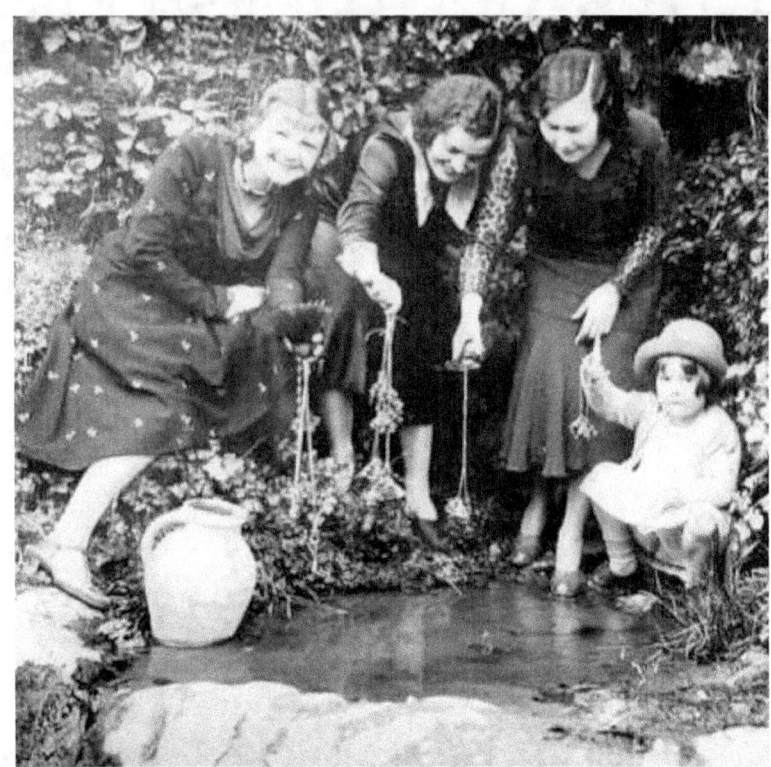
Another image of charms being dipped in the 'Saint's Well' from the 1930s (digitally recoloured)

In 1934 business partner Douglas Sargeant sought damages from a newspaper that had described him and his involvement with Joan the Wad as dishonest. In the course of the proceedings he admitted: *'The charms are manufactured in Birmingham and then they are taken to Cornwall and dipped in a certain well'*.[92]

That year Nettleinghame moved to St Benet's Abbey in Lanivet near Bodmin with a new wife, Marion Puckey, by which time he was

---

[92] Nettleinghame's charms were manufactured by the Peerage Brass Company in Birmingham (known prior to 1946 as Pearson-Page).

investing proportionally less in the charms business: *...we still had income coming in from 'goodwill'. And this income we spent consistently and at great velocity in developing the St Benet's Abbey estate in two separate occupations. One a roadhouse and the other a nursery.*

The nursery evolved into a successful bamboo-growing business which was well established by the outbreak of the war, but even after the move to Lanivet, Nettleinghame found new ways to promote Joan the Wad to more lucky customers[93]. A tiny stapled pamphlet, whimsical and not much larger than a postage stamp, was published during this period. It explains an obvious debt to Jonathan Couch, and bears the title 'A Short History of Joan the Wad'.

The opening section states: *Cornwall is not merely the land of Pilchards and Craime, of Blue Seas and Sunny Skies, of Quaint Villages and Beauteous Maidens, of Love and Health. It is the Land of Giants and Piskies. It is the luckiest County in England. It has less unemployment and more health, and where will you find a Cornishman who is not firmly convinced, that this is due to the good offices of the little piskey folk with whom he makes a point of keeping on good terms? Rare indeed it is that you will find a Cornishman who does not carry with him a metal replica of the Queen of the Piskies....The Piskey folk, according to Couch's History of Polperro, are "about a span long, clad in green, and wearing straw hats or little red caps on their heads." Two only are known by name, 'Jack o the Lantern " and "Joan the Wad."*[94]

Interestingly artist-occultist Ithell Colquhoun mentions St Benet's in her much-loved book on Cornwall 'The Living Stones', published in 1957. Colquhoun's account of Nettleinghame is as follows: *(He) advertised widely in the press particularly in popular 'occult' magazines, with an impressive array of testimonials from satisfied customers claiming that their luck had changed dramatically once they possessed 'Joan the Wad,' 'who sees all, hears all, does all.'*

---

[93] The author recently spotted a bus ticket from Manchester advertising Nettlingehame's Joan the Wad, though the exact date is not clear.

[94] It was T.Q.Couch (Q's father) that was the folklorist. It was he that added chapters of folklore to Jonathan Couch's original manuscript of 'History of Polperro'.

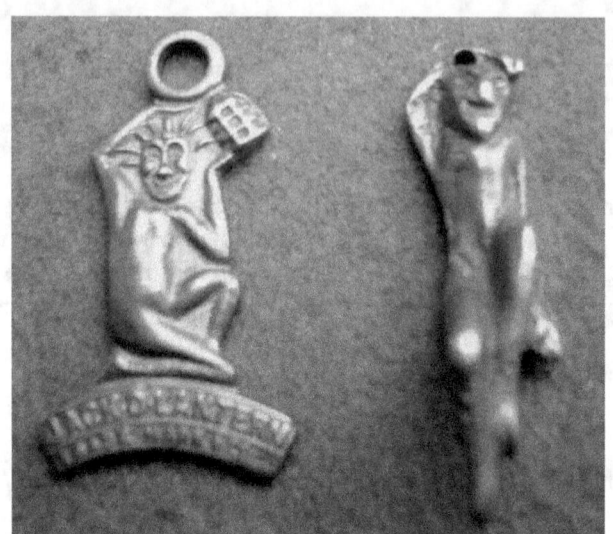

'Jack 'O' Lantern' and early 'Joan the Wad' charms. Later versions of Joan the Wad have her name written above her head.

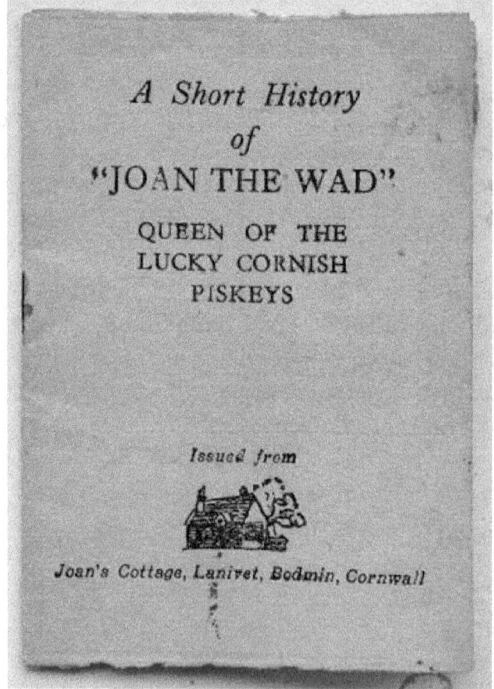

'A Short History of Joan the Wad'. Produced by Nettleinghame when he was in Lanivet.

The small metal figure...represented her as an elf - the conventional Cornish 'piskey' who appears on many objects offered for sale to tourists; Vulgarised now as a 'souvenir,' this image may yet perpetuate some genuine tradition about the look of the 'small folk.' But was 'Joan the Wad' a piskey at all? She may have been all too human, a witch who could cast spells for good or ill. 'Joan,' as Professor Margaret Murray has shown, was a favourite name among the witch-covens.

Colquhoun, who was an astute observer of such matters, implies that Nettleinghame's Cornish venture inspired several copycat businesses and something of a craze for charms in the late 1950s. She says: *St. Bennet's*

Joan the Wad ad (1947) in 'New Frontiers' an early sci-fi magazine. These are the ads that Ithell Colquhoun describes in her book 'The Living Stones'

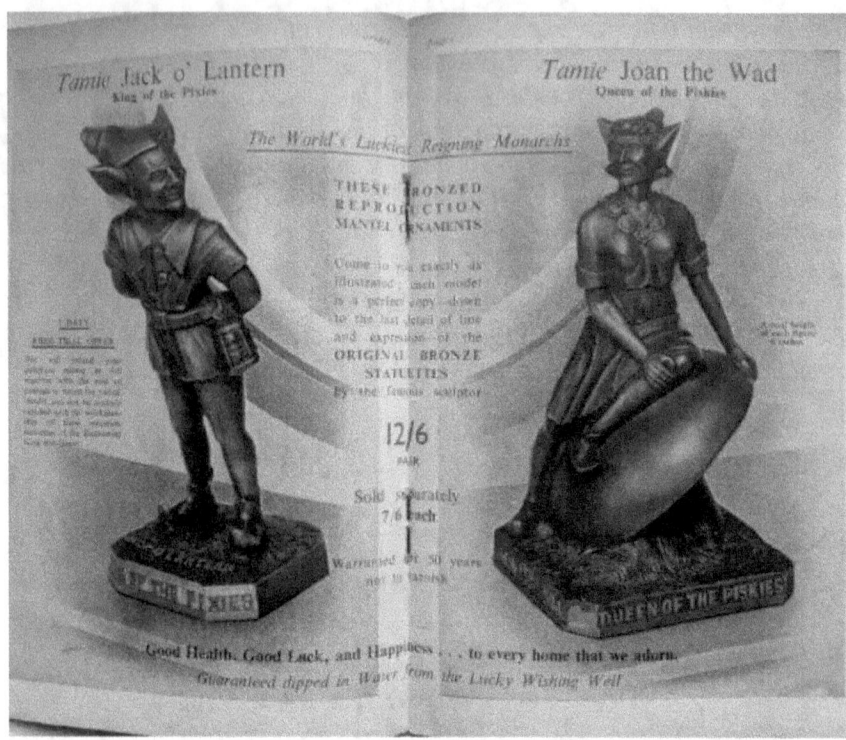

'Bronze-reproduction' mantel ornaments as depicted in Kendall Bailey's 'Astonishing History of the Lucky Cornish Piskies' (1950). Photo Laura Coulson.

is empty again, and Joan is now distributed from Polperro, whence also hails 'Glama, the oriental charm of luck and love.' When Joan appeared at Lanivet some years ago, she seemed to be the only luck-bringer of this type in the field; but she heralded a bevy of others, and now besides Glama, there is Lady Luck, the Lucky Seroom, Beppo's Little Man, the Horn of Plenty and the Wheel of Life, not to mention such die-hards as the Rabbit's Foot and the Four-leaved Clover to choose from, most of them with a 'legend' or 'history' thrown in, for about the same price as Joan.

One of the copycat businesses was based only a few miles further west. After the war 'The Queen's Parlour, Mevagissey', based in Market Square, started selling their own unique piskey charms - and larger plaster figurines - using similar sales tactics, though with more limited success. The business owner Kendall Bailey, as author of 'The Astonishing History of the Lucky Cornish Piskies' (1950), also describes his charms being as dipped in 'a lucky wishing well'. Though referring to several (badly spelt) holy wells in Cornwall, he is very vague about which one in particular was used to confer its magic, however.[95].

Meanwhile, given Colquhoun's book was published in 1957, it seems Nettleinghame quit the abbey in Lanivet and returned to Polperro in the mid 50s. Certainly, in 1959 he was doorstepped at Joan's Cottage in Polperro by an inquisitive, and highly sceptical, reporter from 'Weekend' Magazine[96]. In the article Nettleinghame - who answers the door of the shop whilst 'munching on his breakfast' - is portrayed disparagingly as an unscrupulous sixty-five year old married to an ex-employee called Doreen who is thirty years his junior[97].

The reporter doesn't get to speak to Nettleinghame, but his wife admits that the business used to receive around 300 letters a day requesting charms, many from as far afield as Africa and Australia. A local shopkeeper also describes the 'lucky Saint's well' in which the charms were, allegedly, dipped: *It's not really a well. It used to be an old horse trough…there was a little ceremony there twenty or thirty years ago. Dipping lucky charm pixies in the water. But it was just a publicity stunt…*

Sadly, the reporter manages to locate the well in Landivvidy Lane, but finds it in a state of disrepair: dried up, filled with gravel and overgrown with weeds.

---

[95] As a businessman Bailey had a few brushes with the law. In 1954, for example he was ordered by a local magistrate to destroy 2271 postcards sold in Mevagissey that were deemed obscene and liable to 'corrupt and deprave'. He was even given a prison sentence in 1961 after allowing a chip shop to operate on his premises. In 1967 he appeared again in the newspapers following a complaint regarding a macaroon. At the time he is reported as owning a café in St Ives, and a shop in Mevagissey.
[96] 'Weekend' March 11th -16th 1959 (from the DoreenValiente Scrapbooks). Nettleinghame is also described as owning a prestige car - an Austin Sheerline - and living in 'Little Warren' a large detached house overlooking the sea in Polperro.
[97] Tovey (2021) suggests that he married a third wife, Doreen Sobye, in 1947.

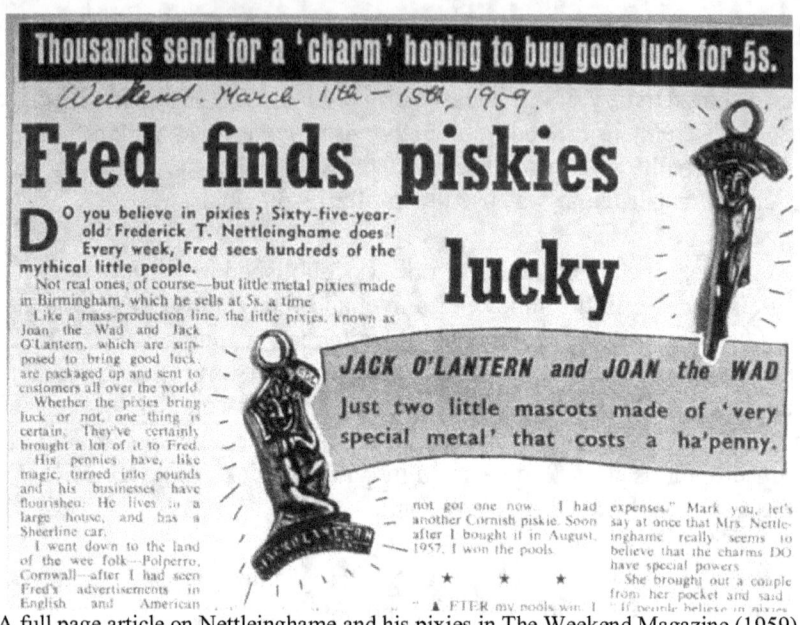

A full page article on Nettleinghame and his pixies in The Weekend Magazine (1959). From the Doreen Valiente Scrapbooks.

However, by 1959 Polperro had Cornwall's first model village[98]. It was made immediately after the war by a local entrepreneur, Jim Beddoes, with help from local builders. It is a representation of Polperro itself, to a scale of about 1:24, and having opened in spring 1948, it is still open to the public now, largely unchanged (Salter, 2014).

---

[98] Model villages started to become a visitor attraction in the 1920s and 1930s, though the other well-known model villages in Cornwall - at St Agnes and Lelant - didn't open until the 70s. The latter was created by commercial artist and Slade alumnus Leslie Caswell. Caswell was known in the 50s for the illustrations he provided to magazines like 'John Bull', 'Homes Notes' and 'Everybody's'. His house models were later taken to Land's End.

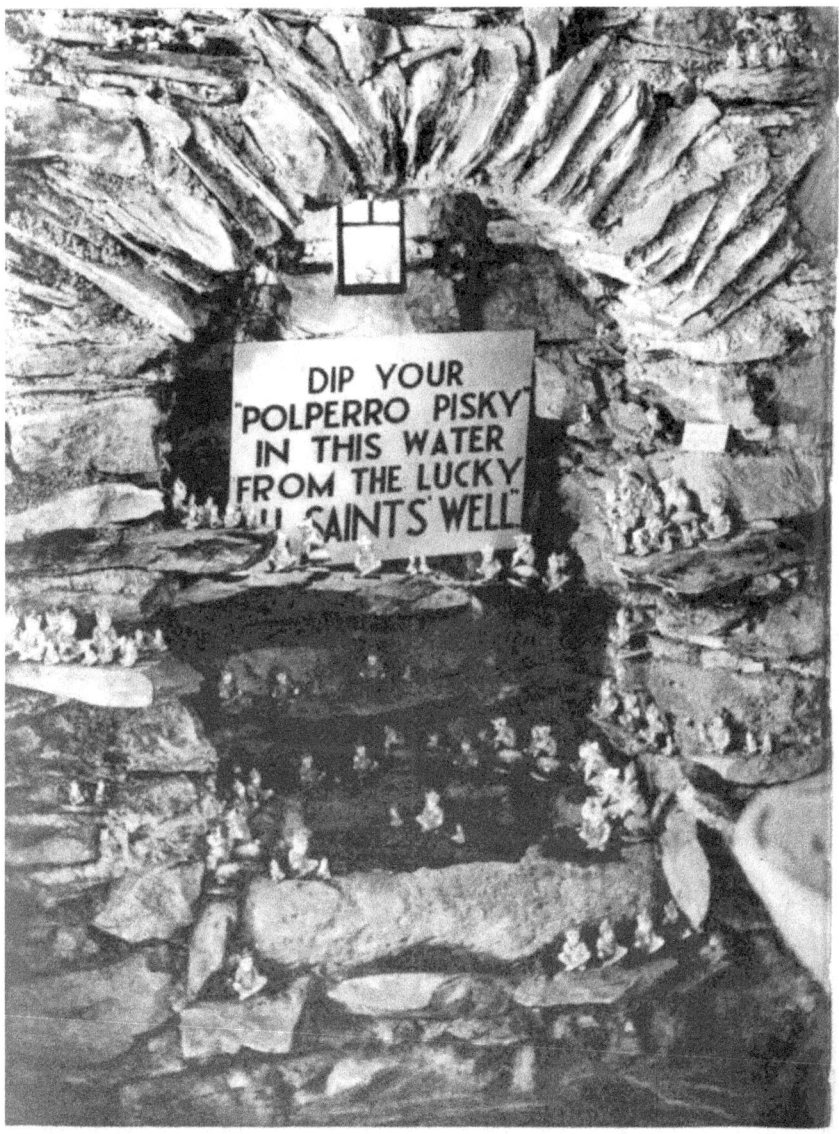

The Pisky Well, Polperro [Valentine

Photo from 'In the Steps of Pilgrims' by Sidney Heath (1953). The pisky well (a converted fireplace?) is still in the present shop in Lansallos Street.

12. The Land of the Gods

The period between the wars saw a re-evaluation of common-sense views regarding the religious history of Britain. In Cornwall, no-one was more outspoken in this regard than Thomas F G Dexter who, in promoting the pagan legacy of the Duchy, was considered something of a heretic by his peers.

Not much is known of Dexter's early life and career. Born in 1860 in South London, he had a wife called Eulalie, and between 1898 and 1905 was the author of four textbooks for trainee teachers, as well as a pioneering work on educational psychology (Dexter and Garlick, 1902). In an advert for one of these titles he is described as the Headmaster of Finsbury Pupil Teacher's School in Barnsbury, Islington (cf Cornishman Obituary, October 1933)[99].

Having first visited Cornwall at the age of 30 (Dexter & Dexter, 1938) Dexter started taking an interest in its antiquities and became convinced that the remains of the old church of Perranzabuloe could be found somewhere in the sand dunes to the east of Perranporth beach.

The old church was last used in 1790 before being dismantled and moved to its current site further inland. It had been built in the 11th century to replace the even older oratory of St Piran, which was an early medieval stone building a few hundred metres away. Despite their historic importance, both oratory and church had fallen victim to the shifting sands even though, in 1910, attempts had been made to protect the oratory by placing a concrete shell over it[100].

---

[99] In 1908 the Educational Times indicates that, that year, he moved to become Principal of Islington Day College in Offord Road.
[100] The oratory was first uncovered in the mid-1800s. The protective shell was removed again in 1980, and the oratory reburied before once again being exposed in 2014. Many skeletal remains were also discovered.

In the summer of 1917 Dexter started work at a site in the dunes above the oratory, and, sure enough successfully dug out - largely by hand - the remains of the old church with the help of a small band of trusty volunteers[101]. Based on his efforts, he was awarded a PhD by St Andrews, and his carefully written report on the excavation can be seen at the Royal Cornwall Museum (RIC).

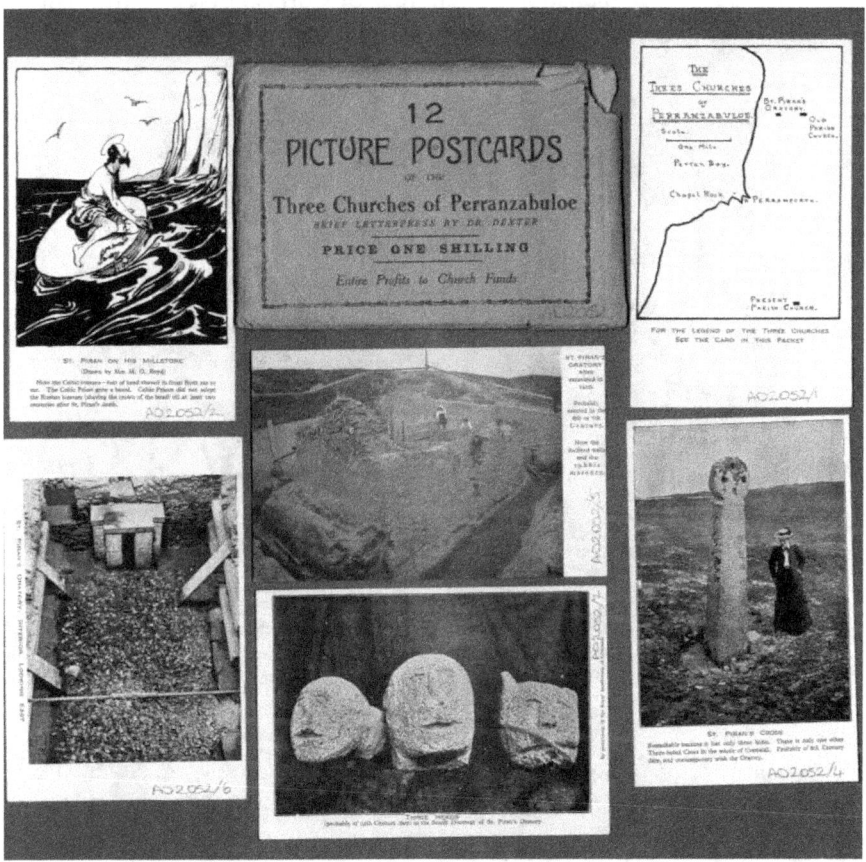

Six of the twelve postcards published by Dexter. Photo Kresen Kernow.

---

[101] This, together with the fact that Dexter can be shown to have become more involved in the RIC and RCPS in 1919, suggests he retired early to Cornwall either during or immediately after WW1.

For a few years Dexter offered his services as a guide to both the oratory and the old church. No doubt concerned by the poor condition of both sites - the oratory was (and still is) particularly prone to flooding - he published a set of 12 picture postcards that between them tell the story of the three churches, and their travails. The money raised was donated to the church funds.

Shortly afterwards, under the auspices of the Royal Institution of Cornwall (RIC), Longmans published Dexter's 'Cornish names' (Dexter, 1926), a detailed explanation of hundreds of Cornish place-names that draws on an extensive knowledge of the Cornish language.

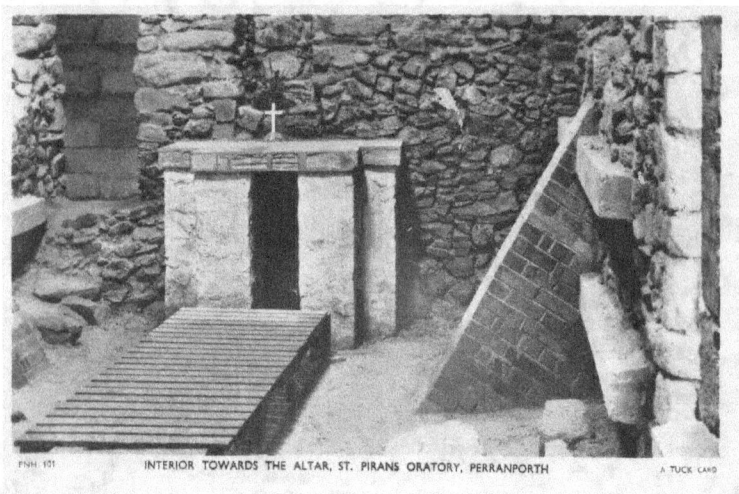

Mid-century postcard showing the partially restored interior of St Piran's Oratory, with original stonework thought to date to the 6th century CE. The protective concrete shell can be glimpsed through the doorway in the top left corner.

It was in the last few years of his life that Dexter's books on paganism were published, however, and in what appears a complete volte-face given his previous work[102], in all of them he seems determined to demonstrate that Christianity in Britain was but a thin veneer over a much more substantial pagan history. It was an idea that was considered subversive at the time.

---

[102] His work on place-names appears to have helped uncover this hidden history.

In 1929 a quartet of self-published works appeared. 'Civilisation in Britain', 'The Sacred Stone', 'The Pagan Origin of Fairs' and 'Fire Worship in Britain' all ask probing questions about Britain's pagan past. The latter, for example, describes the Celtic and solar fire festivals and notes their survival into modern times. Not only does Dexter explain that some of the most important dates in the Christian calendar are derived from these festivals, but that several saints, most obviously St Bridget, are in fact pagan gods. He even suggests, for example, that the names St Anne and St Antony actually refer to Tan the pagan fire-god. Referring to St Anthony in Roseland says: *it may be that we have here another Lan-tinn-ey, 'Enclosure of the Fire' and this surmise receives support from the fact that there is today a lighthouse on the point, for it would seem that man of old like man today saw the necessity of a beacon light on this promontory....The Cornish Anthonys just noted would seem to be but clerical equations for the fire-god Tin, Ten, Tan in his sacred enclosure.*

'The Sacred Stone', adopts a similar approach, and refers to Dexter's preferred theory that settlers from the Mediterranean built some of our most famous monuments. Supporting this Dexter notes a possible physical resemblance between some Celtic crosses and the Egyptian ankh.

A fifth 'pagan' publication, 'Cornwall: Land of the Gods' (1932), takes up the same themes but addresses Cornish prehistory more specifically, challenging accounts by the likes of Baring-Gould and other hagiographers regarding the nature of the Celtic Saints: *Cornwall has about 4000 years of history. It is generally supposed that Christianity was introduced into Cornwall sometime in the fifth century. So of the 4000 years of Cornish history 2,500 are pagan and only 1,500 Christian...*

Dexter goes on to explore the possible origin of Cornish saint-days, pointing out that nothing is known of the biography of St Wenep of Gwennap, but that her name, in Cornish, means 'white horse': *Gwennap Feast with its 'saint' Wenep is in origin a pagan festival of the White Horse. Saint Wenep is the pagan White Horse masquerading as a Christian saint, nothing more, nothing less.*

Most of the rest of the book draws on his knowledge of Cornish placenames in a similar way: *St Michael Penkevil means 'The Sun as represented by the Horse's Head'. There is no doubt that this Church is one of many on a pagan site, in this case a site of sun- and horse-worship.*

There is a lengthy exposition relating to Liskeard, and a number of other places: *The Welsh Kerridwen was among other things a moon goddess. The Cornish Kerid seems also to have been one for her fair at Liskeard (Lis-kerid means 'Kerids Court') is on the eve of the autumnal equinox, which was originally a moon date...*

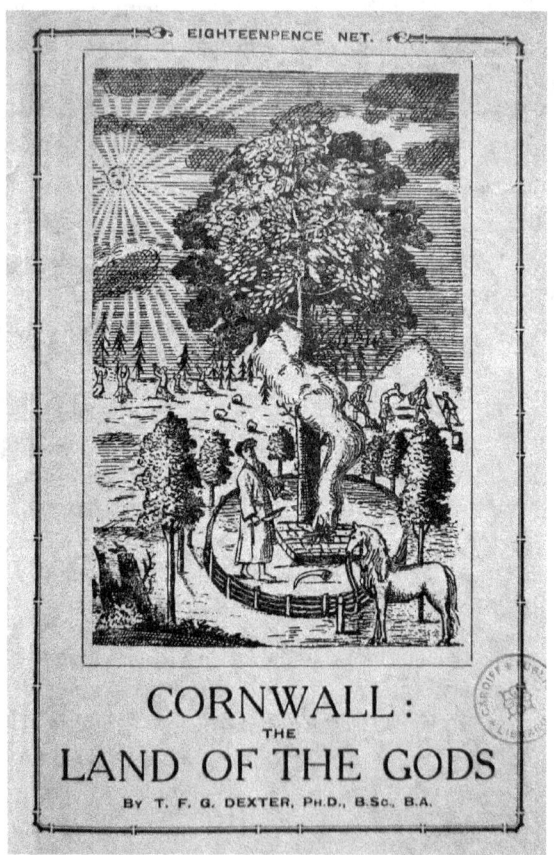

Dexter's 'Cornwall: Land of the Gods' (1932)

Din-sul 'Sun-hill' is said by a medieval commentator to be an old name for St Michaels Mount....there is much in favour of the ideas that St Michael is the successor of the sun-god and that St Michaels Mount was once a place of sun-worship...

Dexter takes a swipe at Jenner and Morton-Nance, leaders of the Cornish revival who, like a number of his peers, were sceptical of his theories: *In this hour of revival of medievalism, the man who dares to hint at a doubt concerning any one of the Cornish saints becomes according to the devotees of a certain school of thought an outcast fit only for the society of heretics, cranks and other impossible people.*

'Cornish Crosses - Christian and Pagan', which resumes the same approach, was published by Longmans in 1938, five years after TFG Dexter had died. Dexter's brother, Henry, compiled this more substantial book from Thomas' notes and manuscripts, and the result is a brave attempt to challenge existing wisdom regarding the many hundred stone crosses scattered across the Cornish countryside.

The book refers to Arthur Langdon's 'Old Cornish Crosses' (1896), and indeed borrows many of its illustrations. Dexter, however, believes that most of them shouldn't even be thought of as crosses, and are better referred to as 'monoliths': *The cross at Grampound is not a cross but a thinly-veiled phallic symbol'....There is a strange looking monument called the Crowz-an-Wra in Buryan. Crowz-an-Wra means 'the witches Cross', and the witch is generally the successor of the pagan priestess; perchance we have in the name, a folk memory of pagan rites once celebrated at this monolith, the head of which forms a crude wheel: a Sun-symbol.*

Dexter points out that crosses were used as symbols for many hundreds of years before Christianity: *The Greek cross symbolised the four directions of space, whilst for the Chaldo Assyrians, it was a symbol of the sun. Many other cultures used a four-spoked wheel as a sun-symbol, the wheel probably represented the radiant progressing power of the sun'.* According to Dexter many such cultures used imitative magic (eg using flaming wheels) in a magical attempt to make the sun brighter and more vigorous.

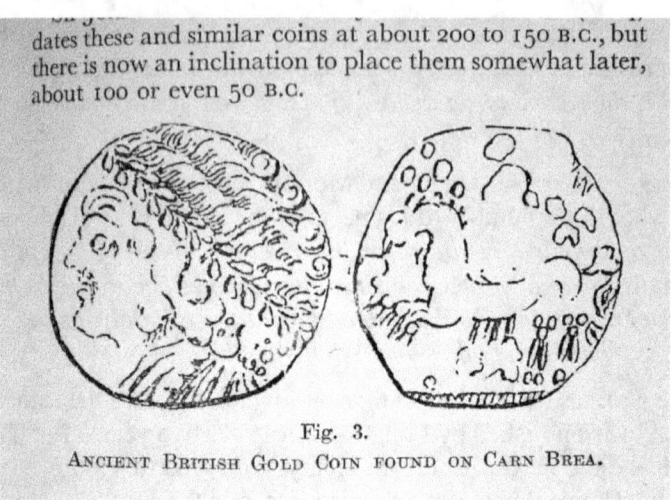

Fig. 3.
ANCIENT BRITISH GOLD COIN FOUND ON CARN BREA.

In 'Land of the Gods' TFG Dexter suggests the horse on the reverse of this coin found on Carn Brea has the head of a chicken and the legs of a greyhound, and is therefore a representation of Kerid, the pagan goddess associated with Liskeard in North Cornwall.

Dexter, referring to Langdon, identifies fifty wheel crosses in Cornwall, some of which have slanting spokes, and some a central boss representing the axle of the wheel. In fact Dexter identifies no less than 7 crosses indicating sun-worship in the village of Lanivet alone, and comments that the name itself perhaps derives from the word Lan-eu-et meaning enclosure of Hu (a sun god identified in Welsh literature by Iolo Morgawng).

Whilst Dexter's comments on wheel crosses have some credibility, much of the rest of the book is interesting but more speculative. For example, in looking for traces of pagan religious practice, Dexter identifies two crosses bearing images of men with tails (in Morrab Gardens and Lanivet churchyard) suggesting, that they might have been *'worn for ceremonial purposes'*.

13. Pat Doherty and the Beast

In March 1947 The Cornishman newspaper reported on the death of one of Cornwall's most important artists: *Stanhope Forbes RA was buried last Thursday amongst the primroses and snowdrops in Sancreed Churchyard. The sun shone as if paying a tribute of beauty to the artist who filled so many canvases with the sunshine of Cornwall....*

Forbes' passing represented the end of an era for the Newlyn colony, and amongst the long list of mourners were many members of the art community including Pat Doherty who was the grand-daughter of Newlyn painter Thomas Cooper Gotch[103].

But this was not the only funeral Doherty attended in 1947. At the end of the year, she and her son Gair were also amongst the handful of mourners at Aleister Crowley's funeral in Brighton, where they would have witnessed Crowley's defiant 'Hymn to Pan' being exclaimed by his executor, Louis Wilkinson. Indeed it has even been suggested that Doherty was also the only person present at the very moment of Crowley's passing in a nursing home in Hastings[104].

---

[103] Gotch first visited Newlyn in 1879 and became best known for his Pre-Raphaelite paintings of women and children, for which he often used his only daughter Phyllis (Pat Doherty's mother) as a model.

[104] Aleister Crowley's links with Cornwall have often been overstated, and for example, there is little evidence that he owned the house that Bryan Wynter, the painter, lived in. However because of his connections within the literary and bohemian community of Londons Fitzrovia and Café Royal he left his mark on many who came to see Cornwall as London's rural 'other'. To summarise this: 1) As discussed, he was a close friend to Duncombe Jewell 2) He worked closely with Meredith Starr, the man who introduced Peter Warlock to Black Magic in Zennor 3) Mary Butts who stayed in the Abbey of Thelema and helped him write 'Magick' lived in Sennen 4) The man that he considered his heir, Randall Gair MacAlpine, grew up in Newlyn. Crowley's biological son, he was also Thomas Gotch's great-grandson.

Doherty and Crowley's unlikely relationship, which resulted in Crowley at the age of 61 becoming a father to Gair, is explored in a previously unpublished essay by Ithell Colquhoun[105].

It seems that T C Gotch's daughter, Phyllis, having married a Patrick Doherty, gave birth to Pat at Gotch's house in Newlyn in 1915[106]. As a teenager Pat developed an interest in the occult after attending classes in the Kabalah held by Robin Thynne, another of Crowley's acolytes, who was living in Trevithal just outside Mousehole.

Thynne, along with psychoanalyst-painter Grace Pailthorpe who will appear in the next chapter, had provided financial support to Crowley's publisher, Mandrake Press in the early 30s. Based in Museum Street, their offices had been, in 1929, raided by police, after they had been used to exhibit DH Lawrence's paintings (Kaczynski, 2010).

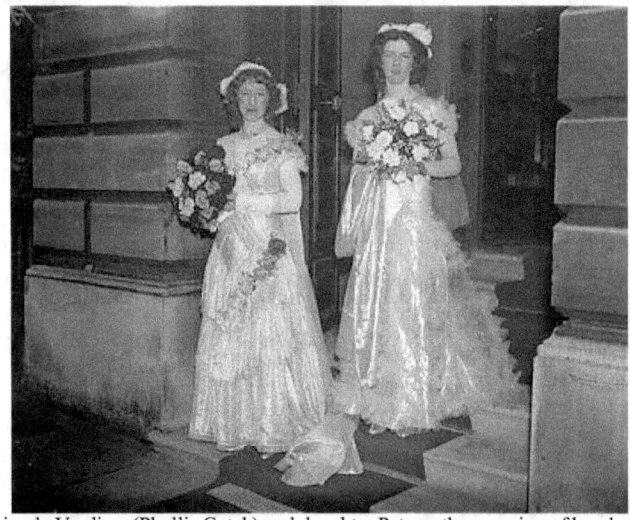

The Marquise de Verdiere (Phyllis Gotch) and daughter Pat, on the occasion of her daughter's first presentation at court (1933). Four years later Pat would give birth to a son by occultist Aleister Crowley.

---

[105] See 'The Torso Laughs' on artcornwall.org (Colquhoun, 2021). Des Hannigan has also written some personal memories of Gair on artcornwall.org.

[106] Phyllis subsequently married a Belgian Marquis, and, as the exotically named Marquise de Verdiere, was active both as an author and, in Penzance, as a local councillor for many years.

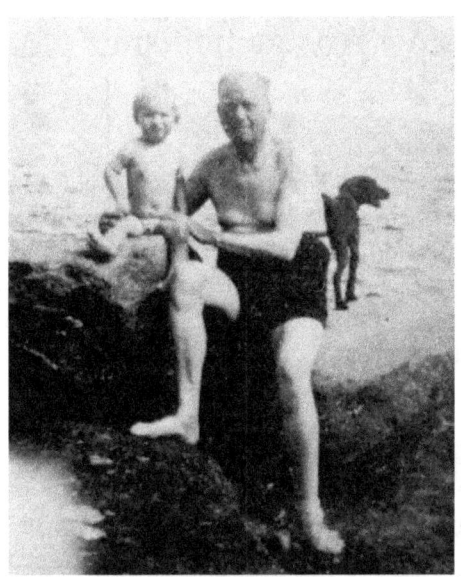
Occult holiday-maker: the Beast Aleister Crowley on the beach in Cornwall 1938 with his son Gair. From Colquhoun's 'Sword of Wisdom'

Newlyn was scandalised when Thynne and the young Pat Doherty started having an affair. Then in 1934, during the 'Laughing Torso' libel case, Thynne introduced the 19 year old Doherty to Aleister Crowley. Ithell Colquhoun, who knew Pat Doherty in the 60s, describes their subsequent relationship: *Pat was longing, in the most starry-eyed fashion, to become the mother of a magickal child and, convinced of Crowley's praeternatural powers, she felt he was the man most likely to give her one.... Pat's relationship with Crowley was intermittent but she was with him whenever she could steal a few days or weeks in London...On one of these occasions the sign of Leo – the Mansion of the Sun in zodiacal parlance – was in course and together they planned to produce a Sun child...*

Gair was subsequently born in Newcastle in May 1937, and, as proven by a grainy black and white holiday snap, was visited by his father in Cornwall the following year.

14: Surrealism v Abstractionism

In 1934, six years after Ben Nicholson 'discovered' Alfred Wallis in St Ives, he and Barbara Hepworth were married. By this time the power couple of British Modernism, they became outspoken advocates of abstract art which had slowly begun to gain support amongst the cognoscenti in Britain. But then, in the mid-1930s Abstractionism was suddenly outflanked by a different and, arguably, more alluring alternative.

The term 'Surrealism' was first coined by the French poet Guillaume Apollinaire, but it was given a more tangible identity, initially as a literary movement, by poet Andre Breton who wrote its first manifesto as early as 1924[107]. Adopting a bombastic tone, reminiscent of DH Lawrence and the English socialists, he denounces rationalism:
...experience itself has found itself increasingly circumscribed. It paces back and forth in a cage from which it is more and more difficult to make it emerge. It too leans for support on what is most immediately expedient, and it is protected by the sentinels of common sense. Under the pretense of civilization and progress, we have managed to banish from the mind everything that may rightly or wrongly be termed superstition, or fancy; forbidden is any kind of search for truth which is not in conformance with accepted practices.

Breton goes on to define Surrealism as: *Pure psychic automatism by whose means it is intended to express, verbally or in writing, or in any other manner, the actual functioning of thought. Dictation of thought, in the absence of all control by reason, and outside of all aesthetic or moral preoccupations....Surrealism is based on the belief in the superior reality of certain forms of association hitherto neglected, in the omnipotence of dream, in the disinterested play of thought.*

---

[107] Surrealism had a number of antecedents, most notably the Dada movement, a loose affiliation of artists based primarily in Zurich and Berlin.

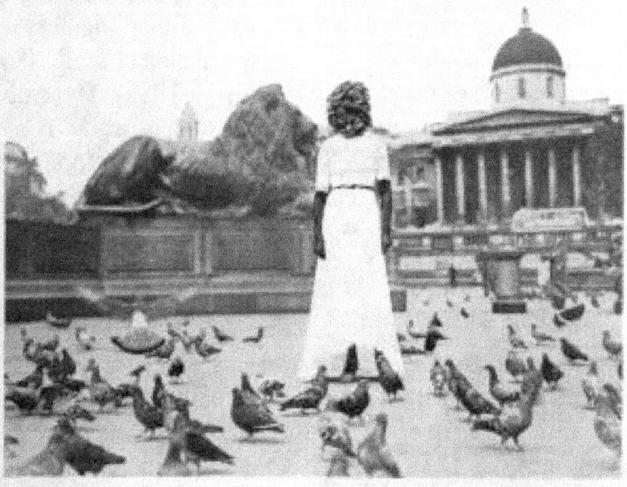

Cover of the 'International Surrealist Bulletin' No.4 September 1936 which reports on the International Surrealist Exhibition and its '390 exhibits'.

It tends to ruin, once and for all, all other psychic mechanisms, and to replace them in solving the main problems of life.

Surrealism did not make much of an impact on British art until June 1936, when the International Surrealist Exhibition opened in The New Burlington Galleries in London[108].

The show had been initiated by two Englishmen, poet David Gascoyne and painter Roland Penrose. The British artists were selected by Penrose and art-critic Herbert Read, and the continental by Breton and Paul Eluard (Remy, 1999). Nearly 400 works were jammed together on the walls of the gallery, and talks were given by artists including, famously, Dali dressed in a deep-sea diver's suit (Harrison, 1983). The exhibition attracted great publicity, though was received with hostility by a conservative British press. Herbert Read gave a less reactionary view: *June 1936: the International Surrealist Exhibition broke over London electrifying the dry intellectual atmosphere, stirring our sluggish minds to wonder, enchantment and derision.*

British artists had been slow to pick up on Surrealism. Neither of Cornwall's best-loved Surrealist artists, John Tunnard and Ithell Colquhoun, for example, fully embraced Surrealism until after the 1936 exhibition. In fact it is even doubtful that there were many true Surrealists amongst the 27 British artists that were included in the exhibition. Most had simply adopted the look, or aspects of it, without fully buying into the philosophy[109].

---

[108] None of the visual artists mentioned by Breton in the 1924 manifesto were British, however many modernists, like Henry Moore and Roland Penrose, travelled to Paris and were exposed to Surrealist works throughout the 20's. Surrealist films were shown in London in the late 20's, and there were exhibitions by Surrealist artists, like Max Ernst, at the Mayor Gallery in the early 30's. Surrealist influences thus inevitably found their way into the paintings of some of the British artists who formed the membership of Unit One in 1934 and exhibited alongside Nicholson and Hepworth, notably Paul Nash, Tristam Hillier, John Armstrong, and Edward Burra.

[109] Plymouth-born Cecil Collins, whose parents were both Cornish, is a good example. At around the time he moved to live in Dartington, two examples of his visionary paintings were included in the exhibition, even though he tended to actively distance himself from the movement.

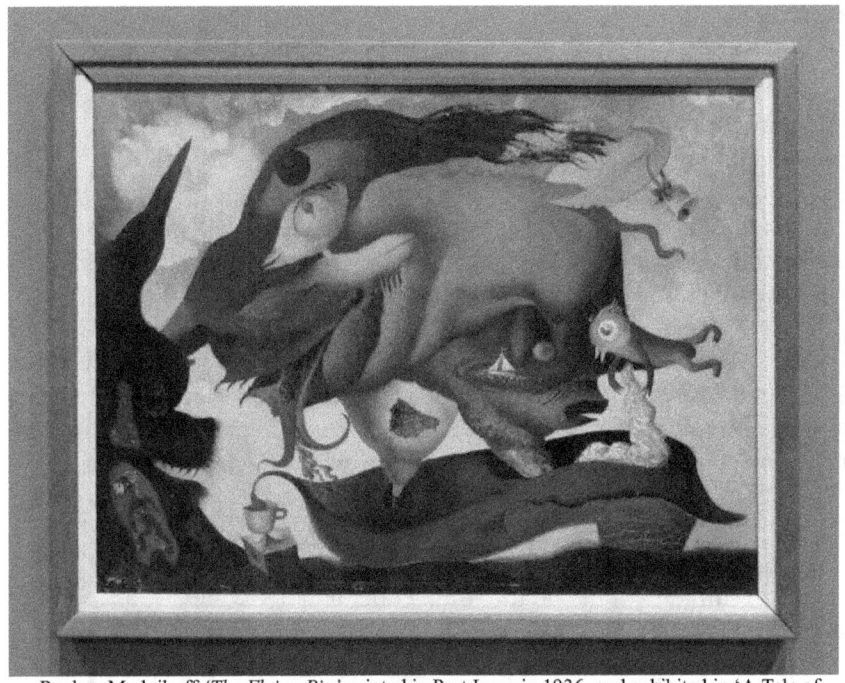

Reuben Mednikoff *'The Flying Pig'* painted in Port Isaac in 1936, and exhibited in 'A Tale of Mothers Bones' at The Exchange, Penzance in 2019. Photo the author.

However, probably because of their involvement with psychoanalysis and their unflinching ideological commitment to psychic automatism, Breton later singled out two of the British contingent: Grace Pailthorpe and Rueben Mednikoff. He regarded their contribution as *'the best and most truly Surrealist of the works exhibited by the British artists'*. Others have said that *'they were the haunting conscience of British Surrealism because they explored the unconscious in the most thorough tenacious and uncompromising way'* (Remy, 1999).

Since May 1935, Pailthorpe and Mednikoff had been working in a modest bungalow in Port Isaac[110], an isolated fishing village near Wadebridge a few miles up the North Cornwall coast from DH

---

[110] Garrick (or Garrick House), Trewetha Lane, on a hill on the outskirts of the village.

Lawrence's wartime getaway in Porthcothan. Theirs was a rather strange relationship, to put it mildly, and the art they produced even more so.

Pailthorpe was a surgeon-turned-psychoanalyst who had received prolonged Freudian analysis from Dr Ernest Jones, later Freud's biographer. Although she was subsequently scathing of the experience, she went on publish research on delinquency that led to the foundation of the Institute for the Scientific Treatment of Delinquency (later The Portman Clinic).

Pailthorpe met Mednikoff in London on February 1935 via their mutual friend and Crowley's former magickal partner, Victor Neuburg (Neuburg and other luminaries like Havelock Ellis were co-founders of the Institute of Delinquency)[111]. At the time Pailthorpe, who was tall, severe and formidable, was 44, and Mednikoff, who was shorter and rounder, only 28.

Initially Pailthorpe took the role of the doctor and Mednikoff, as her full-time patient, would provide her with strange, nightmarish images to interpret. At times he too would analyse them (eg referring to April 21st, 1935): *Here all my savagery plays the part of defending mother. Escape again – meaning that by pretending to defend mother I was escaping having my real motives discovered. The bent, double-ended penis symbol is toothed, but in defence of mother [...] the desecrated walls of the womb, in turn, protect the breast symbol. This I realise is now no longer a defence of mother but me viciously attacking mother. My savage teeth are really savage – defending myself. Fear of castration. That which is to be protected (the stolen breast) is sheltered within the protectiveness of mother"s shattered womb [...]*(Montanaro, 2010).

---

[111] In 1930, Pailthorpe, is known to have given £500 to the Mandrake press to pay for her research to be printed, and so it is possible that it was through this link that she knew Neuburg. Neuburg, since meeting Aleister Crowley in 1907 and contributing to his Equinox Magazine, was well connected in literary circles. As editor for Sunday Referee, he had published poems by Mednikoff, as well as other up-and-coming writers like David Gascoyne and Dylan Thomas.

After moving to Cornwall together in order to continue their work in seclusion, the boundary between doctor and patient became much more blurred. Pailthorpe herself started painting, with positive results that refuted her experience with Ernest Jones:...*it was undoubtedly what I had been looking for, viz another method of reaching the unconscious and of bringing it up into consciousness. My own fruitless experience of seven years of psychoanalysis by the strict Freudian method had left me a complete wreck physically and psychologically. Others I knew had suffered in the same way. I had been a most efficient doctor and surgeon and came to analysis as a necessary part of my equipment when I decided to specialise in psychological medicine. My career had been everywhere successful. In the process of analysis my sublimations were all broken down, but there was the conscious realization of what was causing this, and the wrecking of my physical health, except the unrelieved tension and strain of unproductive [.....] over a continuous period of 7 years* (Montanaro, 2010).

Pailthorpe became more interested in the object-relations theory of Melanie Klein, and the couple's research primarily concerned with the recovery of their *'earliest experiences, even [going back] to those before we could talk. If that repressed child within us is to be revived, we shall find it still the infant with the infant's mode of expression'.*

As a published poet himself, Mednikoff already knew David Gascoyne at the time he met Grace Pailthorpe, and through Gascoyne, was familiar with continental Surrealist art. It is therefore no surprise that despite their penetrating forays into the unconscious, the couple's work is not truly spontaneous and instead retains visual echoes of Surrealists like Andre Masson. Nor is it surprising that, despite having never shown together before, they were asked to be included in the 1936 exhibition (Montanaro 2010).

It should be said that, as a professional draftsman and one-time commercial artist, Mednikoff's work is generally more finished and more complete in its structure and design, but both artists use the same convulsing amoeboid shapes, and scatological references to bodily functions.

Letters written during this period indicate that Pailthorpe and Mednikoff remained in touch with Gascoyne after the close of the International Surrealist exhibition, and he is likely to have visited them in Port Isaac. (eg Gascoyne to Mednikoff, 20th July, 1936): *I imagine you both to be hard at work in your seclusion, and am most interested to know how it is all going [...] Taking you at your word, I am wondering whether it would be possible for you and Dr. Pailthorpe to take me as a paying-guest for a few weeks, if convenient just now. You were kind enough to offer me your hospitality and, feeling in need of a change of air and scene, it would be most pleasant to stay with people with whom I share so much interest in common, and in such a congenial part of the country.*

Dylan Thomas, the writer, was one of many present at the opening of the 1936 Surrealist show. Legend has it that, getting into the spirit of the exhibition he offered visitors cups of boiled string asking 'weak or strong?'

Another indication of Cornwall's continuing attraction to London's bohemia, immediately prior to attending the exhibition in June 1936, Thomas, too, had spent a couple of months in Cornwall with Wyn Henderson, an older, fiery, red-headed libertine with whom he had a brief affair. In the late 20's, Henderson had worked for Nancy Cunard's 'Hours Press' in Paris, where, as the general manager she published Havelock Ellis' 'The Re-evaluation of Obscenity'. In fact she apparently told Dylan Thomas, proudly, that Ellis had taught her to urinate standing up (Lycett, 2003).

Returning to London to live next door to Virginia Woolf's brother Adrian Stephen in Gordon Square, she had subsequently helped put Antonia White into print (Frost in May, 1933). However by 1936 she had been declared bankrupt and retreated to Polgigga near Land's End, to run a B&B.

By the time Dylan Thomas returned to Cornwall again a year later, in the summer of 1937, he had fallen in love with Caitlin Thomas. With the help of board and lodging from Wyn Henderson, who (along with Max Chapman, a Newlyn painter) by then had taken on the Lobster Pot in Mousehole, he and Caitlin were married in Penzance Registry Office on

11th July[112]. Caitlin and Dylan had their honeymoon in Cornwall and are known to have met Dod Procter and Indian novelist Mulk Raj Anand, who cooked them a fiery curry (Lycett, 2003).

There were other notable Surrealist comings and goings that year. In June the painter Roland Penrose organised a month's holiday for some of his friends in Cornwall at a house between Truro and Falmouth, called Lambe Creek. The party included several artists who had taken part in the 1936 exhibition. ELT Mesens, Eileen Agar, Max Ernst, Leonora Carrington (his younger, English girlfriend), Paul Eluard, Lee Miller and Man Ray, all managed to squeeze into an elegant white, creekside property looking upriver towards Truro.

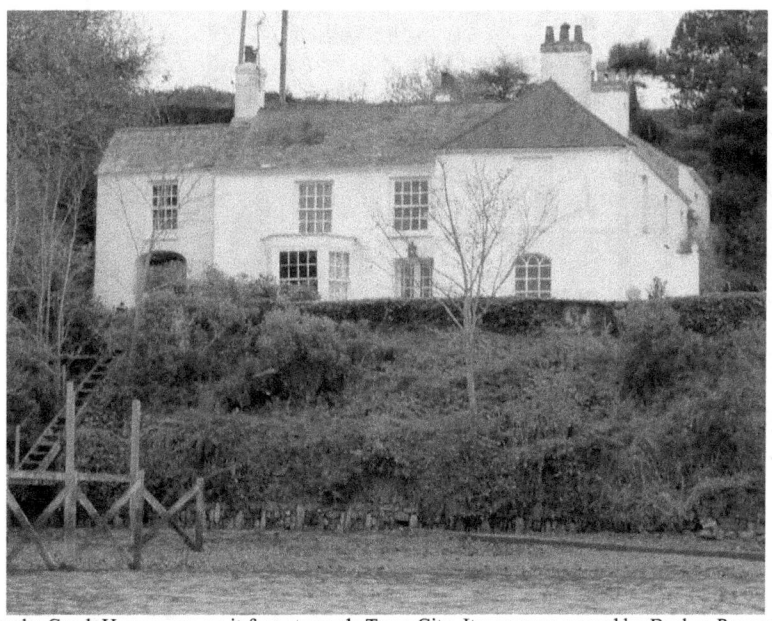

Lambe Creek House now, as it faces towards Truro City. It was once owned by Beakus Penrose, brother of Roland.

---

[112] In August 1938, Aleister Crowley stayed in the Lobster Pot in Mousehole whilst visiting Pat Doherty and his son Ataturk (or Gair). Extremely tenuous rumours persist that whilst in Cornwall he performed magickal rituals with Bernard Walke and Quiller Couch in the woods near Paul.

The police had issued an arrest warrant for Max Ernst on the basis that his recent exhibition at The Mayor Gallery was pornographic. Despite this, the artists did little to try to avoid detection, and engaged in plenty of playful exhibitionism in the garden on the bank of the Truro River: pulling shapes, and posing for two of the century's most renowned photographers, Lee Miller and Man Ray (Penrose, 2004).

By this time Wyn Henderson, who had known Peggy Guggenheim earlier in the 30s, was back in London. Early in 1938 she was asked by Guggenheim to run a new gallery. Henderson suggested the name - Guggenheim Jeune - and designed the branding. By a strange twist of fate it would be important to the careers of a number of British Surrealist artists.

Pailthorpe and Mednikoff were amongst the first to be asked, by Henderson, to show there, and would have travelled up from Cornwall for meetings:
Dear Wyn Henderson,
Many thanks for your letter and the enclosed Bulletin. I expect to be up in London the last week of July (1938) and would like very much to come to lunch with you and meet Miss Guggenheim. Is this Peggy or another Guggenheim?
R. Mednikoff and I have been asked to show our pictures at all surrealist shows since the International in 1936, both at home and abroad - New York, Chicago, Washington, Boston. We were asked to show in the Belgium show, but the show eventually did not come off, I forgot why. I am interested to see that you are showing surrealist works.
I shall look forward to seeing you soon.

Extended correspondence, particularly letters from summer 1938, indicate that Pailthorpe also visited Andre Breton in Paris at around this time.

John Tunnard was another artist living in Cornwall who visited Guggenheim Jeune in 1938, and was offered an exhibition there the following year. Born in 1900, Tunnard enrolled as a student at The Royal College in 1919, where he became acquainted with sculptor Henry Moore. Tunnard married Mary 'Bob' Robertson in 1926, and in 1929 gave up a promising career as a commercial artist to become a full-time painter. He spent most of the next few years in West Cornwall, and when he was offered a show at the Redfern Gallery in 1933, most of the exhibits were landscape paintings of the area: naive and expressionistic and similar in their feel to the 7 and 5 Society era paintings (Glazebrook, 1977).

Tunnard and 'Bob' went on to buy a gypsy caravan in which they lived in Cadgwith on the Lizard peninsula, and he is known to have been given a copy of Herbert Read's 'Surrealism' by Bob for Christmas, 1936. He is reputed to have said *'it's all in there, it's all in there'*.

In fact Tunnard drew equally from abstract art, and artists like Juan Miro, Alexander Calder and Ben Nicholson, in arriving at his mature style. However his use of space, and his tendency to place biomorphic modernist forms in front of a long featureless horizon, so they appear to float within a strange futuristic landscape, has always suggested a strong affinity with Surrealism, and accordingly he was included in several Surrealist shows in the late 30s.

In 1938 he presented himself to Peggy Guggenheim: *One day a marvelous man in a highly elaborate tweed coat walked into the gallery. He looked like Groucho Marx. He was as animated as a jazz band leader, which he turned out to be. He showed us his gouaches which were as musical as Kandinsky's, as delicate as Klees and as gay as Miros. His name was John Tunnard. He asked me very modestly if I thought I could give him a show, and then and there I fixed a date'* (Guggenheim, 1998).

Whilst Tunnard may have only been obliquely influenced by the 1936 International Surrealist exhibition, the same cannot be said to be true of another artist who later would be his near neighbour in Cornwall, namely Ithell Colquhoun.

Colquhoun was born in India in 1906. She attended Cheltenham Ladies College before gaining entry to the Slade School of Art in 1927. Whilst there, she painted classical and mythological subjects in a modernist, figurative style and made some precocious forays into the occult by getting involved, and contributing to Quest Magazine. (Hale, 2020; Shillitoe, 2010).

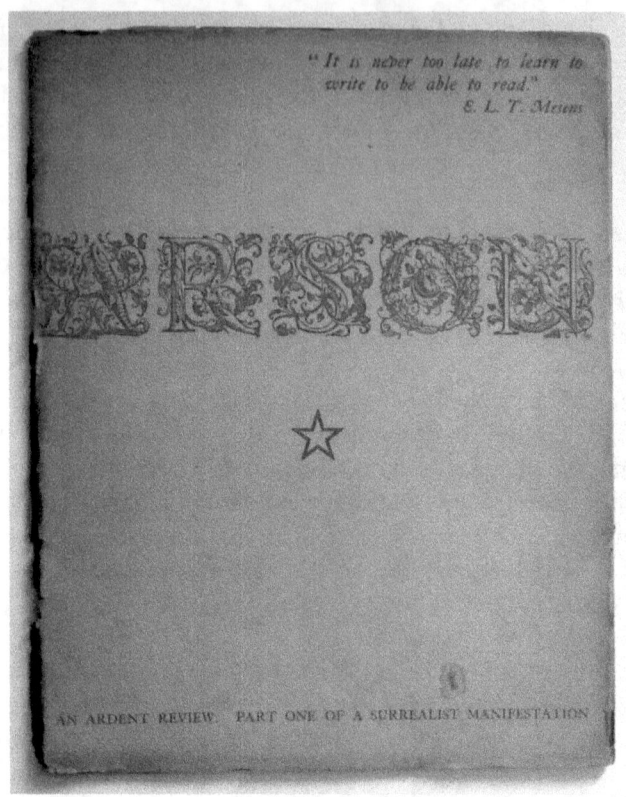
Arson: a one off publication produced in 1942 by Ithell Colquhoun's husband Toni Del Renzio

After leaving the Slade she went travelling throughout Europe, and managed to have a formal portrait taken by Man Ray in Paris in 1932. However Colquhoun only really got turned onto Surrealism after witnessing the 1936 exhibition in London: *When I went to Paris in 1931 I read a booklet called what is Surrealism by Peter Negoe – and American, I think, of whom I have never subsequently heard. I saw paintings by Salvador Dali in small mixed exhibitions. Dali had not then been excommunicated by Breton. Only in 1936 did the movement (Surrealism) make its full impact on me.....Andre Breton, robust and thickset, with wavy hair of a length at that time conspicuous, and other also spoke, but who could follow Dali? It seemed that he did actually evoke phantasmic presences which generated a tense atmosphere; the white cloth stretched to form a lowered ceiling vibrated as in a strong wind, though the weather was still and sultry. Dali was minute, feverish, with bones brittle as a birds a mop of dark hair and greenish eyes*[113].

Responding to the provocation and radical edge of Surrealism, and its problematisation of sexuality, between 1937 and 1942 Colquhoun produced her most archetypal surrealist works. She subsequently referred to this as her 'Dali phase'. In June 1939 she had a joint show with Roland Penrose at the Mayor Gallery, and shortly afterwards visited Paris to see Breton. She formally joined the Surrealists late in 1939.

When war was declared in September 1939, Pailthorpe and Mednikoff moved from Cornwall to Hertfordshire, and attempted to organise a Surrealist exhibition at the British Art Centre. The gallery had been recently established by Guggenheim and Herbert Read. Previously the British Surrealists had rather relied on the London Gallery and the London Bulletin for exposure, and their demise at the outbreak of war had very much threatened the survival of the group.

During the lead-up to the event, Mednikoff sent a letter to the Surrealists inviting them to dinner at the Barcelona Restaurant:
At a meeting between Dr Pailthorpe, Roland Penrose, W Hayter and myself, it was decided that arrangements be made for a gathering of Surrealists for the purpose of planning the reforming of the Surrealist Group in England.

Dr Pailthorpe and I suggested the reforming of the group with freedom from political bias or activity as part of its constitution. As it was felt by us all that Surrealism's vital purpose would benefit considerably by the reforming of the group, it was agreed that arrangements be made for a dinner, to be followed by a discussion in which all views could be made known and a constitution formulated.

---

[113] This is taken from the essay Colquhoun wrote for her retrospective exhibition at The Newlyn Gallery in 1976.

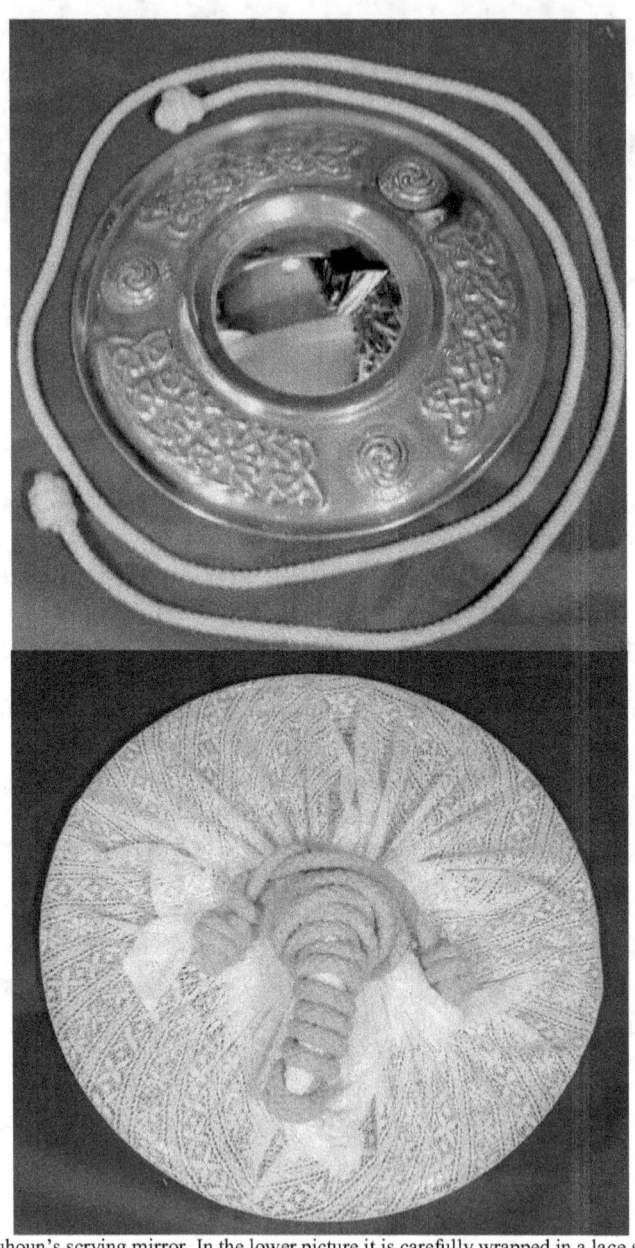

Ithell Colquhoun's scrying mirror. In the lower picture it is carefully wrapped in a lace shawl. Photo Ben Fernee.

The plans for this are now in progress. The dinner will be held on Thursday, April 11th, at 7.15pm, and the price will be 3/6 per person... Yours sincerely

Ithell Colquhoun supported the couple's arrangements for the meeting. In a handwritten letter dated 5th April 1940, she wrote: *I shall be very pleased to come to the dinner you and Dr Pailthorpe are arranging to discuss the future of Surrealism in England. As you know I am in agreement with your idea of the non-political basis of any group which may be formed.*

ELT Mesens, however, was committed to retaining a much more principled political stance, prompted by the rise of Fascism, and Breton's recent endorsement of Marxism. As the leader he demanded that anyone wishing to remain in the British Surrealist group would have to commit to the following rules:
1. Adherence to the proletarian revolution
2. Agreement not to join any group or association, professional or other, including any secret society, other than the surrealist
3. Agreement not to exhibit or publish except under surrealist auspices.

Intent on pursuing their studies in psychoanalysis and the occult respectively Pailthorpe, Mednikoff and Colquhoun, along with Eileen Agar and Henry Moore, could not agree to Mesens' demands, and left the group.

Paithorpe and Mednikoff ended up moving to the US. Colquhoun, on the other hand, visited Cornwall, and in 1940 painted the 'Dance of the Nine Maidens' series of watercolours, a response to the Merry Maidens circle between Lamorna and St Buryan[114].

On July 10th, 1943 Colquhoun married a Russian/Italian, Toni Del Renzio who the previous year had published a one-off Surrealist journal 'Arson', which included an interview with Andre Breton. It incurred debts, however, that Colquhoun had to help pay off.

---

[114] It is assumed this was her first visit to the Duchy (See White, 2017).

Colquhoun and Del Renzio believed that the British Surrealists had strayed from Breton's original principles, but for their pains, suffered abuse from them at a series of poetry-readings that they organised at the International Arts Centre.

Colquhoun divorced Del Renzio in 1947, and is thought to have visited the Scilly Isles that same year. Intending to spend more time in Cornwall, she also bought Vow Cave, a small studio with corrugated iron walls in Lamorna valley, at around this time.

Unlike several other artists Colquhoun was never herself made into a bard, but, alongside her occult studies, she became very engaged with Cornwall, and Cornish culture, writing for the Cornish Review and related publications, for example.

A few years ago, her precious scrying mirror came up for sale. A convex mirror decorated with Celtic knotwork, she would fixate on her own reflected image whilst connected to it by a yellow rope, which she called the 'um' (short for umbilicus) (Colquhoun, 2015). Interestingly it was made for her by Francis Cargeeg (1893-1981), who had set up as a copper-worker after moving back to his home town of Hayle in 1939. Cargeeg is now best known for creating the copper regalia used by the Cornish Gorsedh, and indeed one of his first commissions was the Grand Bard's crown itself, which was completed during the WW2 and uses an ornate oak-leaf design[115].

In 1949 Colquhoun shared an exhibition in Mousehole, at the Arra Gallery, with Marlow Moss[116] and John Armstrong, but by then she seemed to prefer working in relative isolation on the leafier, southern side of West Cornwall. Whilst artists with Neo-Romantic tendencies, like Bryan Wynter and Sven Berlin, were readily accepted into the St Ives colony, Colquhoun, Tunnard and the other Cornish surrealists never integrated with it as it grew in size and influence after the war.

---

[115] Robert Morton Nance recalls watching Herkhomer making a similar crown at Bushey School of Art. Francis Cargeeg's own bardic name was 'Tan Dyvarow'.

[116] Moss lived in Paris from 1927, and whilst there made her reputation as an abstract artist and friend of Piet Mondrian. She moved to Cornwall, having visited on many previous occasions, at the outbreak of WW2.

This may well be attributed to Ben Nicholson's antipathy to Surrealism, which was enflamed by the 1936 exhibition. Certainly following the exhibition, the British avant garde became caught up in what Henry Moore called *'a violent quarrel between the abstractionists and the surrealists'* (The Listener, August 1937).

Ben Nicholson was seen as the natural leader of the abstractionist faction. As Charles Harrison explains (Harrison, 1983): *the development of an explicit interest in Surrealism in England generally marked a process of polarisation within the ranks of the avant garde... between the abstractionists (or 'Ben boys' as Paul Nash was wont to call them) and those that saw Surrealism as an alternative'*

According to Harrison the two arguments were perfectly counterpoised: *The abstract and constructivist artists on the whole idealized the artist as the typical designer of the forms of a new and harmonious world of which he was an important instigator....the Surrealists saw the artist as*

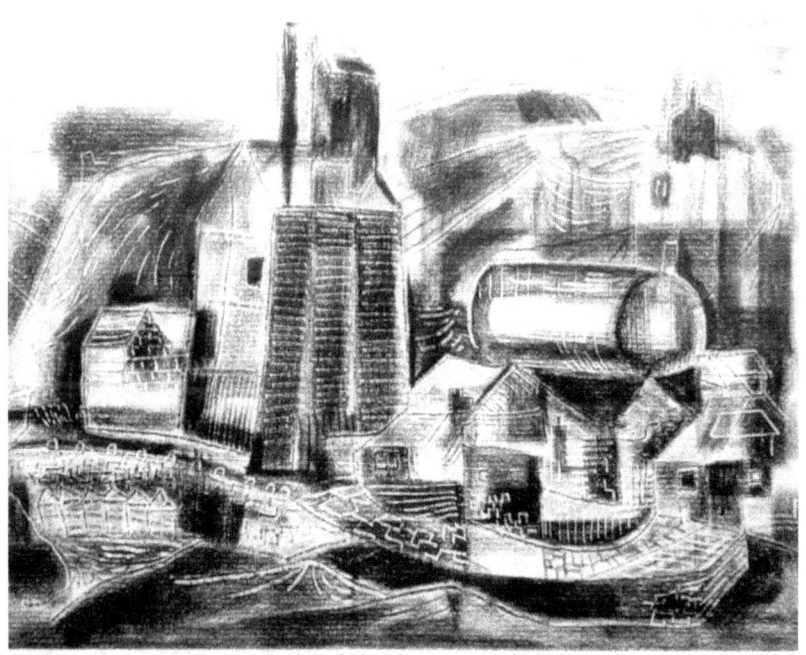

A monotype by Bryan Wynter (1945) depicting the gas works in St Ives, where Tate St Ives is now situated. Photo Rosemary White.

the anarchic and unafraid guardian of the values of an uncensored humanity and as an informed critic of the bourgeois world...on the one hand the theoria of abstract art....proposed ideal harmony as a critique of the lack of spiritual satisfaction and of progressive planning in modern society....on the other surrealism proposed irrationality and disorder as means of criticizing and subverting prevailing bourgeois concepts of reason and order...

The two approaches were clearly, on many levels, irreconcilable, and the intensity of the stand-off was heightened by the approach of the Second World War.

In the end, when the war came, many - particularly those avant garde artists associated with Hampstead - ended up leaving London. Piet Mondrian went to the US, as did Walter Gropius, whilst Naum Gabo followed Nicholson and Hepworth to St Ives.

It was under these extraordinary, never-to-be-repeated circumstances, that the art colony in St Ives became 'modernised'. Certainly, for well over two decades the town became a centre for abstract and constructivist art known across the world. After Nicholson, Hepworth and Gabo, it became possible to talk of second and even third generation St Ives artists. These included Terry Frost, Peter Lanyon, Bryan Wynter and Patrick Heron all of whom benefitted from the spotlight that Bernard Leach together with Gabo, Hepworth and Nicholson caused to be cast on West Cornwall.

The colony's contribution over several decades was considerable, and was rightly recognised in 1993 when the Tate opened a gallery in St Ives.

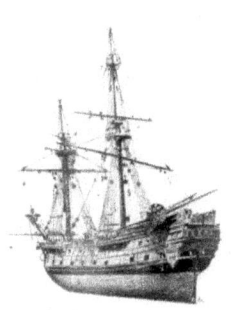

Select Bibliography

Andrews, M. (1999) *Landscape and Western Art* Oxford

Blondel, Nathalie (1998) *Mary Butts: Scenes from the Life* MacPherson

Borlase, William (1754) *Antiquities, Historical and Monumental, of the County of Cornwall (incl Vocabulary of the Cornu-British Language)*

Borlase, William (1756) *Observations of the Ancient and Present State of the Islands of Scilly*

Borlase, William (1758) *The Natural History of Cornwall*

Bottrell, William (1870, 1873 and 1880) *Traditions and Hearthside Stories of West Cornwall*

Button, Virginia (2000) *Christopher Wood: St Ives Artists* Tate

Burke, E.(1759) *A philosophical enquiry into the origin of our ideas of the sublime and beautiful.*

Cardew, Michael (1988) *Pioneer Potter: An Autobiography* Collins

Carpenter, Edward (1891) *Civilisation: its cause and cure*

Carter, Eileen (2001) *In the Shadow of Saint Piran* Lodenek

Colquhoun, Ithell (1957) *The Living Stones* Peter Owen

Colquhoun, Ithell (1975) *Sword of Wisdom: MacGregor Mathers and the Golden Dawn* Putnam's

Colquhoun, Ithell (2021) *The Torso Laughs* artcornwall.org

Colquhoun, Ithell (2015) *I Saw Water* Pennsylvania State University

Couch, Jonathan (1871) *History of Polperro*

Courtney, Margaret (1890) *Cornish Feasts and Folklore*

Cross, Tom (1994) *The Shining Sands: Artists in Newlyn and St Ives 1880-1930* Lutterworth Press

Crowley (1989) *The Confessions of Aleister Crowley: An Autohagiography* Arkana

Cunliffe, B. (2003) *The Celts: A very short Introduction* Oxford U P

Deacon, Bernard (1993) *And Shall Trelawney Die? The Cornish* identity (in Cornwall Since the War ed Payton) Truran

Dexter, T.F.G. and Garlick, A.H. (1902) *Psychology In The Schoolroom* Longmans, Green and Co, London

Dexter, T.F.G. (1926) *Cornish Names - An Attempt to Explain over 1600 Cornish Names* (republished as Cornish Names) London; Longmans Green and Co

Dexter T.F.G. (undated) *Civilisation In Britain 2000 B.C.* New Knowledge Press, Perranporth, Cornwall

Dexter, T. F. G. (undated) *The Pagan Origin of Fairs* New Knowledge Press, Perranporth, Cornwall

Dexter, T F G (1929) *The Sacred Stone* New Knowledge Press, Treberran, Perranporth, Cornwall

Dexter, T.F.G. (1931) *Fire Worship in Britain* [New Knowledge Series No. 4] Watts & Co, London, United Kingdom

Dexter T.F.G. (1932) *Cornwall: The Land Of The Gods* Jordan's Bookshop, Truro Cornwall, 1932

Dexter, T.F.G. (1933) *A Pre-History Reader or History from Things not Books. (World of Youth Library No. 14)* Watts, London

Dexter, T.F.G & Dexter, Henry (1938) *Cornish Crosses - Christian and Pagan* London; Longmans Green & Co.

Dorson, Richard M. (1968) *The British Folklorists A History* University of Chicago

Ellis, Havelock (1914) *Impressions and Comments* Stella Browne

Ellis, Havelock (1939) *My Life: The autobiography of Havelock Ellis*

Evans-Wentz, W.Y. (1911*) The Fairy Faith in Celtic Countries*

Forbes, Stanhope A. (1898) *A Newlyn Retrospect (in The Cornish Magazine Vol1)* Pollard

Gilpin, W. (1794) *Three Essays* Blamire

Glazebrook, Mark (1977) *John Tunnard 1900- 1971* Arts Council, London

Gray, Cecil (1934) *Peter Warlock: A Memoir of Philip Heseltine* Jonathan Cape

Gray, Cecil (1948) *Musical Chairs: Between Two Stools* Home & Van Thal

Grosskurth, Phyllis (1980) *Havelock Ellis: a Biography* Knopf

Guggenheim, Peggy (1998) *Confessions of an Art Addict* Ecco Press

Hale, Amy (2020) *Genius of the Fern Loved Gully* Strange Attractor

Hardie, M (2009) *Artists in Newlyn and West Cornwall 1880-1940* Art Dictionaries

Harrison, Charles (1983) *English Art and Modernism* Yale

Harrod, Tanya (2013) *The Last Sane Man: Michael Cardew* Yale University Press

Hepburn, Nathaniel (2012) *Cedric Morris and Christopher Wood: A Forgotten Friendship* Unicorn

Hendra, Viv (2007) *The Cornish Wonder: A Portrait of John Opie* Truran

Hunt, Robert (1865) *Popular Romances of the West of England*

Hutton, Ronald (1999) *The Triumph of the Moon* Oxford U P

Hutton, Ronald (2009) *Blood and Mistletoe: History of the Druids in Britain* Yale University Press

Jacobs, Michael (1985) *The Good and Simple Life: Artist Colonies in Europe and America* Phaidon

Jenner, Henry (1904) *A Handbook of the Cornish Language*

Kaczynski, Richard (2010) *Perdurabo: The Life of Aleister Crowley* North Atlantic Books

Kent, Alan M (2000) *The Literature of Cornwall: Continuity, Identity, Difference 1000-2000* Redcliffe

Kinkead-Weekes, Mark (1996) *D H Lawrence Vol2 Triumph to Exile* Cambridge University Press

Leach, Bernard (1940) *A Potter's Book* Faber & Faber

Lowenna, Sharon (2005) *Noscitur a Sociis:Jenner, Duncombe-Jewell and their milieu* in Cornish Studies #12

Lycett, Andrew (2003) *Dylan Thomas: A New Life* Orion

Marsh, Jan. (1982) *Back to the Land: The Pastoral Impulse in Victorian England 1880-1914* Faber

Martin, Mary (1979) *Wayward Genius: Neville Northy Burnard, Cornish Sculptor 1818-1878* Lodenek Press

McMahon, Brendan (2015) *A Wreck Upon the Ocean: Cornish Folklore in the Age of the Industrial Revolution* Evertype

Michell, John (1977) *A Short Life at The Land's End*

Montanaro, Lee Ann (2010) *Surrealism and Psychoanalysis in the work of Grace Pailthorpe and Reuben Mednikoff: 1935-1940* PhD thesis (Edinburgh) available from artcornwall.org

Nettleingham, FT (1917) *Tommy's Tunes* Erskine Macdonald

Nettleinghame, FT (1926) *Polperro Proverbs and Others* Polperro Press

Nettleinghame, FT (1948) *The Romance of a New Cornish Industry* British Bamboo Cane Company

Newman, Paul (2005) *The Tregerthen Horror* Abraxas

Newman, Paul (2010) *The Man who Unleashed the Birds* Abraxas

Payton, Philip (2004) *Cornwall, A History* CE Ltd

Payton, Philip (2009) *D H Lawrence & Cornwall* Truran

Penrose, Anthony (2004) *The Surrealists in Cornwall* Falmouth Art Gallery

Polwhele, Richard (1806) *History of Cornwall*

Pool, P.A.S (1986) *William Borlase* RIC

Pycroft, George (1883) *Art in Devonshire* Exeter: Eland

Quiller-Couch, A (1898 & 1899) *The Cornish Magazine Vols 1 & 2* Pollard

Raymont, C Morton (1962) *The Early Life of Robert Morton Nance* New Cornwall

Remy, Michael (1999) *Surrealism in Britain* Lund Humphries

Ruskin, J. (1851-1853) *Stones of Venice Vols 1-3*

Salter, Brian (2014) *Model Towns and Villages*

Sagar, Keith (1975) *DH Lawrence Life into Art* Penguin

Shillitoe, Richard (2010) *Ithell Colquhoun: Magician Born of Nature* Lulu

Smiles, Sam (2006) *Light into Colour: Turner in the South West* Tate Publications

Souhami, Diana (1988) *Gluck: Her Autobiography* Quercus

Speight E. E. (1905) *Hakluyt's English Voyages* Horace Marshall

Speight E E & Nance, R. Morton (1905) *Britain's Sea Story* Hodder & Stoughton

Speight E E & Nance, R Morton (1906) *The Romance of the Merchant Venturers* Hodder & Stoughton
Stukeley, William (1740) *History of the Ancient Celts*

Thomas, P W & Williams D R (2007) *Setting Cornwall on its Feet: Robert Morton Nance 1873-1959* Francis Boutle

Tolstoy, Leo (1882) *A Confession*

Tolstoy, Leo (1897) *What is Art?*

Tovey, David (2021) *Polperro: Cornwall's Forgotten Art Centre* Wilson Books

Val Baker, Denys (1973) *The Timeless Land*

Walke, Bernard (1935) *Twenty Years at St Hilary*

White, Rupert (2017) *The Reenchanted Landscape* Antenna

White, Rupert (2019) *Physick and Folk Medicine* Antenna

Wiener, M (1981) *English Culture and the Decline of the Industrial Spirit 1850-1980* Penguin

Yeats, William Butler (1921) *Four Years*

Yeats, William Butler (1897) *The Celtic Element in Literature (in 'Ideas of Good and Evil')* Bullen

Yorke, Malcolm (1997) *Matthew Smith His Life and Reputation* Faber

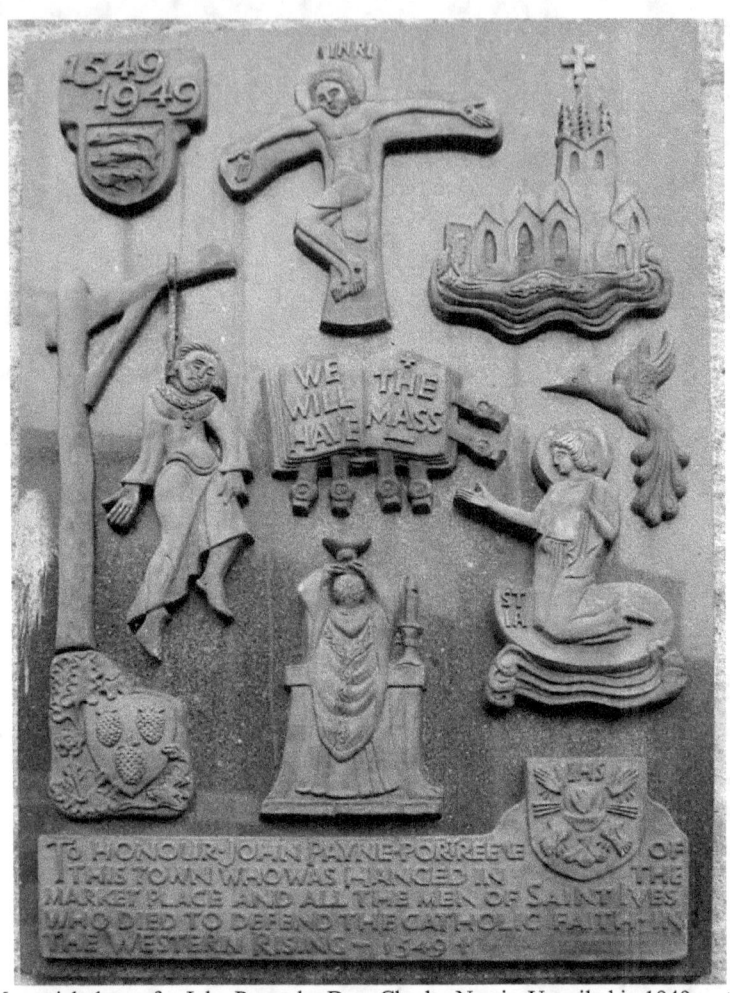

Memorial plaque for John Payne by Dom Charles Norris. Unveiled in 1949 on the outside wall of the Catholic church on Tregenna Hill, St Ives, it marked the 400th anniversary of the 'Western Rising'. Charles Norris, from Buckfast Abbey, was best known for his 'dalle de verre' windows made for Catholic churches all over Britain including, in Cornwall, St Agnes, Falmouth, Tintagel, Truro and Perranporth.

www.ingramcontent.com/pod-product-compliance
Lightning Source LLC
Chambersburg PA
CBHW071400210526
45465CB00001B/191